THE JOY OF PAIN

THE JOY

of

PAIN

SCHADENFREUDE AND THE DARK SIDE
OF HUMAN NATURE

Richard H. Smith

OXFORD
UNIVERSITY PRESS

OXFORD

UNIVERSITY PRESS

Oxford University Press is a department of the University of Oxford.
It furthers the University's objective of excellence in research, scholarship,
and education by publishing worldwide.

Oxford   New York

Auckland   Cape Town   Dar es Salaam   Hong Kong   Karachi
Kuala Lumpur   Madrid   Melbourne   Mexico City   Nairobi
New Delhi   Shanghai   Taipei   Toronto

With offices in

Argentina   Austria   Brazil   Chile   Czech Republic   France   Greece
Guatemala   Hungary   Italy   Japan   Poland   Portugal   Singapore
South Korea   Switzerland   Thailand   Turkey   Ukraine   Vietnam

Oxford is a registered trade mark of Oxford University Press
in the UK and certain other countries.

Published in the United States of America by
Oxford University Press
198 Madison Avenue, New York, NY 10016

Library of Congress Cataloging-in-Publication Data
Smith, Richard H.
The joy of pain : schadenfreude and the dark side of human nature / Richard H. Smith.
pages cm
ISBN 978–0–19–973454–2 (hardcover); 978–0–19–939371–8 (paperback)
1. Envy.   2. Failure (Psychology)   3. Humiliation.   I. Title.
BF575.E65S65 2013
152.4—dc23   2012044930

CONTENTS

ACKNOWLEDGMENTS

Lori Handelman was my first editor at Oxford University Press. Do you know someone whose judgment is so keen that you hang on her every word? You know that whatever your own understanding might be, it is necessarily incomplete until you have consulted her. Lori is in this category. Lori gave the first draft of the book an initial thumbs up, and she began the tough task of helping me turn a sow's ear into something of better quality. Chance favored me a second time when Abby Gross took over the project. Upon these two rocks of Handelman and Gross, I could start a publishing company. I was very far from solving the problems with the first draft, but Abby rolled up her editorial sleeves and went to work on guiding it toward the copy editing stage. Like Lori, her wisdom is extraordinary. As with Lori, I was incapable of a confident judgment on any issue until I got her opinion. If this final product misses the mark in any way, it is because I was unable to act on Abby's suggestions. I should add that the whole operation at Oxford was superb. The group of folks, together with Abby, who thought through the cover of the book did an exceptional job. I had imagined any number of designs for the cover, but none was close to what the Oxford team created. It was perfect, really. Suzanne Walker, Karen Kwak, Coleen Hatrick, and Pam Hanley expertly guided the final draft through to its completion as book in hand.

This book is partly a story of empirical work, done by myself and a group of other psychologists, including Norman Feather, Shlomo Hareli, Wilco van Dijk, Jaap Ouwerkerk, Masato Sawada, Hidehiko Takahashi, Zlatan Krizan, Omesh Johar, Colin Leach, Russell Spears, Niels van de Ven, Seger Breugelmans, Jill Sundie, Terry Turner, Mina Cikara, and Susan Fiske—as well as some of my current and former students, Ron Garonzik, David Combs, Caitlin Powell, Ryan Schurtz, Charles Hoogland, Mark Jackson, Matt Webster, Nancy Brigham, and Chelsea Cooper. Much of this work I summarize in this book, and I am indebted to these scholars for all their efforts to make conceptual and empirical headway in understanding *schadenfreude*.

Many friends and colleagues have contributed directly to my thinking or have simply given me the support of their friendship, which indirectly made this book possible. John Thibaut and Chet Insko at the University of North Carolina, where I did my graduate work, and Ed Diener at the University of Illinois, where I enjoyed a postdoc, were my first academic mentors. They each made me a much better researcher and thinker. The first study on *schadenfreude* that I was part of was done at Boston University, my first academic home. Much thanks to Ed Krupat, Len Saxe, Fabio Idrobo, Jean Berko Gleason, Henry Marcucella, Hilda Perlitsh, Mary Perry, and Joanne Hebden for their constant goodwill during the four years I was in the department—and to the late Phil Kubzansky, a marvelous human being of many parts who gave me so much good advice, including these words from A. E. Housman: "Get you the sons your fathers got, and God will save the Queen." What a mensch he was.

I am lucky currently to work at a place, the Psychology Department at the University of Kentucky, that provides a friendly, respectful, and intellectually vibrant environment conducive to getting good work done. A special thanks to Bob Lorch, Betty Lorch, Jonathan Golding, Ron Taylor, Art Beaman, Phil Berger, Monica Kern, Larry Gottlob, Charley Carlson, Ruth Baer, Rich Milich, Tom Zentall, Mike Bardo, Phil Kraemer, Mary Sue Johnson, Jenny Casey, Erin Norton, Melanie Kelley, Jeremy Popkin, Richard Greissman, Steve Voss, and Mark Peffley.

A number of people read and gave me feedback on one or more chapters. Mark Alicke, Phil Berger, Zlatan Krizan, Rich Milich, Jeremy Popkin,

Peter Glick, and Stephen Thielke read early versions of Chapters 9 or 10, and their comments greatly improved each. Mark Alicke, Phil Berger, and Stephen Thielke also read Chapters 5 and 6, and, here again, their comments were very, very helpful. Stephen was a constant source of astute observations about *schadenfreude* and other social emotions. Phil supplied me with many pertinent newspaper clippings and magazine articles. Claire Renzetti read Chapter 7 and gave me useful sociological references. Heidi Breiger provided me with a judge's perspective on assessing emotional reactions to criminal behavior. Jerry Parrott clarified much of my thinking about envy. Late in the process, Charley Carlson read the penultimate draft of the entire book. This was an enormous help in fine-tuning points. Before submitting the last draft of the book, Jon Martin, Sarah Braun, Alex Bianchi, and Allie Martin, the undergraduates in my lab at the time, read parts or all of the book. They also made very helpful suggestions and caught many writing glitches. A former honors student, Edward Brown, read the entire book and gave me especially useful comments.

My sisters, Gillian Murrell and Helen Smith, read the first draft of the book. Their comments were extremely helpful in my being able to take a sober assessment of where things were—what was working and what was not. I very much appreciated their enthusiasm for what I was trying to accomplish. My brother-in-law, Arch Johnson, who has a lot of horse sense, was always ready as a sounding board. And my sensible and fair-minded niece, Julia Smith, read early versions of Chapters 5, 6, and 10. Her comments greatly assisted my efforts to clarify these sections.

There are a few people I want to single out for extra thanks. My good friend, Mark Alicke, has had my back ever since we were in graduate school together, when he accepted my citing the Bard rather than the latest social psychological research. He has followed this project from its inception, sometimes reading chapters, but always, and with inimitable humor, giving me frank, constructive suggestions for how to get it done. Thanks, Mark.

My brother, Eric Smith, read several drafts and helped at all stages, from pleading with me to write the book in the first place to volunteering to do the figures. I am not the only person who has benefited from his willingness to help others, professionally and personally, in hugely substantial ways.

I am blessed with a family who has remained loving, patient, and optimistic as I worked to complete the book. My younger daughter, Caroline Smith, who shares my proclivity for punning, rather than groaning at them, simply came up with reciprocal puns of her own. This pun-upmanship was a sure energy boost when my vigor lagged. My older daughter, Rosanna Smith, despite her many other activities, did the drawings for the book. Working with her on ideas for these drawings was by far the most fun part of this project. My wife, Sung Hee Kim, painstakingly read the book at least five times at critical junctures. So gladly forbearing, she also created guilt-free conditions in our home to make it easier to complete it. More than anyone, by a country mile, she is the reason this thing got done. Finally, I thank my parents. I owe my love of reading and of scholarly pursuits to both. My mother, Hilary Smith, spent many years as an editorial assistant in the English Department at Duke University, and, during that time, helped edit the collected letters of Thomas and Jane Carlyle. She is still quick with an adapted line of poetry for any occasion. With rings on her fingers and bells on her toes, she shall have music wherever she goes. My late father, Peter Smith, who was a professor of chemistry at Duke for several decades and the son of a flower and seed shop owner in Manchester, England, knew and valued his Shakespeare, and this rubbed off on me as well. "Lay on, Macduff, and damn'd be him that first cries, 'Hold! enough!'"

INTRODUCTION

Homer Simpson's neighbor, Ned Flanders, announces during a backyard barbecue that he will quit his sales job to start a business called the "Leftorium," catering to left-handed people. Ned and Homer break the wishbone from a turkey carcass, and Homer gets the bigger piece and the right to make a wish. "Read it and weep!!" he exclaims, imagining a scene of the business failing. It turns out that it does start poorly, as Homer discovers when he passes by the store some weeks later. It is "deeeserted," he happily reports to the family at dinner. Lisa Simpson, ever the erudite daughter, labels and defines the emotion he is feeling.

> LISA SIMPSON: Dad, do you know what *schadenfreude* is?
>
> HOMER SIMPSON: No, I do not know what *schadenfreude* is. Please tell me because I'm dying to know.
>
> LISA: It's a German word for shameful joy, taking pleasure in the suffering of others.[1]

There is no English word for what Homer's feeling, but as Lisa tells him, there is one in German: *schadenfreude*. It comes from the joining of two words, "*schaden*" meaning "harm" and "*freude*" meaning "joy," and it indeed refers to the pleasure derived from another person's misfortune.[2] This book is about *schadenfreude*, an emotion that most of us can feel despite its shameful associations.

GAIN FROM OTHERS' MISFORTUNE

Although most of us feel uncomfortable admitting it, we often feel *schadenfreude* because we can gain from another person's misfortune. What does Homer gain from the failure of Ned Flanders's business? Actually, quite a lot. Homer envies Ned. Although Ned is a good neighbor, he still has it better than Homer in just about every way, from his well-equipped recreation room with foreign beers on tap to his superior family bliss. The envy Homer feels runs deep and takes its typical inferiority-tinged and hostile form. When Ned fails, Homer feels less inferior. Ned's failure also satisfies Homer's hostile feelings. These are heady psychological dividends and should make Homer feel pretty good as a result. What better tranquilizer for Homer's inadequacy and ill will than Ned's failure?

Perhaps you have heard this joke: two campers come across a grizzly bear while hiking in the forest. One immediately drops to the ground, takes off his hiking boots, and starts putting on his running shoes. The other says, "What are you doing? You can't outrun a bear!" His friend replies, "I don't have to outrun the bear, I only have to outrun you!" While this example is cartoonish, similar but lower-stakes scenarios like this one play out in relationships every day. In Chapters 1 and 2, I examine the link between *schadenfreude* and personal gain and show that a large part of our emotional life results from how we compare with others. We gain from another person's misfortune when this "downward comparison" boosts our rank and self-worth. We shall see that this is no small benefit.

The benefits to Homer from Ned's failing are largely intangible, but *schadenfreude* also results from tangible things. As I will stress in Chapter 3, much of life involves competition. One side must lose for the other to win. This is captured well in *Apollo 13*, the film based on the near-fatal NASA lunar mission. In this film version of events, Jim Lovell is unhappy because fellow astronaut Alan Shepard and the others on Shepard's crew have the latest coveted opportunity to travel to the moon. But Shepard develops an ear problem, and his crew is replaced by Lovell's. This is painful for Shepard, but Lovell's reaction is exuberant when he rushes home to give the news to his family. Lovell shows no hint of sympathy for Shepard as he tells his wife what has happened.[3]

As viewers of *Apollo 13*, we are watching from Lovell's perspective and, with him, we experience the good news. We see that when an outcome is so desired, its value for ourselves eclipses other factors. The extra detail that our gain comes at another person's expense recedes in relevance and does little to reduce the pleasure involved. Notice, however, that Lovell would have had no reason to delight in Shepard's ear infection had it not furthered his own goals. He was not happy "in" Shepard's misfortune, but rather "because of" it. Does this mean his joy was not *schadenfreude* at all? In this book, I take a broad definition of *schadenfreude*. The distinction between types of gain is easily blurred in our experience. For example, Lovell may well have envied Shepard. As I will explore later in the book, Homer Simpson is an exaggerated version of all of us. Envy can produce deep satisfaction in another's misfortune, especially in competitive situations, and there may be few pure cases of gain uncontaminated by such features. Plus, would we see Lovell showing his joy outside the family? Taking any pleasure from another's misfortune simply because we are gaining from it seems illicit and shameful. This gives it the clear stamp of *schadenfreude*.

If *schadenfreude* arises to the extent that we gain from another person's misfortune, then any natural tendencies we have to favor our own self-interests should further this pleasure. In Chapter 4, I address how human nature pulls us in at least two directions, one toward narrow self-interest and the other toward concern for others. Our capacity to feel *schadenfreude* highlights the self-interested, darker side of human nature. Without ignoring our compassionate instincts, I consider some of the evidence for our self-interested side and suggest that this evidence indeed reveals our capacity for *schadenfreude*.

PLEASURE FROM DESERVED MISFORTUNES

How about deservingness? Sometimes misfortunes suffered by others satisfy our sense of justice. In Chapters 5 and 6, I shift to this important reason why we can feel *schadenfreude*. Examples are everywhere. Take the case of Baptist minister and clinical psychologist, George Rekers. He made headlines in May of 2010 for using a Web site, Rentboy.com, to hire a 20-year-old male to accompany him on a short trip to Europe.[4] On the surface, this doesn't sound like news, but Rekers quickly became the focus of jokes on the internet and on late-night TV.[5] Rekers, as *The New York Times* columnist Frank Rich argued, is "the Zelig of homophobia, having played a significant role in many of the ugliest assaults on gay people and their civil rights over the last three decades."[6] His hiring of the Rentboy.com employee was viewed as a case of pure hypocrisy when the hired man claimed that he had given Rekers intimate massages during the trip. As Joe Coscarelli noted in his blog for *The Village Voice* soon after the event made news: "Please excuse most of the forward-thinking, tolerant world for being a bit excited and snide about the news…."[7]

As shameful as *schadenfreude* can be, the more a misfortune seems deserved, the more likely *schadenfreude* is out in the open, free of shame. This is true especially if the standards for judging deservingness are clear cut—for instance, if someone has committed crimes—or has behaved so hypocritically, as with George Rekers. The pleasure is collective and free-flowing.

I will emphasize that the desire for justice is a strong human motive, so strong that we are *biased* in our perceptions of deservingness. We are particularly biased in our reactions to being personally wronged. Our pleasure in a wrongdoer's misfortune is sweet indeed if we are lucky enough to have this *hoped-for* event occur. Here, the desire for justice merges with a desire for revenge against someone we dislike, even hate.

THE AGE OF *SCHADENFREUDE?*

Are we living in the age of *schadenfreude?* Just glance at the checkout lanes in the grocery store: some of the best-selling magazines will have break-ups, scandals, and other personal tragedies emblazoned on their colorful covers. The reality TV industry flourishes by developing programs that pit people against each other in difficult situations; ratings and advertising spending speak for themselves. Of course, the internet multiplies these trends many times over, which is why we speak of information going "viral." I was not surprised to find out what happens if you insert the word *"schadenfreude"* in the search tool Google NGram Viewer. Figure I.1 shows the percentage of times that *schadenfreude* is used among all words in books published in English from 1800 to 2008. Starting in the late 1980s, its use begins to increase and then rockets upward by the mid-1990s. An analysis of the use of the word in *The New York Times* nicely mirrors this pattern: in 1980, there were no instances; in 1985, only one; three in 1990; seven in 1995; twenty-eight in 2000; and sixty-two in 2008.[8] Perhaps this upsurge in usage comes as trends in media also shift toward a focus on people suffering all variety of misfortunes.

In Chapter 7, I examine two distinctive examples of reality TV, *American Idol* and *To Catch a Predator.* Both shows, in memorable ways, pioneered the pleasures of humiliation as entertainment—or "humilitainment," a term coined by media researchers Brad Waite and Sarah Booker.[9] Why are these shows so popular? We shall see that humilitainment, when heightened by the way a show is edited and structured, often arises within narratives of deservingness. These shows provide a steady diet of pleasing downward comparisons for viewers.

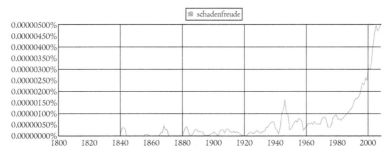

Figure I.1. Google NGram for usage of *"schadenfreude"* in thousands of books published from 1800 to 2008.

A BALM AND CURE FOR ENVY

I give envy its due in the next three chapters. Although envy is a painful emotion and *schadenfreude* is a pleasing one, the two emotions often travel in tandem. As Homer experiences it and as Lisa helps him understand, I detail in Chapter 8 how misfortunes befalling those whom we envy transform pain into a special joy. This is why definitions of envy often include the readiness to feel pleasure if the envied person suffers.

Much can be said about envy and its link with *schadenfreude*. Because envy is such a repugnant emotion, most of us are in fact more like Homer than Lisa. We are so threatened by the feeling that we suppress awareness of it. Even if we are aware of it, we rarely want to admit to it. In Chapter 9, I show that this often causes envy to transmute into other emotions, ones more palatable to ourselves and to others. In this altered form, *schadenfreude* resulting from an envied person's misfortune can seem justified, sometimes even decent. Moreover, envy is usually hostile at its roots. Hostility may breed dissatisfaction with passive forms of *schadenfreude*. When we feel envy, strong envy especially, we not only hope for misfortunes to befall those whom we envy; we may sometimes find ways to bring the misfortune about.

ENVY, *SCHADENFREUDE*, AND HUMAN DEPRAVITY

In Chapter 10, I take envy's transmutational nature into especially dark territory. I examine the special case of anti-Semitism and the Nazis' pleasure in the brutal treatment of the Jews. I claim that this extreme example of *schadenfreude* is partly explained by unconscious envy transmuted into resentment. When this happens, the envious person can rationalize and justify extreme forms of *schadenfreude*, as well as aggression. This is the outer range of *schadenfreude*, where crimes occur that go "beyond denunciation."[10]

ARE THERE ANTIDOTES?

As natural as *schadenfreude* is, should we encourage it? Who would argue this way, especially if we see that it can trend toward hurtful actions? I won't try to claim that we can snuff out this feeling, but I will suggest in Chapter 11 at least one way that we might moderate its likelihood. I will elaborate on our psychological tendency to prefer personality explanations when explaining other people's behavior. This "fundamental attribution error" enhances *schadenfreude* over empathy when we see people suffer misfortunes. People will seem to deserve their misfortunes because their internal qualities will appear to cause them. If we can curb this tendency, then empathy might trump *schadenfreude*—as we will see was true for Abraham Lincoln.

Let me be doubly clear from the start. By focusing on *schadenfreude* in this book I do not mean to suggest that human beings lack a strong capacity for empathy when others suffer. Of course we do. Some recent evolutionary thinking suggests that human nature disposes us *more* toward compassionate responses than hostile ones. We see this in titles of recent books. The primatologist Frans de Waal labels this shift in how we view human nature as *The Age of Empathy*. The emotion researcher Dacher Keltner uses the phrase *Born to Be Good* to capture this shift in zeitgeist. And, just as we have instinct for revenge, we also have an instinct for forgiveness, as psychologist Michael McCullough argues in *Beyond Revenge: The Evolution of the Forgiveness Instinct*.[11] We see the embracing of the good in human nature in the speedy ascent of positive psychology and its focus on healthy human functioning rather than mental illness. Important studies on understanding happiness by psychologists Ed Diener, Robert Emmons, and Martin Seligman are examples.[12] One theme of the positive psychology movement is that compassion leads more to personal happiness than does self-focused gratifications. Nonetheless, our capacity to feel *schadenfreude* resonates with our less compassionate side.

In sum, we will see that *schadenfreude* arises because there are varied ways that we can gain from other people's misfortunes. The primacy of our own self-interests in competitive situations and our keen preference for superiority over inferiority ensure a place for *schadenfreude* in our repertoire of feelings. We have a passion for justice, and it happens that many misfortunes seem deserved. *Schadenfreude* is intimately linked with deservingness, particularly when the suffering person has wronged *us*, and I will also examine the basis for this important link. An envied person's fall brings a special pleasure, and I will explore the many reasons for this frequent cause of *schadenfreude* as well. More than we realize, *schadenfreude* is a natural human emotion, and it pervades our experience. It is worth taking a very close look at why it is so prevalent because it will tell us a lot about human nature—and should help redirect us toward, in Lincoln's words, "the better angels of our nature."[13]

CHAPTER 1

_____

THE HIGHS OF SUPERIORITY

To feel one's well-being stronger when the misfortune of other people is put under our own well-being like a background to set it into brighter light, is founded in nature according to the laws of the imagination, namely that of contrast.
    —IMMANUEL KANT[1]

For a few days I brought along Saul Bellow's novel Herzog *so I could feel a little better than everyone else in line.*
    —DON J. SNYDER, *THE CLIFF WALK*[2]

I'm Chevy Chase…and you're not.
    —CHEVY CHASE, "WEEKEND UPDATE" FROM *SATURDAY NIGHT LIVE*[3]

When my eldest daughter was four years old, she attended a day care center close to where I worked. One day, I came into the center to pick her up and saw her drawing with a piece of chalk on a low-slung chalkboard. She saw me and immediately begged me to help her sketch some people. I did, but, coincidentally, one of her friends had been drawing right next to her. Just as my daughter began to draw again, the girl's mom showed up. The first thing her mom saw were my drawings next to her own daughter's age-appropriate stick figures. Never have I seen a look of shock and confusion appear so forcefully on a person's face.

"Did she do that…did she do that??!!!!"

"No, no, I drew them."

Her expression swiftly changed to embarrassed relief.

I often think of this incident when considering the effects of how we compare with others on our everyday emotions.[4] Identified as she was with her daughter, the gulf in apparent performance between her daughter and mine jolted her. The sudden knowledge that my daughter was blessed with so much greater talent than hers was painful. And if you think about it, revealing my contribution was a kind of *bad* news for me and *good* news for her. The diminishment in my daughter's talents brought her relief and, I sensed, a touch of *schadenfreude*.

Comparisons with others, the conclusions we make about ourselves based on them, and the resulting emotions pervade much of our lives. As much as inferiority makes us feel bad, superiority makes us feel good. The simple truth is that misfortunes happening to others are one path to the joys of superiority and help explain many instances of *schadenfreude*.

This sometimes disquieting fact is more easily digested when we see it at arm's length, in the context of entertainment. There are many examples from *Frasier*, the long-running sitcom that starred Kelsey Grammer as a neurotic, endearingly snobbish psychiatrist, Dr. Frasier Crane. In one episode, "The Perfect Guy," Frasier is intensely envious because the radio station where he has his own call-in show has hired a new health expert, Dr. Clint Webber—who is extraordinarily talented and handsome. Along with an irritating, modest charm, Clint effortlessly outshines Frasier and gets the lustful attention of all the women. To convince people that he is not envious, Frasier throws a party for Clint. The event evolves into yet another showcase for Clint's staggering set of talents. When Frasier tries to impress a Chinese woman with his (woefully rudimentary) Mandarin Chinese, he compliments her by trying to say that she looks "absolutely beautiful," but his pronunciation translates this to "lovely as a chicken beak"—as she is quick to point out. Clint has partially overheard the conversation and interjects, "Who is as lovely as chicken beak?" He then proceeds to have a smooth conversation with the woman in perfect Mandarin.

Frasier, thoroughly defeated, concedes to his brother Niles that Clint must be entirely free of defects. But later, he finds himself alone in the kitchen with Clint, who thanks Frasier for arranging the party in his honor. In the background, a hired pianist is playing "Isn't It Romantic" on Frasier's grand piano, and Clint says how much he loves the song. Anticipating yet another domain in which Clint is superior to top off the evening, Frasier exits the kitchen as Clint begins to sing—way off-key! Frasier immediately recognizes this unexpected good fortune and turns with keen anticipation back into the kitchen. Clint apologizes for singing too loudly, but Frasier, now grinning broadly, says, "No, no, not at all. I can't tell you how much I'm enjoying hearing it."

Clint admits to being a bit of ham when he has a glass of wine in him and asks if he might "serenade" the guests. Frasier seizes this opportunity, leading Clint to the piano. As Clint prepares to sing, Frasier rushes over to Niles to tell him the *good* news: "Oh Niles, Niles, I've done it. I have found his Achilles' heel....I just heard him singing, the man's completely tone deaf. He's about to launch into a rendition of 'Isn't It Romantic' that will simply peel the enamel from your teeth!"

Niles objects to the plan: "Are you sure you want to let him do that?...You have your victory, you're a wonderful singer. Isn't it enough to know that? Do you really need to see him humiliate himself?"

Frasier pauses for a moment, then says, "Yes."

Humiliation is precisely what Frasier wants. He has had it with feeling inferior to Clint and is thrilled to discover his rival's "Achilles' heel." Frasier gleefully anticipates the added pleasure of seeing Clint expose this flaw to all the guests. When Clint starts singing, Frasier is triumphant, delighted with the results. The guests try to be polite, but they are almost made ill by the horrid performance. And Frasier says with an ironic, rebuking air, "Please, everybody—nobody's perfect."[5]

It is funny and entertaining, but it is also just a sitcom. Even if, in identifying with Frasier, we half recognize his feelings in ourselves, we can also keep this recognition at a comfortable distance. And yet is Frasier more like ourselves than we want to admit?

HOW GOOD AM I? COMPARED TO WHOM?

Social comparisons not only help tell us whether we are succeeding or failing, but they also help *explain the cause* of our success or failure. If we "fail" because most people are performing better than we are, we infer low ability; if we "succeed" because most people do worse than we do, we infer high ability. Social comparisons deliver a double influence by defining whether a performance is a success or a failure and by suggesting that the cause probably results from high or low ability. No wonder misfortunes happening to others can be pleasing. They increase our relative fortunes and upgrade our self-evaluations.

It is worth stressing how much social comparisons can contribute to *defining* our talents and abilities. How do you know whether you are a fast runner? Is it enough to time how fast you can run a lap? No. You must compare this time with the times of other people who are similar to you in age, gender, and practice level. If you run faster, *then* you can say you are a fast runner.

Many have tried to capture the powerful role of social comparisons in human experience. Sometimes it comes through in a quip inspired by a lifetime of experiences, such as, "I've been rich and I've been poor. Believe me, honey, rich is better," attributed to the American singer and actress Sophie Tucker.[6] Or, it comes from a transforming event, such as when entertainer Walter O'Keefe was replaced by young Frank Sinatra at a New York nightclub in 1943. O'Keefe summed it up this way: "When I came to this place, I was the star.…Then a steamroller came along and knocked me flat."[7] Stand-up comedian Brian Regan once fantasized about what it would be like to be one of the few people in the world to have walked on the moon; then, in social situations involving "me-monsters" who like to dominate conversations by bragging about their accomplishments, he could break in and say, "I walked on the moon."[8] No one could beat this comparison.

A slew of utopian novels, such *Walden Two* by B. F. Skinner and *Facial Justice* by L. P. Hartley, reveal how people's common use of social comparisons challenges societal efforts to maximize happiness. But I doubt anyone has been as effective in showing the importance of social comparisons in everyday life as 18th-century philosopher Jean-Jacques Rousseau. In his classic work, *A Discourse on Inequality*,[9] Rousseau imagines what life might have been like early in human history and speculates that people may have lived in a relatively solitary state. If this were so, the implications for our sense of self and our emotional life would have been huge. Natural differences among people in intelligence and strength, often the stuff of social comparison, would have carried little weight in this "state of nature." As long as people were smart and strong enough to procure food and shelter, they would have needed no greater talents—nor would they have felt lacking. Rousseau suggests that with greater contact among people in our more recent history, an increase in social comparisons resulted, yielding likely effects. Rousseau writes:

> People become accustomed to judging different objects and to making comparisons; gradually they acquire ideas of merit and of beauty, which in turn produce feelings of preference.…Each began to look at the others and to want to be looked at himself; and public esteem came to be prized. He who sang or danced the best; he who was the most handsome, the strongest, the most adroit or the most eloquent became the most highly regarded, and this was the first step toward inequality.[10]

Feelings about ourselves would also change. In a solitary state, we would feel good about ourselves if we had food in our bellies, a roof over our heads, and the absence of physical injury. Not so when living among others. Now, a kind of self-pride or "*amour propre*" takes over, inspired by a newfound desire to be superior to others and to be recognized as such. Rousseau highlights the feelings that dominate when self-feelings are powered by relative differences—shame and envy if we are inferior and vanity and scorn if we are superior.[11]

SOCIAL COMPARISON AND SELF-ESTEEM: WHAT IS THE EXPERIMENTAL EVIDENCE?

Psychologists, beginning with the pioneering work of Leon Festinger in the 1950s that linked social comparison with a basic drive to evaluate ourselves, have found many ways to give empirical weight to claims about the importance of social comparison in self-evaluations.[12] Susan Fiske, in her recent book, *Envy Up, Scorn Down: How Status Divides Us*, provides an excellent distillation of this research done by her and many others.[13] I am most fond of a study done in the late 1960s by Stan Morse and Ken Gergen.[14] The design was simple, but the implications of the findings are far reaching. Participants who were students at the University of Michigan showed up in response to an ad for a job. The job promised good pay, so the stakes were higher than for a typical experiment. On arriving, they were placed in a room and asked to fill out a questionnaire as part of the application. After the students had completed half of the questionnaire, which contained an indirect measure of self-esteem, the experimenters arranged for another apparent applicant to enter the room and also begin completing the application. The appearance and behavior of this person were adjusted to create two conditions. In the Mr. Clean condition, this person was impressively dressed, well-groomed, and self-confident. He carried with him a college philosophy text and began completing the application with efficient ease. In a contrasting, Mr. Dirty condition, this person was shabbily dressed, smelly, and seemed a little dazed. While working on his application, he would occasionally stop and scratch his head, as if he needed help.

Participants then completed the final part of the application, which contained another embedded self-esteem measure. By subtracting the participants' self-esteem scores before and after the second applicant entered the room, Morse and Gergen were able to test a number of possible predictions. One possibility was that comparing with "Mr. Clean" would decrease self-esteem, but comparing with "Mr. Dirty" would not increase it. This would suggest that an "upward" comparison typically affects self-esteem, but a "downward" comparison does not. Superiority in others makes us feel bad, but we may be indifferent to inferiority in others. A second possibility was that Mr. Dirty would increase self-esteem, but Mr. Clean would not decrease it. This would suggest that a downward comparison can affect self-esteem, but an upward one may not. We are indifferent to superiority in others, but inferiority in others gives us a boost. A final possibility—the one that actually occurred—was that *both* conditions would affect self-esteem. Applicants felt worse about themselves when the other applicant was superior *and* better about themselves when the other applicant was inferior. Superiority in others often decreases our self-esteem, but their inferiority provides a boost, especially in competitive circumstances—as many other subsequent studies have shown since this one by Morse and Gergen.

The results were revealing in other interesting ways. A staff person rated how similar the participants were to the accomplice in terms of demeanor, grooming, and overall appearance and confidence. As illustrated in Figure 1.1, most of the movement in self-esteem occurred for those participants who resembled Mr. Dirty—that is, those who appeared to have "inferior" characteristics themselves. They must have felt the contrast with the superior applicant most acutely, as their reports of self-esteem, when compared to

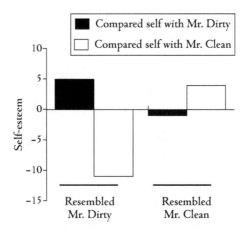

Figure 1.1. The association of resembling Mr. Clean or Mr. Dirty with self-esteem. Participants resembling Mr. Dirty had lower self-esteem after comparing themselves with Mr. Clean and higher self-esteem after comparing themselves with Mr. Dirty. In contrast, participants resembling Mr. Clean had no change in self-esteem after comparing themselves with Mr. Dirty and slightly greater self-esteem after comparing themselves with Mr. Clean.

Mr. Clean, took a big hit. But they also *benefited* most if they were lucky enough to be in the Mr. Dirty condition—comparing themselves to someone at least equally inferior appeared to give them a much-needed boost. Interestingly, participants rated as having superior characteristics were little affected by either accomplice. If anything, comparison with the superior applicant made them feel better. Perhaps the comparison confirmed their own feelings of superiority.

INFERIORITY IN OTHERS AND *SCHADENFREUDE*

It is hard to overstate the far-reaching advantages of superiority, as well as the obvious disadvantages of inferiority. The implications for understanding many instances of *schadenfreude* are important as well. Most of us are motivated to feel good about ourselves; we look for ways to maintain a positive sense of self.[15] One reliable way to do this is to discover that we are better than others on valued attributes. When our self-esteem is shaky, comparing ourselves with someone inferior can help us feel better.

A series of studies by Dutch social psychologists Wilco van Dijk, Jaap Ouwerkerk, Yoka Wesseling, and Guido van Koningsbruggen gives strong support for this way of thinking.[16] In one study, participants read an interview with a high-achieving student who was later found to have done a poor job on her thesis. Before reading the interview, as part of what appeared to be a separate study, they also filled out a standard self-esteem scale. Participants' feelings about themselves were very much related to how much pleasure they later felt after learning about the student's failure (items such as "I couldn't resist a little smile" or "I enjoyed what happened"): the worse they felt about themselves, the more pleasing was this student's failure. The explanation for these findings was reinforced by a closer analysis using a different measure. Immediately after reading about the high-achieving student, participants indicated whether reading about the student made them feel worse about themselves by comparison. The analysis showed that the tendency for participants with low self-esteem to feel pleased over the student's poorly done thesis was linked precisely with *also* feeling that they compared poorly with this student. In other words, when the participants with low self-esteem felt *schadenfreude*, they had also felt the earlier sting of comparing poorly with the student.

A second study added further evidence. The procedure was exactly the same, except that half of the participants, immediately after reading the interview with the high-achieving student but before learning about her academic misfortune, were given a prompt to think "self-affirming" thoughts about their important values. The other half did not get this opportunity. Only this latter group showed the same pattern of reaction as in the first study. Participants in the first group, because self-affirming thoughts may have prevented the unpleasant effects of the social comparison, were less inclined to find the student's academic misfortune pleasing.

There is nothing like a little success to blunt the influence of low self-esteem. I noted earlier that Frank Sinatra had the kind of talent to flatten the hopes of other singers. But even Sinatra went through a rough period in his career, and his self-esteem was at a low ebb by the end of the 1940s. Then he got the role of Maggio in the 1953 film *From Here to Eternity* and won the Oscar for best supporting actor. His psychiatrist, Dr. Ralph Greenson, watched on television as Sinatra received it, and said to his wife, "That's it, then. I won't be seeing him anymore!" And he never did. Winning the Oscar was hugely self-affirming and was the start of a lasting comeback.

A third study by the Dutch researchers (van Dijk et al.) added yet another wrinkle. The starting point of the first two studies was existing variations in self-esteem. This time, the researchers "created" variations in self-esteem by giving false performance feedback to participants and then examined how they responded to others' misfortune. Each participant performed a task described as highly linked with intellectual ability and was told that he or she scored among the worst 10 percent of the population (a control group received no feedback). Then the participant read a national magazine article that described a student who had tried to impress people at a party by renting an expensive car. But, after arriving and while trying to park the car, the student drove it into a nearby canal, causing severe damage to the car. Sure enough, participants receiving the negative feedback on intellectual ability found the misfortune more enjoyable than did those in the control condition who did not receive such feedback.[17] As the 17th-century writer François de la Rochefoucauld expressed in a maxim, "If we had no faults of our own, we would not take so much pleasure in noticing those of others."[18]

Thanks to the ingenuity of these researchers, we have a store of evidence demonstrating that people who stand to gain psychologically from another person's misfortune indeed get a boost to self-esteem from comparing themselves with someone suffering a setback. People with low self-esteem and those who have experienced threat to self-esteem seem especially likely to benefit. *Schadenfreude* provides one way of spotting this process.

THE EVOLUTIONARY ROOTS
OF SOCIAL COMPARISON

Evolutionary psychology highlights the important role of social comparisons in everyday life and also helps explain why inferiority in others should be pleasing. A simple fact crucial to understanding how evolution works is that people *differ* in ways that consistently matter in terms of survival and reproduction. Differences that provide advantages for survival contribute to natural selection. Much of life comes down to a competitive striving for superiority on culturally prized dimensions: to gain the status and many-splendored spoils following from such status. Superiority, literally, makes the difference. Attributes that underlie greater dominance or prestige compared to rivals allow us to rise in the pecking order and accrue benefits as a result. For these reasons alone, human beings should be highly attuned to variations in rank on any attributes that grant them advantages. And, given the huge adaptive implications of rank and status, inferiority *should* feel bad and superiority *should* feel good.[19]

How much we attend to social comparisons is nowhere more obvious than in the mating game. This makes sense in evolutionary terms because reproductive advantage is the bottom line. Survival means that our genetic material survives us (in our offspring), not so much that we survive individually. Thus, we must mate—and mating with those who give our offspring adaptive superiority is the name of this competitive game.[20]

Interestingly, couples are usually matched in terms of physical attractiveness. Why is it so? As much as we may desire to mate with the most attractive person around, we are competing against others with the same goal. Any overture we make must be reciprocated if the relationship is to proceed, and overreaching on this valued dimension usually doesn't work. It leads to rejection.

In a graduate course I teach, I use a classroom demonstration to dramatize this point.[21] The 15 or so students in the class are randomly given folded index cards that have their physical attractiveness "mate value" indicated inside (ranging from 1 to 15). They open up the cards and place them on their foreheads such that only others are aware of the value on the card. Ignoring their sex, they are told to pair up with someone with the highest mate value they can find. The pairing is initiated by offering to shake a potential mate's hand. If the offer is accepted, then the pair is complete. Rejected offers require that the person keep making offers until an offer is accepted.

As things progress, a small number of unhappy people wander about until, finally, even they find a mate. Then everyone guesses their own mate value and writes it down before seeing the actual value. They also rate their satisfaction with their pairing. Using a computer, I quickly enter actual and perceived values and ratings of mate satisfaction. Simply correlating these values is instructive. First, actual values are highly correlated. People pair up with those of similar value. Second, actual and perceived mate values are also highly correlated. It only takes a rejection or two to realize that one is not high on the attractiveness totem pole. Finally, mate values, both perceived and actual, are highly correlated with satisfaction. Attractive pairs are pleased; unattractive pairs are not. The demonstration is artificial, of course, but it dramatizes the consequences of ranking in one important area of life. People easily sense their mate value from how they are treated by others, and their feelings of satisfaction parallel actual and perceived mate values.

For our primitive ancestors living in closely knit tribes, it would have been important to be superior *relative* to other group members because it would have enhanced competitive advantage. Economist Robert Frank notes an interesting benefit to relativistic thinking. He argues that the rule of thumb, "do the best you can," leads to a quandary. When can you conclude that you have done enough? Frank suggests that the *relativistic* rule "do better than your nearest competitor" solves this problem in an efficient way.[22] The adaptive goal is to be better than your competitor, not to keep on achieving ad infinitum. Having a natural focus on social comparisons should lead to efficient actions: stop striving when you have a clear relative advantage; this is the signal to get off the treadmill. The process of evolution is likely to disfavor those who are fully at ease having low status because those with low status have less access to resources and are less preferred by potential mates.[23] No wonder there is mounting evidence that lower status is related to an array of ill effects on health and longevity.[24] Most people are unhappy with low status, and this is adaptive to a degree—a signal to do something about it. Similarly, most people are happy with high status. This is also adaptive—a signal of having achieved the benefits of high status. This happy feeling is something to anticipate and seek, as well as to relish.

One route to high status and its pleasures is through the reduction in status of others, especially those of higher status. As the pioneering evolutionary psychologist David Buss suggests, the anticipated pleasure of seeing higher status people fail serves an adaptive goal as well: to bring about these misfortunes, the relative gain that results, and the experience of this pleasure.[25]

The adaptive benefits of a keen sensitivity to relative differences are supported by observing a parallel tendency in primates, who share great genetic similarity to humans. Researchers at the Yerkes National Primate Research Center at Emory University trained a group of capuchin monkeys in what they called a "no-fair" game.[26] The monkeys were trained in pairs to hand a small rock to a researcher in exchange for a food reward, either a slice of cucumber or a grape, their much preferred food. When both received cucumber slices, both seemed satisfied. But when one received a cucumber slice and the other received a grape, the monkey receiving the cucumber became upset. The *relative* quality of rewards appeared as important as their presence versus their absence. As the lead researcher Sarah Brosnan noted, these disadvantaged monkeys "would literally take the cucumber from me and then drop it on the ground or throw it on the ground, or when I offered it to them they would simply turn around and refuse to accept it."[27] These monkeys' reactions seemed to mirror what we see in ourselves when we are unfairly treated, relatively speaking: if we can't have the best, don't bother us with second best.

Even canines appear to show a concern over unequal treatment. The celebrated 18th-century scholar Samuel Johnson suggested that some people are superficial in their thinking and, in this sense, that they are like dogs and "have not the power of comparing." They snatch the piece next to them, taking "a small bit of meat as readily as a large" even when they are side by side.[28] A study on dog behavior indicates that Johnson may have underestimated canine abilities. A group of researchers at the University of Vienna examined domestic canines' behavior. Paired dogs were given either a high-quality reward (sausage) or a low-quality reward (brown bread) if they placed a paw in the experimenter's hand. Consistent with Johnson's claims, the dogs seemed indifferent to the reward quality, even when they received the brown bread rather than the sausage. However, one procedural variation created a different reaction. When one dog received *either* of these rewards and the other got *nothing*, this seemed to make the disadvantaged dog much slower at offering his paws and more likely to disobey the command entirely. The disadvantaged dogs became more agitated and appeared to avoid the gaze of their advantaged partners. The researchers inferred from these findings that the dogs were having a negative "emotional" reaction to the unequal distribution—at least if being disadvantaged meant getting nothing. One piece was as good as the next, but "nothing" was upsetting when the other dog got something.[29] If dogs appear bothered by disadvantage, we can easily infer that most humans will be at least as concerned.

There are important cultural variations in how much social comparisons affect people's emotions.[30] But if I meet people who doubt how powerful social comparisons can be, I often put aside the research evidence and evolutionary theory and ask them if they have kids. If they do, I ask what would happen if they treated one child more favorably than another. Their faces usually animate with instant memories of family clashes caused by making this mistake. They remember the fireworks, the wails of unfairness, and the leftover resentments. They typically need no more convincing, but, primed in this way, I complete the point by telling them of the challenges my wife and I had in giving out popcorn to our two daughters when they were very young. Popcorn and movies were a compulsory pairing, and, from the beginning of this tradition, our daughters often quarreled over who received more popcorn. The only way to avoid an argument was to take delicate care in making sure the mound of popped kernels in each matching bowl was exactly equal. Nevertheless, one often would claim the other was getting more and was "always" favored. Sometimes we tried to snatch a teaching moment out of the sibling conflict: "Does it really matter who gets more? And why not ask for the bowl with the smaller amount? Be happy that your sister is getting more," and so on. As readers might expect, our teaching moments were usually no match for what our daughters perceived as favoritism. Now that they are grown, we laugh about these times. But the raw distress over disadvantage they showed when they were young is good evidence for the natural concerns people have over social comparisons.

In my introductory social psychology course, I take a different tack to show the importance of social comparisons. As social psychologist Mark Alicke demonstrates in many experiments, people are usually self-serving in their beliefs about how they compare with others. This "better-than-average effect" is *very* easily demonstrated.[31] One classroom activity that works spectacularly well begins by asking two questions, answered anonymously by each student, on a single sheet of paper:

1. How good is your sense of humor?

1   *2*   *3*   *4*   *5*   *6*   *7*

much worse   *much better*
than the average   *than the average*
college student   *college student*

2. How good is your math ability?

1   2   3   4   5   6   7

much worse   much better

than the average   than the average

college student   college student

After collecting the responses, I ask a few volunteers to do a quick tally of the responses. Figure 1.2 shows roughly what emerged when I conducted the exercise in a class of more than 100 students. For sense of humor, the distribution describes a near impossibility. Just about *everyone* in the class is reporting themselves above average. Most students see themselves as *way* above average. When it comes to sense of humor, this is easy to do. A highly subjective

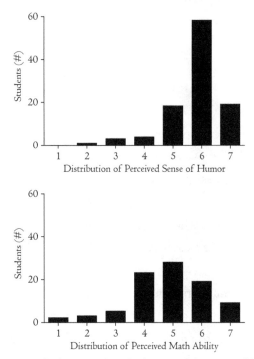

Figure 1.2. Biased perceptions of relative standing. Students rated their sense of humor (top panel) and their math ability (bottom panel) compared to the average college student. Most rated themselves at or above the midpoint (number 4 on the scale).

judgment lends itself to bias, and we seize the opportunity to see ourselves in a flattering way. The second distribution for perceived math ability shows the bias as well, but it is not nearly as extreme. Math ability is more objectively determined than sense of humor, and our judgments on such domains are more likely to be anchored by actual standing. And yet, even so, most people manage to see themselves as above average here as well.

Why are these perceptions so skewed? I think it is mainly because most of us like the idea of being superior to others, and we search for ways to come to this view whenever we can. The late comedian George Carlin captured the craving: "Have you ever noticed that anybody driving slower than you is an idiot, and anyone going faster than you is a maniac?"[32] Such illusions help us maintain a sufficiently robust self-esteem.[33] If superiority was superfluous for self-judgments, then there would be no need for biased construal. But we don't throw objectivity completely out the window.[34] On traits and abilities that are less subjective, we are more responsive to the realities of our actual relative standing, even though we may still give ourselves the benefit of the doubt.

SOCIAL COMPARISONS AND *SCHADENFREUDE* IN FICTION: *THE RED BADGE OF COURAGE*

The more we recognize how profoundly social comparisons permeate everyday judgments about ourselves—whether we are talented or mediocre, whether we are successful or unsuccessful, whether we are noticed or ignored by others— the clearer it becomes why another person's misfortune might be pleasing. Not surprisingly, great novelists who understand the human condition bear out this pattern. In Stephen Crane's Civil War novel, *The Red Badge of Courage*, the main character, Henry Fleming, eagerly joins the Union Army near the start of the war.[35] But his excitement soon turns to dread when he confronts the possibility of dying. Naively, he had felt superior to his school friends who had not joined the army. All it took was to see the first dead soldier to reverse this perception. His friends were now the lucky ones. He also worries that he will run when he gets his first taste of battle, and this causes him to compare his worries with those of the other soldiers "to measure himself by his comrades."[36] Fleming's fears get the better of him in his first battle: he speeds "toward the rear in great leaps"[37] and soon feels ashamed and inferior because of his cowardly behavior. Of course, upward comparisons are hard for Fleming to ignore. He notices a proud group of soldiers marching toward the battle front, which makes him feel even more inadequate, as well as envious. He slips into another group of soldiers who have just come from a battle but soon feels acute shame because so many of these men, unlike himself, have wounds or "red badges of cour-age." Happily for Fleming, he also meets other soldiers whose difficulties help him regain self-worth—sometimes leading to *schadenfreude*. Fleming notices a struggling friend, and this makes him feel "more strong and stout."[38] During the first battle, when he acted so cowardly, he takes some comfort in learning that many other soldiers also fled. Later, he notices a group of fearful, retreat-ing troops and likens them to "soft, ungainly animals."[39] He takes pleasure in the flattering comparison and concludes that "perhaps, he was not so bad after all."[40] By the end of the novel, Fleming finds redemption in showing that he can act bravely in battle, but not before his sense of self is rehabilitated through pleasing comparisons with other soldiers.[41] It is extraordinary how much social comparisons regulate Fleming's emotional life, their influence on *schadenfreude* being just one example.

SOCIAL COMPARISONS AND *SCHADENFREUDE* IN BIOGRAPHY: NATHAN McCALL'S *MAKES ME WANNA HOLLER*

It is easy to find biographical examples conveying a similar pervasive role for social comparison in people's everyday emotions, with *schadenfreude* inevi-tably punctuating the emotional landscape as a result. Born and raised in working-class Portsmouth, Virginia, journalist Nathan McCall illuminated the troubled terrain of racial comparison in his memoir, *Makes Me Wanna Holler: A Young Black Man in America*.[42] Although McCall grew up in a largely stable family and did well in school, by the time he was 15 he was carrying a gun and engag-ing in a range of criminal behavior from gang rape to armed robbery. He nar-rowly avoided a murder charge when a man he shot managed to pull through and survive, but, by his late teens, he was arrested for robbing a McDonald's. McCall finds himself in prison, which, despite its challenges, helps him turn himself around. By the time he left prison, he had completed a degree in journalism. After several disappointments, he landed a job as a reporter for *The Atlanta-Journal Constitution*, and, eventually, *The Washington Post*.

The memoir takes the reader through a territory unfamiliar to most people. Few of us know what it is like to commit armed robbery or to engage in gang rape, and the people who commit such acts are rarely in the position to write about them with McCall's effectiveness. His honesty is blistering, but for the reader interested in human psychology, the dividends are rich.

McCall is hyper-aware of social comparisons, especially those that involve race. Much of his downward spiral toward cruel behavior and crime can be traced to feelings of inferiority linked to his black identity. As a child of about seven or eight, he would watch TV and be "enchanted" by white people. He would think how much more fun white people seemed to have. In various ways, he got the message that white people were superior to blacks, such as when his mother would tell him to "Stop showing your color. Stop acting like a *nigger!*"[43] Or his grandmother would compare his bad behavior with the good behavior of the kids from an affluent Jewish family for whom she did domestic work. These white boys were "*nice*" and did everything she told them to do—why didn't he act like them also?[44] Once, he tried to straighten his hair with some of his grandfather's pomade, but it didn't last. Within minutes, his hair went from "straight, to curly, and back to nappy."[45] He received a whack on the back of his head from his mother when she discovered what he had done and endured the scalding effects of washing out the pomade. Worst of all, he suffered the pride-wounding recognition that his hair would never be as straight as the privileged and superior white people around him.

Painful longings and confused frustrations ruled his life. Envy and resentment plagued him. McCall summed up this time in his life this way:

> I'm certain that that period marked my realization of something it seemed white folks had been trying to get across to me for most of my young life—that there were two distinct worlds in America, and a different set of rules for each: The white one was full of possibilities of life. The dark one was just that—dark and limited.[46]

The accumulating toll of these experiences had corrosive effects on his psyche, and McCall suffered bitterly from consuming, explosive anger. He could hardly see straight well enough to make good decisions, which partly explained why he turned to various unhealthy and ultimately criminal behaviors.

One way he coped was by finding ways to see himself, and black folks in general, as superior to whites. During his time in prison, he learned how to play chess, conscious that white inmates considered themselves better at chess because it involved thinking. Thus, McCall approached any game against a white inmate as a war rather than a game. He focused every fiber of his being and every ounce of his concentration on winning. And he usually did win.

> The win and the trophy (I still have it) were especially sweet because I beat an egotistical white inmate in the finals. I fasted for two days in preparation for that match and beat that white boy like he stole something.[47]

Later, as a reporter, he would constantly examine the behavior of his white colleagues and note when it seemed better or worse than the behavior of black folks. He was depressed by their superiority and was elevated by their inferiority. He attended a party at which "constipated-looking white folks" discuss politics and tell "corny jokes.[48] While working at *The Atlanta Journal-Constitution*, he concluded that many of the white reporters were terrible at choosing clothing, having selected uncoordinated colors and patterns. He notes that they "couldn't dress as sharp as the brothers and they felt insecure about it."[49] He enjoyed their ineptitude.

McCall also found satisfaction when the owners of the *Journal-Constitution* hired Bill Kovach, a former Washington bureau chief of *The New York Times*, to run the paper and upgrade its quality. Kovach brought in his own team and shook the place up. Many reporters were comfortable with the old ways and resented a "Yankee" coming in and changing things. It was as though they still hadn't accepted the outcome of the Civil War. McCall could understand why his colleagues reacted this way and, to a degree, felt a kinship with them. He sensed that many Southerners suffered an inferiority complex that ran deep. Whites from the North had "worked a *mojo* number on their minds"[50] that continued across many generations. Maybe there was a parallel in the ways black people had coped with the degrading legacy of slavery. Kovach's actions, by suggesting that these white reporters couldn't run a newspaper in a competent way, aggravated past wounds. McCall imagined that the stereotype of the

"hick" Southerner was humiliating in ways not so very different from stereotypes of intellectual inferiority that black people had suffered. But this understanding did not take the edge off McCall's *schadenfreude.*

> Watching some of those good ol' boys huddling conspiratorially in their clus-
> ters, grumbling all the time about "them damned Yankees coming in and
> taking over," you would have thought they were planning to fight the fucking
> Civil War all over again. Some got mad and quit. Kovach fired others. It was
> interesting seeing white people warring against each other like that. I enjoyed
> watching the carnage.[51]

McCall's sentiments are raw, but they are not mysterious. They come as no
surprise in the light of the laboratory evidence that van Dijk and his colleagues
provide. The pleasure that McCall experienced when he perceived inferiority in
whites was fine-tuned by the insults to his racial dignity suffered as a child and
the continued challenge of confronting racial stereotypes of black inferiority.

McCall enjoyed the highs of superiority. But notice that a big part of his
enjoyment came from focusing on another person's inferiority as much as on
his own superiority. Perceptions of superiority and inferiority are interlinked,
but our attention can be directed at either pole. As we'll learn in Chapter 2,
this second direction of focus, downward comparisons, provides many opportunities for *schadenfreude.* Indeed, they explain why many events hit an ingrained
funny bone.

CHAPTER 2

Looking Up by Looking Down

"Ain't no reason to cry, George," Dub said. "We're a lot better off than the grasshoppers."
—W. T. "Dub" Scroggins[1]

Let us be thankful for the fools. But for them the rest of us could not succeed.
—Mark Twain[2]

It's not enough that I fly first class...my friends must also fly coach.
—*New Yorker* Cartoon[3]

Writer Susan Cheever describes dinner parties at which people would embarrass themselves with each extra drink. Women would apply their lipstick left of center, and men would crash to the floor among broken dishes. It was, "One tequila, two tequila, three tequila, floor," as George Carlin might have added.[4] Unfortunately for Cheever, this is all in the past. Parties where slurred speech, pratfalls, and shattered crockery can be enjoyed have almost vanished from the social scene in recent years. According to Cheever, people still drink, but they don't get drunk, which means that they behave better and no longer make spectacles of themselves. Social disapproval of overdrinking has even overcome alcohol addiction. Cheever laments the change, because "there is a kind of drunkenfreude to watching others embarrass themselves."[5]

Cheever is an alcoholic, which is why she also avoids drinking at these parties. She knows the ruinous effects of alcoholism. She has authored a book about Bill Wilson, who founded Alcoholics Anonymous, and has written both about the alcoholism suffered by her well-known father, John Cheever, and her own struggles with this addiction. This intimacy with alcoholism moves her to empathize with people who embarrass themselves while drunk, but she also delights in it.[6]

She plays the role of hopeful observer. She longs for replays of the drunken behavior, but refuses the director's chair. Like most people, she is ambivalent enough about taking pleasure in misfortunes in which she plays no role; engineering a misfortune is even more taboo. She takes her downward comparison pick-me-ups as they come, anticipating them, hoping for them, taking the classic passive route to *schadenfreude* rather than an active one. Yet she reveals a certain mischievousness in her heritage when she recalls something her father would do. When he was sober, he would "mix killer martinis" in order to enjoy their effects on his guests.[7]

There are many paths to pleasing downward comparisons. Strategies range from joining groups whose members provide a comparison boost, focusing attention on people who are down and out, exaggerating the inferior qualities in other people who are otherwise superior, dismissing the value of other people's superior qualities to taking actions to bring about others' inferiority—such as making killer martinis. There are unlimited permutations.

DOWNWARD COMPARISON PROSPECTS
IN THE MEDIA

One handy maneuver is simply to look at almost any form of media because so many news outlets home in on scandals and other misfortunes happening to others. So does the ever-expanding genre of reality television that I explore in Chapter 7. Humiliation, or the public bringing "down" of others, is the frequent lure for viewers. And today, with the internet and its various means of providing information, embarrassing behavior becomes instantly available for broad and repeated viewings. What produces hits is often what also provides a gratifying downward comparison.[8] Many readers will recognize this quote:

> I personally believe that U.S. Americans are unable to do so because, uh, some…people out there in our nation don't have maps and, uh, I believe that our, uh, education like such as in South Africa and, uh, the Iraq, everywhere like such as, and, I believe that they should, our education over here in the U.S. should help the U.S., uh, or, uh, should help South Africa and should help the Iraq and the Asian countries, so we will be able to build up our future, for our children.[9]

This was the response by Caitlin Upton, a contestant from South Carolina in the 2007 Miss Teen USA pageant, to the question: "Recent polls have shown a fifth of Americans can't locate the U.S. on a world map. Why do you think this is?" It is not easy to answer any question under a competitive, public glare, and most of us can remember suffering a brain spasm when put on the spot. Later, when interviewed on NBC's *Today Show*, she explained herself much better.[10] She was a good sport about it, even doing self-parodies.[11] But her word salad of an answer was so marvelously convoluted, so replete with unforgettable phrases ("like such as" and "the Iraq") that media outlets replayed it mercilessly, with mocking commentary. This merited multiple viewings and a YouTube link worth forwarding it to others for their sure enjoyment. In fact, it was an instant YouTube sensation, ultimately the second most viewed video of 2007.[12] It won the "stupidest statement of the year award"[13] and was on top or near the top of many lists of memorable quotes of the year.[14] It was second in the "Yale Book of Quotations," just behind "Don't tase me, bro," the plea that a college student used to avoid being tossed out of a college auditorium where Senator John Kerry was giving a speech.[15] It continues to be a favorite downward comparison stimulant, a dependable *schadenfreude* kick.[16]

DOWNWARD COMPARISONS AND THEIR SOMETIMES PLEASING OUTER RANGE

Pleasing downward comparisons can have darker origins. Take the spate of cases in 2005–2006 of brutal assaults on homeless men. Sometimes labeled "sport killings," these acts are typically committed by middle-class teens. One assault, featured on the CBS news show *60 Minutes*, received special attention because it resulted in an unfortunate man's death. The four teens who confessed to the crime came across the man in a wooded area where they had intended to smoke pot. They beat him in three stages for over three hours, off and on, despite his pleas to stop and his cries for help. It was an abhorrent, drawn-out series of actions, beginning with sticks and ending with a two-by-four with a nail at its end. Ed Bradley, the late CBS correspondent for the segment, interviewed the boys after they had been caught, convicted, and sentenced for the crime. The main theme in his questioning was to understand why they did what they did.

The oldest member of the group, 18 at the time of the fatal beating, explained, simply, "I guess for fun." He was ashamed of what he and his friends had done and, in a way, seemed just as puzzled as Bradley. He claimed the man's pleas for help were the main thing he could not "keep out of [his] head…24/7."[17]

Why was it fun? The judge in the case suggested that the helplessness of these men provided someone lower on the pecking order to pick on. Brian Levin, a criminologist and an expert on hate crimes, offered a similar explanation. It would be a mistake to see offenses of this sort as committed by inveterate, hate-filled people. Rather, they are examples of young males looking for cheap thrills. They select targets who are inferior to themselves and who cannot fight back. The vulnerable, inferior status of these homeless men is a psychological boost for the perpetrators, who need to feel superiority. There is "fun" in this process.

But, still, why would these kids need a target in the first place? In this case, the teens were unaware of the DVD series, *Bumfights*, in which homeless people get paid with chump change and alcohol to engage in humiliating behaviors.[18] In other cases of teens attacking homeless people, this series is cited as causing copycat behavior. The judge in the *60 Minutes* case saw one recurring theme. Many of the boys felt that they had been mistreated by others in the past. Perhaps these homeless men presented an opportunity for a kind of payback.

Is it a stretch to interpret these cases as opportunities, at least in part, for pleasing downward comparisons? It is hard to say for sure, but some details of these and other similar cases fit the profile. Psychologist Tom Wills has outlined a theory that explains why comparisons with those less fortunate can enhance a person's subjective sense of well-being.[19] Normally, we feel uncomfortable observing someone's suffering. However, Wills argues that our preferences change when we have suffered, our self-esteem has taken a hit, or we are chronically low in self-esteem. Under these conditions, comparing with someone just as unfortunate or—even better—with someone who is less fortunate has restorative power. Opportunities for downward comparisons can be passive or active. In the former case, we might seek out opportunities that naturally occur all around us, such as stories in the tabloid press or gossip among friends and acquaintances.[20] In the latter case, we actively derogate others or deliberately cause harm to someone, thus *creating* downward comparison opportunities.[21]

According to Wills, downward comparisons tend to be directed at people of lower status, or "safe" targets, who are acceptable to derogate because particular cultural norms seem to give the behavior a free pass.[22]

The beating of the homeless by these teens largely fits Wills's analysis. If the judge who adjudicated the case is right, the boys may indeed have been mistreated by others in the past. In response to their own abuse, and as a means of feeling better about themselves, they may well have sought opportunities to feel superior to others. The homeless were convenient targets. They are at the farthest and most jagged margins of society.

I hesitate to take this analysis too far. At best, downward comparison can explain only part of behavior as extreme as these beatings. That these actions happened in groups may be an another important factor in how the events played out. Extreme antisocial behaviors are more likely to occur in groups in which people become deindividuated and thus feel less responsible for their behaviors and less aware of their motivations.[23] Also, maybe these teens were bored and the simple entertainment value of their behavior contributes to explaining it. But these additional factors seem insufficient for understanding the core motive for these actions; in such cases, downward comparison explanations help provide a plausible reason for actions that can otherwise seem so puzzling. The pleasing enhancement to the self, albeit at the expense of these luckless men, may have been a seductive psychological boost.

Bradley found the teen's explanation of "it was fun" unsatisfactory. We probably resist such explanations because they not only reflect poorly on the boys, but also on human nature, and, therefore, on all of us. Wills also emphasizes that his theory assumes that we are ambivalent about finding gratifications from downward comparisons. Doing this produces mixed feelings, and, certainly, no one is admired for doing so.[24] When a downward comparison explanation fits, we resist it. Wills, however, argues that few people, especially when psychologically primed by their own failure or low status, refuse the opening for self-enhancement through favorable comparison. And we know from the empirical work by Wilco van Dijk and colleagues described in Chapter 1 that *schadenfreude* is more likely if the misfortune happening to another person bolsters our self-esteem—especially when it is in need of a boost. Add the ingredients of group psychology and an especially safe, dehumanized target and downward comparisons, even ones that are engineered, may be a tempting option.

THE SUPERIORITY THEORY OF HUMOR

In a sense, *schadenfreude* implies something funny. The misfortune causes us to smile and sometimes laugh in ways that we would if we heard a good joke— told at another person's or group's expense. In fact, some explanations for humor offer a link between downward social comparisons and *schadenfreude*. Perhaps the longest standing theory of humor has social comparison at its core. Superiority theory assumes that when people laugh, it results from their awareness of superiority over another person. This approach goes back as far as Plato and Aristotle, but the 17th-century philosopher Thomas Hobbes is credited with its full expression. In *The Leviathan*, he wrote that "sudden glory"

> [i]s the passion which maketh those grimaces called laughter; and is caused either by some sudden act of their own that pleaseth them; or by the apprehension of some deformed thing in another, by comparison whereof they suddenly applaud themselves. And it is incident most to them that are conscious of the fewest abilities in themselves; who are forced to keep themselves in their own favour by observing the imperfections of other men.[25]

Laughter, in Hobbes's analysis, often stems from a *sudden* sense of superiority. And, consistent with Wills's ideas, the pleasure in sudden superiority is more likely to occur in those who are "conscious of the fewest abilities in themselves."[26] Indeed, the superiority theory of humor dovetails nicely with the idea of downward comparison. Wills also stresses the connection by noting that humor often entails a negative event happening to another person, causing a pleasurable response in an audience. A downward comparison takes on this incongruent pairing of a negative with a positive in that the negative event is *happening to someone else*.[27]

A downward comparison view on humor assumes that it involves self-enhancement by comparing oneself favorably to another. It also takes threat to self-esteem into account. Wills observes that many examples of humor concern topics about which the audience feels "insecure," such as sexual inadequacies, uneasy relationships with one's boss, ethnic inferiority, and the like. Humor, in social comparison terms, relieves insecurities by providing a flattering social comparison in these and other aspects of life.[28]

As I noted, humor often arises at another person's or group's expense. But at whose expense more specifically? As with downward comparisons, the preference is a safe target. Audiences laugh at jokes that focus on people of lower status, often ethnic, racial, or religious groups usually disliked by the audience. Many comedians more or less make downward comparisons their stock in trade. Insult comics, in the tradition of Groucho Marx ("I never forget a face, but in your case, I'll be glad to make an exception"[29]) and Don Rickles ("Oh my God, look at you. Anyone else hurt in the accident?"[30]), add extreme elements. There is little evidence that we fundamentally object to this approach, even in these extreme forms. We love it. What comedian can waste an opportunity to go for the comic jugular when given examples of anyone displaying a human frailty? Most of the jokes in the opening monologues of late-night talk shows highlight the foolish behaviors of others. Such behaviors are free gifts for a comedian. When people become objects of downward comparison humor because of the exotic nature of their failings, contemporary comedians such as Jon Stewart will show gratitude for the comic material—and wish it a long half-life. Stewart rejoiced in reaction to an extraordinary gaff committed by a politician during a political debate in November 2011: "Are you not entertained? There is so much meat on that bone, and it is all breast meat."[31]

A more recent variant of the superiority theory of humor is advanced by psychologist Charles Gruner. He likens the experience of laughter to winning.[32] Gruner uses "winning" in the broadest sense: "getting what we want." This can mean winning an argument, reaching a goal, or defeating something in nature, such as finally digging up a stubborn tree root. What is funny, in Gruner's view, turns on *who* wins *what*, and *who* loses *what*. Often, when we find something funny, *we* are winning because of someone else's stupidity, clumsiness, or moral or cultural defect.[33]

Gruner's ideas are consistent with evolutionary psychology. Our ancestors' struggles for survival in the competitive conditions of scarcity and competition for mates would have bred emotional reactions to rewards (victory) and loss (defeat). In sports, where norms do not forbid expressing joy in victory, we often see self-assertive, aggressive laughter. One can see examples of the "thrill of victory" in competition events that are captured and preserved in the media. Remember U.S. swimmer Michael Phelps reacting to his 2008 Olympic relay victory? How about Tiger Woods fist pumping after making the clutch putt that catapulted him into a commanding position deep into the fourth round of the 2008 U.S. Open? Gruner claims that the feeling of winning strikes a chord that harkens back to our evolutionary past, where a competitive triumph surely aided survival.[34] Open pleasure, especially when the outcome is sudden and the result of struggle, is a natural reaction to winning. Is it any surprise that hyperbole such as, "Tragedy is when I cut my finger. Comedy is when you fall into an open sewer and die," made by comedian Mel Brooks, can seem more than simply eccentric?[35]

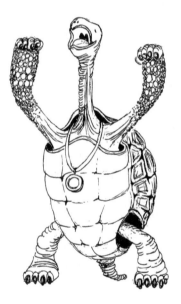

The superiority theory of humor is also supported by research showing how people use social comparisons at the intergroup level to boost self-esteem. Humor that entails disparaging an outgroup is one way of enhancing one's own group and, indirectly, one's own self-esteem. Indeed, studies confirm that we are more likely to laugh at jokes that disparage outgroups rather than ingroups; this makes us feel better about ourselves.[36]

The superiority theory of humor is not an all-encompassing explanation for when and why people find things funny.[37] Other explanations focus on incongruity (a conflict between what is expected and what actually occurs) or release (a relief from strain or stress). But, as Wills argues, a downward comparison perspective implies that such factors are secondary processes and "merely technical devices, serving to obscure the process of presenting another person's misfortune for the enjoyment of the audience."[38] They serve, in part, to circumvent the hesitancy that people feel about making downward comparisons. Similarly, Gruner is undaunted by other approaches to humor and claims that he can see superiority as explaining any example of humor. As someone who often studies the dark side of social comparison, I am less concerned about the debate on the broad origins of humor. What is relevant in explaining *schadenfreude* is that superiority resulting from downward comparisons is present in many cases of humor. It may well be a sufficient condition for humor, if not a necessary one.

THE CODE OF THE WOOSTERS: LIGHT HUMOR IN DOWNWARD COMPARISONS

The unmatched comic writer P. G. Wodehouse set most of his stories in pre–World War I Edwardian England. He populated these stories with upper-class characters who mostly lived lives of leisure and who frequented big country mansions with servants in tow. But the apparent narrowness of the setting and times did not prevent Wodehouse from producing some of the most inspired comic writing in the English language. J. K. Rowling, creator of the Harry Potter books, always places a Wodehouse volume by her bed.[39] A considerable part of Wodehouse's humor involved lighthearted *schadenfreude*. A good example is *The Code of the Woosters*, which the late writer Christopher Hitchens put high on his list of favorite books.[40] Like many Wodehouse novels, the plot of *The Code of the Woosters* is complicated and the narrator, Bertie Wooster, through no major fault of his own, finds himself in all kinds of troubles for which there seem no solutions. Bertie lives a pampered life and has a lazy intellect, but he is a lovable character even so. And, fortunately for Bertie, his uncommonly gifted and skilled valet, Jeeves, finds inspired ways to save the day. The satisfying moments, when those who have tormented Bertie are finally cut down to size, are rich in downward comparison–inspired *schadenfreude*, for Bertie as well as for readers.

Early in *The Code of the Woosters*, we meet Spode, a beefy, threatening character who is intent on physically assaulting both Bertie and one of Bertie's friends. But

Jeeves uses his network of fellow valets to discover an embarrassing secret about Spode.[41] This knowledge gives Bertie the power to reduce this bully to a meek, obsequious lapdog, such that the "red light died out of his eyes."[42] Here is how Bertie analyzes the pleasure he gets from the power he has to humble Spode:

I felt like a new man. And I'll tell you why.

Everyone, I suppose, has experienced the sensation of comfort and relief which comes when you are being given the runaround by forces beyond your control and suddenly discover someone on whom you can work off the pent-up feelings. The merchant prince, when things are going wrong, takes it out on the junior clerk. The junior clerk goes and ticks off the office boy. The office boy kicks the cat. The cat steps down the street to find a smaller cat, which in its turn, the interview concluded, starts scouring the countryside for a mouse.

It was so with me now.[43]

Bertie can be forgiven for actively exhibiting joy from a downward comparison because Spode is a true menace and he is shown to deserve humbling (I will discuss a lot more about the important role of deservingness in *schadenfreude* in later chapters). The novel is alive with other instances of downward comparison, but they are mostly of the standard, passive variety. In another sequence, Jeeves tells Bertie that a police officer, Constable Oates, who has also been unreasonably hostile to Bertie, has been hit on the head. Bertie replies:

"Blood?"

"Yes, sir. The officer had met with an accident."

My momentary pique vanished, and in its place there came a stern joy. Life at Totleigh Towers had hardened me, blunting the gentler emotions, and I derived nothing but gratification from the news that Constable Oates had been meeting with accidents.[44]

The novel ends with the subplots coming together and neatly resolving themselves in a manner not unlike a Shakespearian comedy. Bertie is happy because he is no longer threatened by people like Spode, Constable Oates, and others, and this also eases what has been a string of assaults to his self-esteem and general well-being. He is also gratified because his actions have helped two couples end their love squabbles and because he has found ways of benefiting his aunt and uncle. His aunt avoids losing a coveted servant, and his uncle obtains a much-desired cow creamer. With Jeeves, he reflects on the complex troubles he has suffered *and* Jeeves's brilliant solutions for these troubles. They are in their room in the country house where most of the action has taken place, and they hear a sneeze coming from outside. Earlier, Bertie had been wrongly accused of plotting to steal a prized object from the home (the cow creamer). Constable Oates was ordered to stand guard outside Bertie's window, to prevent him from escaping until morning, when he would be taken to court. But Bertie has been exonerated, and no one has told Oates that his watch is unnecessary. Rain has begun "with some violence." Bertie reacts:

> I sighed contentedly. It needed but this to complete my day. The thought of Constable Oates prowling in the rain like the troops of Midian, when he could have been snug in bed toasting his pink toes on the hot-water bottle, gave me a curiously mellowing sense of happiness.

> "This is the end of a perfect day, Jeeves...."[45]

Using fresh images, incandescent language, and plots impossible to predict and yet so fitting as they unfold, Wodehouse puts a wondrously comic mirror up to nature. A generous portion of his themes relies on the *schadenfreude* felt by his characters, as well as by his readers, but this hardly leaves a mean-spirited taste. There is no real cruelty in his "stern joy" —no beating of the homeless. If Bertie gets pleasure over someone's humiliation, it feels right under the circumstances. Also, it's simply the way of the world to feel this emotion, especially if life has been placing you at a disadvantage and you need a ration of downward comparison.

In the next chapter, I continue to focus on how downward comparisons can create *schadenfreude*, but I add another ingredient: group identity. This is no trivial factor. There is something about "us" and "them" that quickly shifts to "us" *versus* "them." When we are strongly connected to a group, misfortunes happening to the members of rival groups can be thrilling. Examples from sports and politics will provide sufficient proof of this.

CHAPTER 3

OTHERS MUST FAIL

When a nimble Burman tripped me on the football field and the referee (another Burman) looked the other way, the crowd yelled with hideous laughter....The young Buddhist priests were the worst of all.
—GEORGE ORWELL[1]

The object of war is not to die for your country but to make the other guy die for his.
—U.S. GENERAL GEORGE S. PATTON[2]

It's not enough that we succeed. Cats must also fail.
—SAID BY A CANINE IN A *NEW YORKER* CARTOON[3]

If you have ever checkmated someone in chess, you know the experience of winning a zero-sum game, in which one person's gain or loss translates exactly into another person's loss or gain. A clear memory I have from high school is taking my queen and flicking over my friend's king as I said, "checkmate," with understated yet pointed emphasis. Perhaps a small thing, but my friend had beaten me in an earlier match and had *gloated* over the win. This was low-stakes competition among high school kids, but no less intense for this fact. "Gentleman, start your egos," as comedian Billy Crystal once quipped.[4] I can still see the proud smile on his face when he had agreed to the rematch. As a result, beating him was a keener joy.

Although part of why beating him was so satisfying was his gloating, the zero-sum nature of the game told another part of the story. The pleasure I felt was from my winning *and* his losing. Both enabled satisfying gain for me.[5]

Athletic contests are also zero-sum, and emotions are keyed on the outcome. As a parent of two girls, now grown, I spent years engaged in youth sports, sometimes coaching, but usually as a spectator watching the games. I often stepped back to watch myself and the parents of other kids on our team reacting to the ebb and flow of games. Errors by the other side would often receive as many cheers as the successes of our own team, especially as the teams' age group increased. Sometimes, the pleasure over the other side's mistakes more than matched the pleasure of a good play by our own kids. If you think about it, this is hardly a nice thing. When a child commits a turnover in a basketball game, for example, it is a misfortune for the child—maybe a mortifying one. Why should we feel comfortable clapping and cheering? The context of sports seems to make it kosher.

WHEN MEMBERSHIP IN GROUPS AFFECTS SELF-ESTEEM

The triumphs or defeats of our children produce personal gain or loss. Watch the faces of parents when their children perform, especially during unguarded moments, and there is little doubt that our identification with our children is usually total. The best example I can think of occurred during the 2012 Summer Olympic Games. The parents of American gymnast Aly Raisman were in tense synchrony with their daughter as she performed her difficult routine on the uneven bars. The NBC "parent cam" captured their shifting and swaying, and this video quickly spread across the internet. It summed up something that all parents experience.[6] The phrase popularized by ABC Sports, "the thrill of victory and the agony of defeat," applies to our children's performances as much as to our own. And so events that help them succeed, even if they involve another child's failure, can mix pleasure with sympathy.

Spectators feel powerful emotions, even when no family members are playing. The successes and failures of the groups to which we belong affect us perhaps as much as do our individual ups and downs.[7] The attachments we have to groups are quickly cemented and often arbitrary, yet consequential despite these arbitrary origins. The first experiments to hint at this uncanny process were performed by the Polish-born social psychologist Henri Tajfel in the 1960s.[8] Tajfel was as an international student at the Sorbonne at the outbreak of World War II, and he was called into service by the French. He survived imprisonment in Nazi prisoner of war camps only because his Jewish identity remained hidden. Most of his friends and relatives were not so lucky, and the terrible difference in their fates, based simply on ethnicity, spurred him to do his now classic research.

In his early experiments, Tajfel recruited British school boys at the University of Bristol as participants. The boys estimated the number of dots flashed on a screen and were then categorized into groups of either "overestimators" or "underestimators." These categorizations were actually random, so neither group could logically assume any superiority over the other. But when these boys were given the opportunity to either favor their "ingroup" or discriminate against the "outgroup" in distributing rewards, they usually did so.

These findings are easy to replicate using even more arbitrary categorization procedures, such as randomly assigning participants to merely group "A" or group "B." We now understand this phenomenon as the "minimal group paradigm," and it suggests that human beings have an inbuilt tendency to categorize themselves and others into ingroups or outgroups. Why do we do this?

One reason is that it helps us achieve a useful clarity and certainty about our self-concept. Knowing that one is an "overestimator" not an "underestimator" clarifies who one is, and this in itself is useful. It also provides an opportunity to enhance our self-esteem because we mostly conclude that our own groups are superior to others.[9] When it comes to evaluating the groups we belong to, actual objectivity is elusive, and we like it this way.

THE EMOTIONAL LIFE OF THE TRUE FAN

Sports fans know that the wins and losses of their favorite teams affect them in the emotional gut, even when cheering from the sofa. This may seem strange to those who have little interest in sports. But Tajfel's findings, and the decades of research he has inspired, offer a window into the workings of fandom. A savvy and entertaining confirmation of Tajfel's ideas is Warren St. John's book, *Rammer Jammer Yellow Hammer*.[10] St. John, a native of Tuscaloosa, Alabama, took a six-month sabbatical from his job as a reporter for *The New York Times* to tackle one core question: why in the heck did he care so much about Alabama football?

Enrolled at Columbia University in the early 1980s, St. John and his fellow students were experiencing the longest losing streak in modern college football history. But for St. John, the only team that really mattered was the football team of the University of Alabama, the Crimson Tide. Few other Columbia freshmen understood the significance of the poster of Paul "Bear" Bryant, Alabama's legendary coach, displayed proudly in St. John's dorm room. But at home in Alabama, the zeal of the Crimson Tide fans was unsurpassed. And St. John shared this zeal.

St. John collected most of the material for his book by spending the 1999 fall season attending every Alabama game and immersing himself in the tail-gating culture of a group of Alabama fans. He bought a barely functional RV, dubbed the "Hawg," to attend away games and to provide credibility among the group of fans who also drove their RVs to these games. The RV folks were suspicious of St. John at first, but they could soon tell that wins and losses mattered to him as much as they did to them. He was giddy when Alabama won and numb when it lost. As much as anything, this let him gain the trust of these über-fans.

More than 40 years earlier and across the Atlantic Ocean, Tajfel's experiments had suggested that our allegiances to groups have almost astonishingly unplanned origins. St. John's story also offers good evidence. In Tuscaloosa in the 1940s, his then 18-year-old father, Warren St. John Sr., was struggling with the decision of which university to attend. His first preference was Georgia Tech, but his parents were about to divorce because of his father's chronic drinking problem. St. John's father decided to stay near his parents and attend the University of Alabama. He started his own family nearby. And so, for this tangled set of reasons, his son, Warren, would attach his devotion to the Crimson Tide and would be singing the fight song "Rammer Jammer Yellow Hammer," rather than "(I'm a) Ramblin' Wreck from Georgia Tech."[11]

I grew up in Durham, North Carolina, the home of Duke University, because my parents chose to move there for their own set of haphazard reasons. This meant that the Duke Blue Devils became my Crimson Tide; it was as if a mischievous spirit dropped a magic potion on my boyish eyelids while I slept, as in Shakespeare's *Midsummer Night's Dream*. I awoke to see a Duke Blue Devil mascot, and I have rooted for Duke ever since.

It may seem that our emotions follow from a narrow focus on our own team's winning or losing. But the logic of Tajfel's research suggests that it takes two groups to tango. The British boys in Tajfel's studies favored their own group, but they also *discriminated* against the outgroup. The thrill of winning means that we have won *and* a competitor has lost. Interestingly, this can mean that winning *away* from home feels better than winning at home. This accentuates that the rival is now a "loser." St. John noted this when describing how he felt while leaving Florida's stadium, the "Swamp," after Alabama had beaten Florida. Whereas the visiting Alabama fans seemed drawn together by the high of the victory, the losing Florida fans seemed to separate from each other, like wounded animals needing isolation. Away from the noise of the stadium, they could remove the now ridiculous-looking paint that they had applied fastidiously to their faces before the game. For a moment, St. John felt pity for these miserable creatures. But only for a moment, because when he received a hateful look from one of them, he belted out the Alabama victory cry, "Rammer, Jammer, Yellow Hammer," with wild, unself-conscious abandon.

How much of the satisfaction of winning comes from the defeat of the other team? One way to consider this is to focus on situations in which a rival team loses, but not at the hands of one's own team. After Alabama's loss to Louisiana Tech, St. John was relieved to hear the results of another game, this one between Florida and Tennessee. Since Alabama fans dislike *both* teams, there will be some consolation that at least one of them will have to lose.[12]

Any type of misfortune befalling rival teams, such as injury or scandal, is red meat for people highly invested in their own team. In July 2006, J. J. Redick, the two-time National Collegiate Athletic Association (NCAA) basketball player of the year for Duke University, was arrested for driving under the influence (DUI) of alcohol. This was an embarrassment both for Redick and for Duke. Redick had just graduated and was waiting to learn how he would do in the professional draft. The DUI charge would hurt his chances to do well, which would mean a reduced starting salary. The university was also having a tough time, as it was still reeling from the suspension of its lacrosse team for alleged sexual crimes by team members (the charges were ultimately dropped).[13] Redick's misstep was unwelcome news for Duke fans, but how was it received in Lexington, Kentucky, where I now live, home of the University of Kentucky? When I came to work the following day, one of my colleagues stopped by my office early and asked, "Did you hear about Redick?" He pulled a face of fake compassion and wiped away imaginary tears. When I checked my e-mail, there was a message from another colleague wanting to know if I had heard the "bad" news. Exultation powered every typed word.

Why the *schadenfreude*? Alabama fans may dislike Florida, but I doubt it reaches the scorn for which most University of Kentucky basketball fans have for Duke University. Like Duke, Kentucky is a perennially strong team and usually in the running for the national championship (Kentucky won the national championship most recently in 2012; Duke won in 2011), making it a natural rival. There's another reason. In 1992, Kentucky lost in overtime to Duke in the Eastern Regional Finals. The game was won in the last couple of seconds, when Duke player Christian Laettner performed a turnaround jump shot after having received an improbably accurate full court pass from Grant Hill. This shot had snatched away what had appeared to be a sure victory for Kentucky and a place in the coveted "Final Four," the grouping of four teams that compete in the last phase of the National Championship tournament. To the deep irritation of the Kentucky faithful, a clip of this shot replays every spring during each phase of the national tournament (dubbed "March Madness"), and most Kentucky fans have developed a helpless distaste for Duke ever since. And so, as a rare Duke fan in Lexington, I am a target of teasing—or worse—when anything unfortunate happens to the Duke basketball program.

Kentucky rarely plays against Duke. When it does, and when Kentucky wins (as it did in the 1998 Eastern Regionals), the joy is many-fold greater for Kentucky fans than simply learning about an isolated case of Duke's losing. But any Duke loss, misfortune, or scandal will do in a pinch. And, in these cases, the joy is clearly in the loss.

The particulars of the Duke-Kentucky rivalry may be unique, but its underlying dynamics are universal. A study using Dutch participants provided empirical evidence for what one sees in everyday life.[14] The researchers assessed Dutch soccer fans' reactions to an article describing the loss of the German national team, the Dutch team's main rival. Beforehand, the researchers also measured the extent of the fans' interest in soccer. Indeed, most fans found the loss suffered by Germany pleasing, but the loss generated greater pleasure for those most interested in soccer. These were the fans who had the most to gain emotionally from the rival's loss. In another phase of the study, just before describing their emotional reactions to Germany's losing, some of the fans were primed to think about losses that the Dutch team had suffered in the past. This intensified the pleasure over Germany's loss all the more. These fans had even more to gain, psychologically, from learning about their rival's loss. To fans suddenly concerned with their team's inferiority, a rival's loss was welcome news.

WHAT ARE THE LIMITS TO *SCHADENFREUDE* IN SPORTS?

It is extraordinary that the randomness of our team associations fails to render them trivial in their effects on us.[15] But what are the boundaries to what will produce *schadenfreude*? Cultural norms, if not people's capacity for empathy, dictate that claps and cheers stop if an opposing player gets injured. Natural expressions of true concern sweep over every face. Yet there is a distinction between the immediate emotional reaction at the moment of seeing a player injured and the quick realization of the meaning of the injury for one's own team. Compared to a turnover or missed shot, an injury to an important player on the opposing team leads to a greater competitive gain. In addition to feeling bad for the player, is it reasonable to expect the average person to feel no pleasure over this benefit as well?

St. John certainly admits to the impulse. He describes one game against Louisiana Tech in which, toward the end of the game, quarterback Tim Rattay was leading Tech to what appeared to be a go-ahead score. Rattay had been shredding the Alabama defense with accurate passes, and the Tech offense seemed unstoppable.

> A minute forty left. This time Alabama rushes five linemen. Rattay pumps his arm as the pocket collapses on top of him. As he stumbles backward, his cleats bite the turf awkwardly, violently torquing his right ankle. A hulking two-hundred-forty-pound mass of red in the form of linebacker Darius Gilbert smothers Rattay at the thirty-five. He gets up limping. Tech calls time.

> I have an unsporting feeling: I'm happy he's limping.[16]

But Rattay is able to stay in the game, and he continues to move the team forward and very close to a score. Rattay takes the snap again and, before he can set up to pass, finds himself in the grasp of two Alabama linemen. One has him by his tender ankle and the other by his upper body, creating a twisting effect. He is driven to the ground headfirst as his ankle is wrenched a second time. He is badly injured, hobbles off the field, and collapses on the sideline bench. How does St. John feel about this? It is good news. As St. John summarizes the result,

> He has thrown for 368 yards and three touchdowns, and now he's finished.

> Hallelujah and amen.[17]

Are St. John's sentiments atypical? I doubt it. Some susceptibility to feel this way is part of what it means to be a true fan. When Tom Brady, the New England Patriots' quarterback, tore his anterior cruciate ligament at the beginning of the 2008 season, few fans outside the New England area seemed to show much sympathy. Some New York Jets' fans were admonished for voicing open joy. But one Philadelphia blogger, Andrew Perloff, came to their vigorous defense. He argued that it would be absurd *not* to celebrate if a rival quarterback got injured.[18] Perloff may be an outlier, but in the world of spectator sports, emotions run high and frank expressions of *schadenfreude* are more common than in other areas of life.[19] In sports, people are freer to voice their darker feelings—the same feelings that in most other contexts would be shameful.

Research shows that the average fan is quite capable of being pleased over injuries to players on opposing teams.[20] Charles Hoogland, Ryan Schurtz, and their fellow researchers at the University of Kentucky asked students to respond anonymously to an article describing either a mild (wrist sprain) or a severe injury (knee tear) to a star player for Duke University's basketball team (later, they were told that the event was fictitious). They also completed a measure assessing how identified they were with Kentucky basketball. The results were illuminating. Students who cared little about basketball felt no *schadenfreude* but considerable sympathy for the player. Naturally, sympathy was greater when the injury was severe. The highly identified fans experienced these events very differently: they tended to be pleased over *both* injuries. The severe injury produced less *schadenfreude* than the mild, but even the severe injury produced a significant amount of pleasure. Most students who reported feeling pleased also indicated that they felt this way because injury would help the Kentucky team and hurt the Duke team. This was the main reason, along with a basic dislike of Duke. With a few extreme exceptions, the pleasure these fans felt was mild, especially when the injury was severe—but that many felt any pleasure at all suggests how "negative" events happening to others are interpreted in the eye of the beholder. Being a highly identified fan flipped the normal meaning of the event: a "bad" thing happening to the rival player was, to a degree, "good."[21]

Other research shows that there may be an evolutionary "wired-in" basis for such reactions to a rival group's suffering. In their Princeton University social neuroscience lab, psychologists Mina Cikara, Matthew Botvinick, and Susan Fiske obtained brain scans of either diehard Boston Red Sox or New York

Yankee fans as they watched simulated baseball plays. These plays featured their own team and their rival playing against each other, against a neutral team, or two neutral teams playing against each other. After each play, the participants reported their levels of pleasure, anger, and pain. Own-team winning, beating the rival, and seeing the rival fail against a neutral team all produced more pleasure than did seeing two neutral teams compete against each other. Losing to any team and seeing the rival succeed produced more anger and pain. The brain scans concurred with self-reports. Activation of brain regions associated with pleasure (the ventral striatum—putamen, nucleus accumbens) was also linked with baseball plays in which participants reported being pleased. Activation associated with pain (anterior cingulate cortex and insula) was linked with plays in which participants reported feeling pain. Thus, how the participants' own group was doing compared to the rival outgroup showed close connections with reward and pain systems in the brain. A rival's failure is a good and pleasing thing, whether our own group is doing the vanquishing or another, neutral group is doing it. It gives a pleasing boost to our ingroup identity, which is an important ingredient in our overall self-feelings. As Cikara and her colleagues argue, because these brain systems respond to basic, rudimentary reward and pain situations, they probably developed very early in our evolutionary history. But they may have further evolved to help us respond adaptively to the beneficial or threatening aspects of intergroup contact.[22]

There was another interesting finding in these researchers' study suggesting the intense motivations that can underlie *schadenfreude*. Their participants were contacted a few weeks after giving their reactions in the scanner. They completed a Web survey designed to assess their willingness to harm rival fans or nonrival fans by heckling, insulting, threatening, and hitting. Participants expressed a greater willingness to do these things to rivals than to nonrivals.

There does seem to be something about intergroup dynamics that brings out competitive instincts. When groups are rivals in sports, competition is a given, but the psychology of intergroup relations suggests many reasons why the competitive mindset will be amplified. Social psychologists Chet Insko, Tim Wildschut, Taya Cohen, and others have done many experiments that compare interactions between two individuals with interactions between two groups. Groups end up being more competitive than individuals.[23] This "individual-group discontinuity effect" is remarkably robust and easily replicated. Why? First, it is easier to serve the interests of our group than our own narrow interests without seeming greedy. Second, we are apt to see it as our *duty* as a loyal group member to favor our group. Far from feeling greedy, we take pride in serving our group's interests. Third, we are much more likely to attribute competitive motives, as well as a host of other negative traits, to outgroups than to individuals; outgroups are more difficult to trust and thus require our vigilance. Finally, any aggressive actions we do take seem to be a collective group action rather than our own individual action, and this diffuses our responsibility for the nastiness that may result. No wonder intergroup relations can be so overloaded with conflict.

If you follow golf, you have probably noticed the difference in both players' and spectators' reactions to Ryder Cup matches compared to regular tournaments. The Ryder Cup is a biennial, three-day event that pits the United States against Europe in a series of competitions between players from each team. As sports go, golf is subdued. Player and spectator norms dictate proper decorum and sportsmanship. The bouncy, Gangnam Style dance that Korean golfer James Hahn displayed after sinking a long birdie putt during the final round of the Phoenix Open in February of 2013 was memorable in part because it was so unprecedented.[24] In regular tournaments, spectators display approval at every good shot made and collective groans at every shot missed. On the back of tickets for one major tournament, the Masters, a sentence reads: "Applauding mistakes is no part of the game of golf and we hope that visitors to the Masters will henceforth observe the etiquette and retain their reputation as among the most knowledgeable and courteous of golfing spectators."[25] Players themselves may be elated if a competitor chokes, but we wouldn't know this from their inscrutable demeanors. However, these norms do not apply quite so consistently for the Ryder Cup matches, especially in recent years.

The 1999 Ryder Cup involved an improbable comeback victory for the United States team.[26] As the drama unfolded, the emotions of both players and spectators intensified and erupted openly. The competition came down to a final pairing between American Justin Leonard and Spaniard José María Olazábal. There were two holes to go (the 17th and 18th), and all Leonard had to do to ensure victory for the U.S. team was to win one of the holes or tie both. On the 17th hole, both golfers made the green on their second shots. Leonard's ball was more than 40 feet away, a very difficult putt. Olazábal's was just over 20 feet away: tough but makeable. Leonard putted first and holed it! Even though Olazábal had yet to putt (and, importantly, making it would have extended the match), American players, some fans, and even wives rushed onto the green in celebration. The green was cleared for Olazábal to putt, but he missed. There was celebration over *this* too! So much for the gentleman's game of golf when play is intergroup.[27]

SCHADENFREUDE AND THE BLOOD SPORT OF POLITICS

There are other arenas in life where partisan instincts carry the day—such as in politics. As in sports, any misfortune befalling an opposing party candidate, from sexual scandal to verbal gaffe, improves the chances of one's own candidate or party winning. In the heat of political campaigns, particularly as election night approaches, most events are interpreted through their implications for victory or defeat, even if a misfortune creates general negative effects for everyone. For example, dispiriting economic news might seem to have no positive outcomes for anyone, and yet for a challenger trying to defeat an incumbent, an economic downturn might be good news indeed—because the blame goes to the incumbent. The prospect of winning is the outcome that matters most and so the "bad news" creates *schadenfreude*.[28]

The partisan interests driving the emotions of those invested in politics can sometimes be difficult to uncover, however. The political costs of appearing to lack empathy over bad news are great—much more so than in sports. Regardless of who is losing politically, both sides are required to put on a long face, their actual feelings notwithstanding. Yet the suspected inconsistency between actual and presented feelings is probably why politicians and their allies often accuse their opponents of experiencing unseemly joy when negative events bring good political news.[29] For example, early in the presidential campaign of 2012, President Barack Obama claimed that Republicans greeted with great enthusiasm the bad news of rising gas prices. They were "licking their chops" over the political opportunity, even though this hurt the average consumer. He added, "Only in politics do people root for bad news."[30] There is little doubt that political motivations can promote *schadenfreude*, often camouflaged by mock concern. A juicy scandal suffered by a political adversary is an unfailing trigger. But is it actually true that *schadenfreude* also occurs when the misfortune is general in its negative impact, affecting more than the specific outcomes of a political adversary? I collaborated on a series of studies led by social psychologist David Combs in which we examined this question.[31] We assessed participants' political party affiliations and the intensity of their affiliation. Approximately two months later, just before the 2004 U.S. presidential election and again just before the 2006 midterm elections, we gauged their reactions to news articles entailing misfortunes of two types. Some were partly comic in nature and embarrassing to either the Republican or Democratic Party (e.g., President George W. Bush falling off his bicycle and Senator John Kerry dressed in a comical outfit during a tour at NASA). Others were objectively hurtful to others regardless of political party, yet had implications for the outcome of an upcoming election (a downturn in the economic news and troop deaths in Iraq). We expected that party affiliation would predict the amount of *schadenfreude* felt by the participants.

This is exactly what happened. For the comic misfortunes, the results were straightforward. Democrats found the article about President Bush much more humorous than did Republicans and vice versa for the article about Senator Kerry. Echoing the findings for sports, this pattern was stronger for those highly identified with their party and thus more concerned about the outcome of the election. Essentially, the "same" event was seen as either very funny or not depending on the political vantage point.

But more interesting were the results from the questions about the two "objectively negative" misfortunes. Democrats found both the economic downturn and the troop deaths more pleasing than did Republicans. Once again, this was all the more true for those highly identified with their party and invested in the outcome of the election. Overall, these feelings of pleasure were not extreme. And yet it was true that these objectively negative misfortunes were pleasing to some degree. Because the pleasure increased with strength of identification, it is likely that this pleasure was linked to resulting political gain. I should note that Democrats felt considerable ambivalence about both the economic downturn and the troop deaths. They seemed to welcome the potential political windfall that might follow from each event, yet they still wrestled with the fact that the news was generally bad for almost everyone. By contrast, Republicans reported less *overall* negative affect as the result of these events. This might be because Republicans were trying to downplay the seriousness of the problem so that they would have less reason to feel troubled by bad things brought about by their party.

In our initial studies, we did not find that Republicans also experienced *schadenfreude* over an objectively negative event. This was a quirk of the period when we ran these studies, a period when scandals were the province of Republicans, not Democrats. Bad news on the economic or military front almost always had negative implications for Republicans, whose party was in power. However, we had no reason to believe that political *schadenfreude* was only something Democrats would feel. In another study, we took the liberty of constructing an article that portrayed a negative event that could be pinned on either Democrats or Republicans. The time period for this study was the tail end of the 2008 primary campaign, after both the Democratic candidate, the then Senator Barack Obama, and the Republican candidate, Senator John McCain, had earned their respective party nominations. The article claimed that during the previous year the candidate had pushed through legislation that directly led to higher mortgage foreclosures that devastated the fortunes of many homeowners. The article stressed these broad, negative effects. As in the previous studies, we assessed party affiliation and party identification. Again, the pattern of findings was strikingly dependent on which candidate was associated with the misfortune and the participants' party affiliation and degree of identification with their party.

As illustrated in Figure 3.1, Republicans were more pleased than Democrats when Obama was the cause of the misfortune. The pattern reversed when McCain had pushed the bad legislation through. Those strongly identified with their party showed the pattern all the more. Just as in the competitive realm of sports, when it comes to political fortune, people naturally focus on their own party's success, regardless of how others' outcomes might be affected. As comedian Stephen Colbert put it during the summer of the 2012 presidential campaign between incumbent President Barack Obama and his challenger, Mitt Romney, "I've got some good news and some bad news.

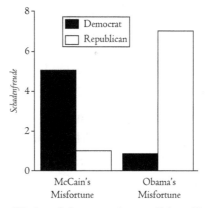

Figure 3.1. The role of party affiliation of observer and party of the sufferer on *schadenfreude*.
Schadenfreude in response to a "misfortune" happening to either McCain or Obama depended on party affiliation of observer.

The good news is there's plenty of bad news, which is great news for Mitt Romney."[32]

The influence of group identification on *schadenfreude* is powerful, but it fits with our inherent social nature. Humans have always lived in groups, and our individual survival has probably been linked with the advantages of being part of a strong group. Group identification is therefore quite automatic and can lead to ingroup favoritism and outgroup antipathy—and *schadenfreude* when a rival outgroup suffers. *Schadenfreude* seems the signature emotion in the competitive rough and tumble of sports and politics, where group allegiances are so intense.

Sometimes sports and politics travel together. Historian Peter Gay grew up in the pre-war Berlin of the 1930s. In his memoir *My German Question*, he describes what it was like to cope with persecutions that he and his family suffered as Jews until they made their escape on a ship to Cuba in 1939.[33] He found refuge from the increasingly vile treatment of the Nazis by immersing himself in sports. He developed passionate attachments to teams and was keenly happy when they did well and miserable when they lost. Also, since he and his father hated the Nazis, they both began identifying with America rather than Germany. By the 1936 Berlin Olympics, they supported "the Americans passionately."[34] They attended most of the events, and their hatred of the Nazis and their love for Americans led to great swings in emotions depending on the outcome of the various games. Gay remembered one event most keenly, the women's 4 × 100-meter relay, in which the highly favored German team lost because they dropped the relay baton:

> As long as I live I shall hear my father's voice as he leaped to his feet… "Die Mädchen haben den Stab verloren!," he shouted, "The girls have dropped the baton!" As Helen Stevens loped to the tape to give the Americans yet another gold medal, the unbeatable models of Nazi womanhood put their arms around each other and cried their German hearts out.… *Schadenfreude* can be one of the greatest joys in life.[35]

Gay is understandably unapologetic about his and his father's *schadenfreude*, and, as I will explore in Chapters 5 and 6, the deservingness of a misfortune can go a long way in disconnecting *schadenfreude* from shame. I am wholly in sync with his experience. I get goosebumps thinking about Jesse Owens defeating the German sprinters as Hitler watched from his stadium seat. Aryan superiority indeed!

Unfortunately, what we see in sports and politics can bring about another sort of chill. The emotions often produced by intergroup relations may also encourage extreme forms of conflict, such as ethnic and religious strife and wars between nations. In this sense, *schadenfreude*, as natural as it is to feel, may be a kind of gateway drug, closing the door on compassion and encouraging darker emotions and actions. Later, in Chapter 10, I venture into this territory.

CHAPTER 4

SELF AND OTHER

We know how little it matters to us whether some *man, a man taken at large and in the abstract, prove a failure or succeed in life,—he may be hanged for aught we care,—but we know the utter momentousness and terribleness of the alternative when the man is the one whose name we ourselves bear. I must not be a failure, is the very loudest of the voices that clamor in each of our breasts: let fail who may, I at least must succeed.*
—WILLIAM JAMES[1]

> *In all Distresses of our Friends*
> *We first consult our private Ends,*
> *While Nature kindly bent to ease us,*
> *Points out some Circumstance to please us.*
> —JONATHAN SWIFT[2]

And afterwards I was very glad that the coolie had been killed; it put me legally in the right and it gave me a sufficient pretext for shooting the elephant.
—GEORGE ORWELL[3]

Suppose you are a woman secretly in love with a man, and you are competing for his love with a good friend of yours. The problem for you is that your friend has many remarkable qualities that make her appealing to this man. But you find out that she has just been fired from the newspaper where she works for plagiarizing someone else's work. How would you feel? Almost certainly you would express public concern for your friend: "Too bad about Betty losing her job. I feel terrible for her."

This is what you are "supposed" to feel, and expressing concern puts you in a flattering light. After all, she is a good friend, and the misfortunes of friends should cause us to feel bad. Part of you undoubtedly does feel bad for her, but you might also add, "Surprising about what Betty did. I guess it's hard to blame the newspaper. She probably needs therapy."

These mild digs at your friend's character and mental health would be a telltale sign that another part of you feels pleased. There might be a touch of the crocodile, crying while eating its victim. Her downfall transforms her from an attractive rival into someone tarnished. Perhaps the critical detail is *exactly* that Betty is now tarnished, a decidedly promising development for you on the romantic front. You might emphasize in your mind the aspect of your feelings that registers concern for her. Perhaps you will convince yourself that compassion is what you are *only* feeling. But in a corner of your being, you may be jumping for joy. The prospect of obtaining your heart's desire may just be the stronger source of your emotions.

Clearly, feeling pleasure because of a friend's troubles leads us into disturbing psychological and moral terrain. We are loath to admit that the *primary* wellspring of our emotions can be raw and narrow self-interest, especially if a friend's well-being is involved. To feel even a momentary secret joy sullies the way we view ourselves. Perhaps we may succeed in falsely convincing the people around us, as well as ourselves, that our motives and the emotions that rest on them are largely selfless. But, in so doing, we may be "strangers to ourselves," as Nietzsche wrote.[4] In the mating game, as in many other competitive arenas of life, self-serving feelings can often go strongly with the grain and overrule our altruistic impulses. The weather vane predicting our stronger emotions in these cases points to the question, "What is in it for me?"

BORN TO BE GOOD OR BAD

In an early episode of *The Simpsons*, Sideshow Bob frames Krusty the Clown for a convenience store robbery and takes over Krusty's show. Sideshow, who fancies himself as far more talented and cultured than Krusty, has been frustrated by playing the minor, sidekick role in what he thinks of as Krusty's crassly produced show. He likes that Krusty is behind bars and enjoys running the show his own way, reading aloud classic literature, making references to Susan Sontag, and singing songs by Cole Porter. After one of his shows, as he walks with a group of toadying staff members, he claims to be feeling sorry for Krusty. He bites his finger and sobs, but after he enters his dressing room and closes the door, his public sobs are transformed into a private, devilish cackle. He has what he wants, full control and the starring role of the show, and he is happy that this came through Krusty's downfall.

Schadenfreude should at least flavor our emotions to the extent that we gain from another person's misfortune, even if empathy arises as well. But Sideshow is a caricature of someone motivated only by self-interest and narrow personal gain; his reaction is pleasure unblended with pity. More typically, our natural tendencies tug us in at least two directions: one toward narrow self-interest and *schadenfreude*, the other toward the interests of others and empathy. Neither direction fully captures human nature.

In the history of psychology, it would be hard to think of someone who had a more razor-sharp and even-handed understanding of human motivation than Harvard psychologist and philosopher William James. Although his landmark work, *The Principles of Psychology*, was published in 1890, contemporary scholars continue to return to his inspired characterizations of how the human mind works. Here is how James captures the two competing sides of human nature:

> In many respects man is the most ruthlessly ferocious of beasts. As with all gregarious animals, "two souls," as Faust says, "dwell with-in his breast," the one of sociability and helpfulness, the other of jealousy and antagonism to his mates. Though in a general way he cannot live without them, yet, as regards to certain individuals, it often falls out that he cannot live with them either.[5]

As contemporary Harvard psychologist Howard Gardner argues, we are neither born to be "good" nor born to be "bad"; we are born to be "good or bad."[6] It is a false dichotomy.

Again, if another person suffers a misfortune that leads to our gain, our feelings usually will be mixed, as the studies on political *schadenfreude* described in Chapter 3 show. And our natural feelings of empathy are likely to be reinforced by cultural norms prescribing this empathy and censuring displays of pleasure over others' suffering. Any secret joys we feel when our rivals lose probably would make most of us feel a little guilty and ashamed.

In the complex interplay between self-interest and other-interest, do emotions connected to self-interest have an edge? Does self-interest have the louder voice—especially in the competitive circumstances that mark many situations in life?[7] Probably. Competition would not lend itself to *schadenfreude* if it did not matter *who* won—"let fail who may, I at least must succeed," as William James put it so well.[8] The 18th-century Irish satirist, Jonathan Swift, made a similar point with these lines:

> Who would not at a crowded Show
> Stand high himself, keep others low?
> I love my Friend as well as you
> But would not have him stop my View.
> Then let him have the higher Post:
> I ask but for an Inch at most.[9]

Most of the time, are we not keenly seeking our own victory? Who among us enters into a competition hoping that the other side wins? When we say "good luck" to an opponent, is it not a contradiction in terms? Competition typically makes our own interests primary. Napoleon advised, "Never interrupt an enemy when he is making a mistake."[10] We may not admit to feeling any happiness over the rival's misfortunes, and it may come blended with empathy and guilt, but at least a trace of the feeling should arise.

Perhaps President Barack Obama shared Napoleon's intuitions during a memorable exchange with Governor Mitt Romney toward the end of the second presidential debate in October 2012. Obama had just finished answering a question about the attack that had occurred the previous month on the U.S. consulate in Benghazi, Libya. This had caused the death of the U.S. ambassador and three other Americans. It was a terrible loss, and it had hit Obama and many in the State Department especially hard because of personal connections with the ambassador. But it had also revealed embarrassing security lapses in the administration's Libya policy, which Romney and other Republicans had been quick to highlight. One theme in their criticisms was that the Obama administration had failed to recognize early enough that the attack had been carried out by terrorists. Romney was expected to score points on this—which he did try to do in response to Obama's answer. Romney focused on Obama's claim, made moments earlier, that on the day after the attack he [Obama] had said that it was "an act of terror." He looked at Obama as if to ask whether this was indeed the president's claim. Obama nodded and said, "That's what I said."

This was a highly charged moment. Romney had thrown down the gauntlet, and Obama responded in kind. Romney appeared absolutely sure that Obama had *not* made the statement, and he said accusingly, "You said in the Rose Garden the day after the attack, it was an act of terror."

Romney then paused, seeming to think that he had the advantage. He raised his eyebrows, gave Obama a look of confident disbelief, and reasserted his position: "It was not a spontaneous demonstration. Is that what you're saying?"

In fact, it was Obama who had the advantage, and Obama knew it. Having calmly completed a sip from a glass of water while Romney was making his assertions, he responded to Romney's allegation by saying, "Please proceed. Please proceed, Governor."

Obama was challenging Romney to keep moving into a trap. The look in his eyes was so intense that the effect was almost physical—and I think there was a whisper of a smile on his face. As comedian Jon Stewart later sized up the moment, when your opponent tells you to proceed, that's "your first clue" that you are in trouble. This is when the door that the Road Runner is offering Wile E. Coyote is "merely paint on a rock."[11] Romney stammered through a few sentences but now seemed to realize that Obama had the upper hand. Indeed, the debate moderator, Candy Crowley, soon confirmed Obama's Rose Garden statement. Obama put an exclamation point on the exchange by saying, "Can you say that a little louder, Candy?"

The debate audience erupted in spontaneous laughter and applause. It was a humiliating moment for Romney, and Obama, no doubt, enjoyed every second of it. Certainly, most Democrats did.[12] It may have been a turning point in the campaign.

THE THEME OF SELF-INTEREST IN HUMAN NATURE

The dual themes of self-interest and other-interest are reflected in any complete analysis of human nature and have been a source of lively debate among thinkers for millennia.[13] But our capacity to feel *schadenfreude* clearly highlights our self-interested side. And so I think that it is worth dwelling briefly here on this theme. There are innumerable scholarly examples to choose from high-lighting the role of self-interest in human actions. In Western philosophy, the British philosopher Thomas Hobbes, mentioned in Chapter 2, argued that a constant desire for power is the prime motivation of human beings.[14] Of course, in psychology, we can turn to Freud, who argued we are essentially self-interested and motivated by pleasure and the desire for sex.[15]

Many well-known maxims capture the idea in succinct ways, such as this one from François de la Rochefoucauld, the 17th-century French writer who I also quoted in Chapter 1: "Few are agreeable in conversation, because each thinks more of what he intends to say than of what others are saying, and listens no more when he himself has a chance to speak."[16] Uncovering people's self-interested ways was a common theme for de la Rochefoucauld, as was *schadenfreude*. Both ideas come through in this axiom: "We all have enough strength to endure the misfortunes of others."[17]

In contemporary popular culture, the ideas proposed by Dale Carnegie are a good example of this theme of self-interest. Carnegie's name is synonymous with simple, common-sense advice on how to get ahead in life. In his long-time best-seller, *How to Win Friends and Influence People*, his main thesis, at which he pounds away in various forms, is that we are primarily motivated to satisfy our own interests, not the interests of others. Carnegie claims that "a person's toothache means more to that person than a famine in China that kills a mil-lion people."[18] He also emphasizes that it is our pride and vanity that cause us to crave appreciation and a sense of our own importance. Therefore, he coun-sels, don't think you will be able to influence others unless you understand that *their* desires and perspectives are what largely motivates them—not your own. His advice is to couch your attempts at influence in terms of the interests of those you are trying to influence, and praise them in any way that is authentic and credible.

Carnegie claims that we show a remarkable capacity to rationalize our behav-ior so that our actions and motives seem noble. No matter the depths of our bad behavior, most of us can produce a positive spin on our motives. He gives the example of Al Capone, the notorious Chicago gangster, who was respon-sible for multiple murders and strong-arm tactics. Did Capone see himself as a criminal? No. He saw himself as "an unappreciated and misunderstood public benefactor"[19] who was simply providing a service to people by giving them access to alcohol during Prohibition. Our self-interest, according to Carnegie, explains why most people are exceedingly prickly when criticized. Far from producing positive changes in behavior, criticism is more likely to inspire defensiveness and retaliatory ill will because it "wounds a person's precious pride, hurts his sense of importance."[20] "Let us remember," Carnegie advises, "we are not dealing with creatures of logic. We are dealing with creatures of emotion, creatures bristling with prejudices and motivated by pride and vanity."[21]

Carnegie's ideas may portray a crude, unbalanced view of human nature, but they have become guiding principles for generations of people wanting to improve their social skills and get ahead in their careers.[22] It seems easy to detect when someone has taken a Dale Carnegie course because he will learn your name, compliment you, and seem to focus on your interests rather than his own. Some are unable to pull off these strategies without coming across as ingratiating and inauthentic. Possession of a native understanding of people may be a necessary ability for Carnegie's advice to work effectively, yet there is merit to his ideas. Many people are so tilted toward their own concerns that they fail to realize that others are similarly focused. But once they take the point of view of those they are trying to influence, they usually become much better at influencing them. Because most people do crave appreciation, they will enjoy any genuine praise that comes their way. Also, they will be most responsive to influence attempts that fit their own interests.[23] When we realize that our own interests are not necessarily the interests of those we are trying to influence, we have taken a huge step toward being more effective in our influence attempts.

Carnegie developed his ideas in the 1920s and '30s, but they never seem to go out of style.[24] Many people, from presidents, coaches, actors, and actresses to scores of successful businesspeople, have taken Dale Carnegie courses and applied his methods to achieve their goals.[25] And Carnegie is far from alone in emphasizing the self-interested side of human nature. A recent example, also in the domain of understanding persuasion and social influence, is the social science approach developed by social psychologist Robert Cialdini, who is perhaps the most respected contemporary expert on these topics. His terrific book, *Influence: Science and Practice*, now in its fifth edition, blends insights from his field experiences with the implications drawn from many laboratory studies done by him and others. He distills this blend into a set of core insights that explain successful persuasion and social influence. Is the principle of self-interest ("the desire to maximize benefits and minimize costs") one of the explanations that he highlights?[26] No—but hardly because he believes it is unimportant. Quite the opposite. He views the principle of self-interest as so fundamental and self-evident that it does not merit a major focus. It is a "motivational given."[27]

SELF-INTEREST WHEN THE CHIPS ARE DOWN

Sometimes, extreme circumstances reveal how self-interest plays a role in our behavior. In November 1959, near a small farming town in Kansas, two small-time ex-cons brutally murdered wealthy farmer Herbert Clutter, his wife, and two children. To detail the crime in his pioneering nonfiction book, *In Cold Blood*, Truman Capote traveled to this town and spent months interviewing residents. He talked with those close to the Clutter family, the law enforcement officers who managed to solve the crime, and, eventually, the murderers themselves, after they were captured and until they were executed.[28] One resident revealed his conflicted reactions to the murders. This was Bob Johnson, Mr. Clutter's life insurance agent. In the months previous to the murders, Mr. Johnson had spent long hours trying to sell a policy to Mr. Clutter, a man very careful with his money. On the very afternoon of the murders, Mr. Johnson had finally convinced Mr. Clutter to buy a policy. It was a $40,000 plan, doubled in the event of accidental death. When Mr. Johnson got word of the murders, he still had Mr. Clutter's signed check to initiate the policy, uncashed in his wallet. His rueful account of his initial reaction on hearing the news suggested more concern about how much money he and his company were going to lose rather than sorrow for the Clutters. He realized that he was the only person still alive who knew about the check. If he destroyed it, no one else would know. Even though Mr. Clutter was a friend, his own wallet was in the forefront of his mind. This concern seemed his first, perhaps primitive, reaction. He did not destroy the check though. By his accounting, his conscience led him to do the right thing, and, after discussing the matter with his manager in Wichita, the company honored the policy. But the tension between self-interest, cleanly entailed by acute monetary concerns, versus the desire to do right by Mr. Clutter was unmistakable.

Another telling incident is described in a World War II memoir, *The Doctor and the Damned*, by French physician and Resistance member Albert Haas. He infiltrated the Nazi High Command of occupied France but was discovered by the Nazis and sent to a series of concentration camps. Because of the awful, barbarous conditions and the enveloping hopelessness among prisoners, these camps did not tend to bring out the most noble, selfless instincts in people. One day, a group of prisoners assaulted one of the guards, and the German officers retaliated by announcing that one in every ten prisoners would be shot. They lined the prisoners up in rows. A guard counted off every ten prisoners and shot the tenth one in succession. Haas was terrified and hoped desperately that he would be lucky to escape selection. As the counting got closer to his position in line, Haas calculated that he would be the next one to die. He noticed that the man just to his left was in weakened physical condition and probably very close to death. Haas eased himself over and pushed the man into his previous place. Within seconds, the German guard placed a gun to the unfortunate man's head and shot him dead. As Haas described it, his "action was so immediate" that he "didn't have time to think it through until after it was done."[29] The memory of this event was fixed in Haas's mind for the rest of his life. Despite the rational thinking girding his decision, feelings of guilt endured. Although Haas's memoir also describes stirring acts of compassion and self-sacrifice, the fearful conditions typically made it difficult for men to see beyond their own survival needs. As Brecht famously wrote, "Food is the first thing—morals follow on."[30]

I have collected anonymous accounts of *schadenfreude* from many people, and the role of self-interest in guiding reactions to others' suffering is a common theme. I am struck by how easily people can come up with powerful experiences—and also how frank they can be about the details—even if these details are unflattering. Many accounts involve competition in its infinite variety. Some echo the conflict experienced by Mr. Johnson when deciding what to do about Mr. Clutter's check, and a few even resonate with Dr. Haas's account. One respondent described a situation in which he had performed poorly at work. He feared a bad evaluation from his supervisor, the person most knowledgeable about his poor performance. Then he heard that the supervisor had taken seriously ill and might have to resign, might even die. On hearing the news, he felt an immediate "yes!" reaction, even though the supervisor was a good person. His honest admission was that a secret joy was his first reaction because this illness might prevent the bad evaluation. Of course, he quickly caught himself and felt a pang of guilt and a surge of sympathy, but his initial reaction sprung from what he stood to gain from the illness.

Because self-interest so often drives our emotional reactions to events, even when these events also entail a misfortune for others, we can feel pleased if we gain from the misfortune.

OUT OF THE MOUTH OF BABES

The unguarded behavior of children can be another window into the self-interested side of human nature. When I was about ten years old, my parents invited a family over for a birthday piñata party. This family had three kids ranging in age from three to eight. They were well behaved until it was time to hit the piñata. First, each wanted to be the first to hit it, and second, each wanted to hit it more than his or her share. My siblings and I backed off and watched them fight over the stick and whack away at the piñata. This was unsettling enough to witness, but nothing compared to what happened when the piñata burst and shot its candy over the ground. All three of these hellions hurled themselves onto the ground and grabbed for the candy. It was a scene worthy of William Golding's *Lord of the Flies*. The eldest of the lot, stout and advantaged in size, soon got the lion's share. I still remember the look on his face as he elbowed aside his smaller siblings. It was unself-conscious and almost brutish, and it revealed how little he cared, in the moment, about their yelps and cries. He wanted more and more, and he was going to get it. Finally, their parents intervened, looking embarrassed.

Most people have seen similar displays in kids. This may be one reason why cultural anthropologist Ernest Becker characterized childhood in this way:

> In childhood we see the struggle for self-esteem at its least disguised. The child is unashamed about what he needs and wants most. His whole organism shouts the claims of his natural narcissism....We like to speak casually about "sibling rivalry," as though it were some kind of byproduct of growing up, a bit of competitiveness and selfishness of children who have been spoiled, who haven't yet grown into a generous social nature. But it is too all-absorbing and relentless to be an aberration, it expresses the heart of the creature: the desire to stand out, to be *the* one in creation. When you combine natural narcissism with the basic need for self-esteem, you create a creature who had to feel himself an object of primary value: first in the universe, representing in himself all of life.[31]

When our younger daughter was four years old, my wife attended a function requiring her to be away and late for dinner. A severe thunderstorm developed by early evening. The sky was purple-black at first, then came the torrents of rain. It was scary. We were characters in *The War of the Worlds,* and the Martians had begun their invasion. My wife called to say she would be delayed because of the storm. My daughter overheard the conversation, and this worried me. Now, the terror of the storm would be compounded by her concern over her mom. And, indeed, the wide-eyed fright in her face seemed to confirm my worry. But, to my surprise she cried out, "What about me?" This really took me aback. After I had a moment to think about it, however, I realized her reaction made a lot of sense. In her young mind, her biggest fear was the implications of her mom not being there for her. What would this mean? Her older sister was also present, and we gave each other bemused looks. Four years her senior, she was more nuanced in her reactions—and could see the humor in it, even as the storm thundered outside. The incident is legend in our family.

When we joke about someone's self-centered behavior, we often blurt out, "What about me?"

In Chapters 1 and 2, I stressed the importance of social comparisons in contributing to our feelings about ourselves and therefore the potential positive effects of downward comparisons—even if they come in the form of misfortunes happening to others. Social comparisons can also reveal the self-interested side of human nature. Becker argues this point as well:

> [T]he child cannot allow himself to be second-best or devalued, much less left out. "You gave him the biggest piece of candy!" "You gave him more juice!" "Here's a little more, then." "Now *she's* got more juice than me!" "You let her light the fire in the fireplace and not me." "Okay, you light a piece of paper." "But this piece of paper is *smaller* than the one she lit." And so on and on....Sibling rivalry is a critical problem that reflects the basic human condition: it is not that children are vicious, selfish, or domineering. It is that they so openly express man's tragic destiny: he must desperately justify himself as an object of primary value in the universe....[32]

HAPPY AND SAD FOR YOU, RELATIVELY SPEAKING

Psychologist Heidi Eyre and I did an experiment that captures some sense of how our reactions to events happening to others are anchored by our own relative experiences.[33] Female undergraduate participants in our study thought that the purpose of the study was to evaluate ways students get feedback on exams. Another student participant would take an IQ test and then be given feedback about her performance using different methods (e.g., oral vs. written). Participants would observe this feedback and evaluate its effectiveness. The actual purpose of the study (revealed when the experiment was over) was to assess how the participants' own *relative* performance on the test would influence their emotional reaction to the other student's performance. To achieve this, we also asked participants to take the test, for the ostensible purpose of their being in a better position to appreciate the experience of the other student. And, as part of their evaluation of the feedback given to the other student, they completed a questionnaire tapping their own emotional reactions (such as "happy for" and "sad for"). In addition, we randomly determined whether the participant and the other student appeared to have done well or poorly on the IQ test (again, at the end of the experiment, the actual nature of what was happening was revealed). We did not measure *schadenfreude* in this study. But it was clear from examining these emotional reactions that participants' sympathy for the other student when she failed, for example, was in part anchored by their own relative performance. Participants' feelings did not simply follow from the objective fact that the other student had "failed." If she failed, participants were less sad for her when they themselves had failed than when they had succeeded. If she succeeded, they were also less happy for her when they themselves had failed than when they had also succeeded.

In sum, participants' reactions to the success and failure of the other student were partly dictated by their own relative performance and not only by the simple fact of the other student's success or failure. It was easy to feel sad for someone else's failure from the vantage point of one's own relative success. It was hard to feel happy for someone's success from the vantage point of one's own relative failure.

THE BALANCE OF SELF-INTEREST AND EMPATHY: A COMPLEX DUALITY

It is important to recognize that even participants who failed usually reported some sympathy for the other failed students—and some happiness for those students who succeeded. That is, they had mixed feelings. None of my suggestions about the self-interested aspect of human nature, let me emphasize once again, aims at cheapening other empathic motivations. I like the way that 18th-century Scottish thinker Adam Smith made a similar point:

> How selfish soever man may be supposed, there are evidently some principles in his nature, which interest him in the fortunes of others, and render their happiness necessary to him, though he derives nothing from it, except the pleasures of seeing it.... That we often derive sorrow from the sorrow of others, is a matter of fact too obvious to require any instances to prove it.... The greatest ruffian, the most hardened violator of the laws of society, is not altogether without it.[34]

It is easy to marshal telling examples of empathy in human beings, and many researchers continue to explore this aspect of human nature.[35] Our dependence on others at all stages of life alone suggests that empathy is itself a product of our evolutionary heritage. Overly self-interested people are likely to be rejected by group members. At the very least, human motivation reflects a complex interplay between concern for self and concern for others.[36] But in trying to comprehend *schadenfreude*, the self-interested side of human nature provides a window into understanding why the misfortunes of others can give us pleasure rather than provoke feelings of empathy.

In Chapter 1, I referred to the research on primates done at the Yerkes National Primate Research Center.[37] When both monkeys were given cucumbers, both seemed satisfied. But when one received a cucumber and the other received a grape, the monkey receiving the cucumber became distressed. These monkeys seemed to show concern over unequal treatment. What I did not mention is that these monkeys appeared unconcerned when getting *more* than their share. Gaining an "unfair" advantage over other monkeys did not seem to cause them distress. Researcher Sarah Brosnan notes: "The capuchins' sense of inequity seems to be very one-sided. It's all about whether or not 'I' got treated unfairly."[38] Not surprisingly, although humans beings are capable of feeling stressed from both unfair *advantage* and unfair *disadvantage*, unfair advantage is generally less troubling than unfair disadvantage.[39]

Psychologists Roy Baumeister and Brad Bushman, in their widely used textbook *Social Psychology and Human Nature*, characterize this duality of self- and other-interest in an interesting way.[40] They emphasize the view that self-interested impulses are especially likely to be rooted in our evolutionary heritage because traits furthering individual survival and reproduction should be favored. This is why Aristotle could suggest that luck is when "a missile hits the next man and misses you."[41] It is hard to imagine living beings surviving without a strong impulse to serve themselves. Baumeister and Bushman also stress that human beings respond to the demands of culture, which typically urges that we adjust our own narrow interests to fit the needs of the group. Even if we want the larger share of the popcorn, we learn to share it equally. This was certainly true as my wife and I watched our daughters mature. As I described in Chapter 1, when they were very young, the disadvantaged one did the protesting and the advantaged one was less perturbed. As they got older, they broadened their concerns, insisted on equality all around, and indeed felt good and took increasing pride in generosity and self-sacrifice. But, even now, if we were to sit down and watch a holiday movie, they would feel puzzled, even a little wounded, if I were to make the mistake of violating the rule equality in distributing popcorn.

Baumeister and Bushman note that many of the rules that we learn, such as turn-taking and respect for the property of others, are based on moral principles that inhibit self-interested behavior. Especially when we are among people we know well, moral emotions such as guilt and shame help in this process. We feel guilty if we satisfy only our own needs and disregard the interests of those in our own group or family, and we feel ashamed when our selfish actions are made public. But our self-interested concerns surface easily. It often requires deliberate, planful efforts on our part to act in culturally appropriate ways. Baumeister and Bushman put it nicely:

> Generally, nature says go, culture says stop....The self is filled with selfish impulses and with the means to restrain them, and many inner conflicts come down to that basic antagonism. That conflict, between selfish impulses and self-control, is probably the most basic conflict in the human psyche.[42]

We can recognize this tension in Mr. Johnson's mind as he struggled with what to do with Mr. Clutter's check, in Dr. Haas's mind as he instinctively changed places with his sick fellow prisoner, and in children's minds when they react to how desired things are divvied out to themselves and others.

Any factor that amplifies the benefits of others' misfortunes for ourselves, such as competition, should promote an "anesthesia of the heart,"[43] to use philosopher Henri Bergson's phrase, and thus intensify our *schadenfreude*. This is one reason we see so much *schadenfreude* in the realms of sports and politics. As the studies I reviewed in Chapter 3 show, misfortunes happening to rival teams and rival political parties produce quick pleasure, especially for people highly identified with their own team or party. This is because when our group identity is important to us, a rival group's loss is good for our own group and thus good for us. In these studies, the perception of self-gain was highly associated with *schadenfreude*. In fact, without this perception, unless our participants had reasons to dislike the rival, there was very little *schadenfreude* reported. Self-interest, through the impact of group identification in these cases, inverted the emotional landscape. For the highly identified fan or political devotee, "bad things" happening to others (if they were rivals) were experienced as good for the group and therefore for the self. In sports, this was true even if the misfortune was a severe injury. In politics, this was true even if the misfortune entailed the death of soldiers. Although *schadenfreude* was typically low in intensity, especially in the case of reactions to troop deaths, and was mixed with concern, misfortunes happening to others created a boost in pleasure to the extent that these events led to self-gain.

In the next chapter, I shift to another important reason why we often feel *schadenfreude*, and this has to do with justice. We care deeply about justice and fairness. Our emotional reactions to both good and bad events happening to others are guided in part by whether these events seem deserved or undeserved, fair or unfair. Misfortunes are bad things, but when we believe that they are deserved, *schadenfreude* is almost sure to follow.

CHAPTER 5

Deserved Misfortunes Are Sweet

When someone who delights in annoying and vexing peace-loving folk receives at last a right good beating, it is certainly an ill, but everyone approves of it and considers it as good in itself, even if nothing further results from it.
—Immanuel Kant[1]

Every decent man will kvell when that sadist goes to jail.
—Leo Rosten[2]

Being an old farm boy myself, chickens coming home to roost never did make me sad; they always made me glad.
—Malcolm X[3]

It is hard to imagine the film industry without the revenge plot. There are inexhaustible variations on the theme, but the basic pattern is simple, predictable—and preferred by viewers. The villain treats the hero badly, and the arc of the story completes itself with the hero taking satisfying revenge. No one is more pleased when justice is served than the eager audience. The villain gets no sympathy. We cheer the outcome. It is highly pleasing to see bad people get what they deserve.

The regular merging in films of justice-inspired revenge with its resulting pleasure suggests a natural link between justice and *schadenfreude*.[4] No manner of bloody end can cause us to blanch. I make this claim confidently because of a two-year stint working as an assistant manager at a movie theater during the late 1970s. The catbird seat in the projectionist booth was a good place for observing audience behavior. We showed many films that made audiences cheer when the villain got what was coming to him, but the one I remember best was the Brian De Palma film, *The Fury*. The villain in this film is an intelligence operative, Ben Childress, played by John Cassavetes, who pitilessly experiments with the lives of two teenagers who happen to have telekinetic powers that could be useful for intelligence purposes. When his actions lead to the death of one of the teens, the other teen turns her telekinetic powers on Childress. Driven by her anger and hatred, she levitates him a few feet off the ground and spins him around with increasing speed until he explodes. The theater audiences were untroubled by the grotesque scene. Some whooped and hollered. They hated this man, played so effectively by Cassavetes. Not only did they want him dead, but they also wanted him minced and pulverized. He *deserved* it. A ghastly end—but pleasing even so.[5]

There seems little question that seeing a just misfortune befalling another causes us to feel pleased, with *schadenfreude* being part of the feeling. Philosopher John Portmann, who has written more on *schadenfreude* than any other scholar, argues it is an emotional corollary of justice.[6] It follows seamlessly from a sense that the misfortune is deserved. And experiments by social psychologists Norman Feather, Wilco van Dijk, and others confirm what one would expect: participants in experiments report more *schadenfreude* over deserved than undeserved misfortunes.[7]

WHAT IS A DESERVED MISFORTUNE?

Typically, we use shared standards to resolve whether a misfortune is deserved. For example, we think people who are *responsible* for their misfortunes also deserve their suffering, and *schadenfreude* is a common response.[8] Brazen swindler Bernie Madoff will go down in history for his Ponzi scheme, breathtaking in scale. Investors appeared to earn returns that were actually generated by later investors. Many high-profile individuals, charities, and nonprofit institutions lost staggering amounts of money, with the tally of the crime reaching $60 billion.[9] In June 2009, when Madoff received his sentence of 150 years, cheers and applause filled the courtroom packed with many of his victims.[10] Even Madoff appeared to finally grasp the enormity of his wrongdoing. After receiving this maximum sentence, he turned to address his victims: "I live in a tormented state knowing the pain and suffering I have created."[11]

Another shared standard for deservingness, often related to responsibility, has to do with balance and fit. We believe that *bad* people deserve a *bad* fate, just as *good* people deserve a *good* fate. We believe that extremely bad behavior deserves extreme punishment, just as extremely good behavior deserves great reward. And so villains such as the character played by Cassavetes in *The Fury* deserve their demise because of their villainous natures and wicked behaviors. They receive their "just desserts." This is pleasing to observe because it agrees with our ideas of how fate should play out. Part of this pleasure is aesthetic. The righting of the balance achieved when bad behavior leads to a bad outcome produces a kind of poetic justice.[12]

Reactions to Madoff's punishment fit this standard as well. He did indeed create extreme suffering and betrayed the trust of many in the process—shamelessly, it seemed—until he was caught.[13] His victims, when given the chance to describe their personal losses before the sentencing, pulled no punches. One victim, Michael Schwartz, whose family used their now lost savings to care for a mentally disabled brother, said, "I only hope that his prison sentence is long enough so that his jail cell will become his coffin."[14] The judge concurred, labeling Madoff's crimes as "extraordinarily evil," which is why for each of the crimes to which Madoff confessed, the maximum sentence was imposed. "It felt good," said Dominic Ambrosino, one of Madoff's many victims, who was outside the courthouse in the crowd when the news of the verdict spread.[15]

One of the most unfortunate tales from the Madoff scandal involved Nobel Peace Prize recipient and Auschwitz survivor Elie Wiesel. Because of Madoff's scheme, Wiesel lost $15 million of funds for his Foundation for Humanity. This was virtually all of the Foundation's endowment. Wiesel was in no forgiving mood. "Psychopath—it's too nice a word for him,"[16] Wiesel said and then went further to recommend a five-year period in a prison cell containing a screen depicting the faces of each of Madoff's victims—presented morning, noon, and night.[17]

Nor was there a trace of sympathy for Madoff when he landed in prison. In fact, some even expressed disappointment that he was sentenced only to a minimum security facility populated largely by other white-collar criminals. The maximum punishment allowed by law seemed hardly enough. Most people took what pleasure they could from the event, nonetheless. This was especially evident on the internet, where most comments were exultant and often crude. A post on one site contained a photo of Madoff's prison bed and included comments such as the following:[18]

Isn't there a bed of nails we could put in there?

There'll be a lot of outrage when people see that he gets a pillow for his head.

I hope those beds are filled with bedbugs.

Madoff's swindle was epoch-making. He betrayed the trust of friends, charities, and, evidently, even his family. He so deserved his punishment by any standard one could point to that no one seemed sorry for him. Rather, just about everyone was openly happy to see this money man with the counterfeit Midas touch reduced to prison inmate.

Schadenfreude clearly thrives when justice is served. As a basis for *schadenfreude*, deservingness has the advantage of seeming to be unrelated to self-interest because the standards for determining justice appear objective rather than personal and thus potentially biased.[19] It is less an "outlaw" emotion, less a shameful feeling. John Portmann describes the example of the influential Roman Catholic theologian Bernard Haring, who declared that *schadenfreude* is an evil, sinful emotion to feel. And yet Haring qualifies this characterization by noting,

Schadenfreude is evil, it is a terrible sin—unless you feel it when the lawful enemies of God are brought low, and then it's a virtue. Why? Because you can then go to the lawful enemies of God and you can say "see, God is making you suffer because you're on a bad path."[20]

I am unaware of any examples in the Gospels of Christ approving of *schadenfreude*. However, Haring's sentiments echo those of other religious thinkers, such as 13th-century Catholic priest St. Thomas Aquinas[21] and 18th-century Christian preacher Jonathan Edwards. The title of one of Edwards's sermons was "Why the Suffering of the Wicked will not be Cause of Grief to the Righteous, but the Contrary."[22] Evil *schadenfreude* may be, but not when the lawful enemies of God get what they deserve. If *sanctified* justice is served, then *schadenfreude* is—well—justified.

THE SINGULAR PLEASURE OF THE FALL
OF A HYPOCRITE

Some types of deservingness produce an especially satisfying *schadenfreude*. I suspect that few things can top the fall of the hypocrite. The archetype of this general category is Jimmy Swaggart, who stands out among a congested group of unforgettable cases. Swaggart, a talented, charismatic entertainer, helped create a particular brand of Christian proselytizing: the TV evangelist. His program, *The Jimmy Swaggart Telecast*, at its peak, was broadcast on hundreds of stations around the globe. Swaggart continues to this day to entertain and attract a large following. He is a remarkable person, a self-made American original. However, he got himself in trouble in the late 1980s. Swaggart not only preached about the consequences of sin, but he also went about exposing the sins of others. Most notably, he accused another well-known evangelist, Jim Bakker, of sexual misconduct. But Swaggart soon lost his high moral footing. A church member, whom Swaggart also accused of sexual misbehavior, hired a private detective to monitor Swaggart's activities. The detective produced photographs showing Swaggart's regular visits to a prostitute. When the leadership of his church, the Assemblies of God, learned of this behavior, they suspended him for three months. In a public confession—a now iconic event in popular culture—Swaggart came before his congregation and television audience to admit his sin and ask for forgiveness.[23]

For many, the image of Swaggart, his face twisted in pain and tears streaming down his cheeks was, and still is, a source of unabashed hilarity. His behavior was full-strength hypocrisy, and his humiliation seemed wholly deserved. Indeed, most media accounts and letters to major papers focused on the hypocrisy of Swaggart's behavior and heaped on the disgust, ridicule, and glee.[24] Making matters worse for Swaggart, and further preserving the likelihood that his confession would persist in cultural memory, was that he returned to the pulpit far from entirely repentant. Thus, the Assemblies of God defrocked him. A few years later, he was caught with yet another prostitute. He didn't bother with contrition this time. He told his congregation, "The Lord told me it's flat none of your business."[25] Confession is one thing; repentance is quite another.[26]

When it comes to hypocrisy and its gratifying exposure, preachers stand out. Many in this line of work seem so quick to point out others' moral failings despite being vulnerable to moral lapses themselves.[27] In the Introduction, I noted the case of George Rekers. His anti-gay initiatives were undone when he was caught hiring a young man from Rentboy.com to accompany him on a trip to Europe. What took Rekers's hypocrisy to its spectacular level—and what made the *schadenfreude* seem so deserved—was that he went out of his way to further policies that harmed gay people for their homosexual behavior—*for more than three decades*. As much as one might feel sorry for Rekers as he combated the white-hot media attention that he received, his prior punishing ways put him at a disadvantage for deflecting *schadenfreude*. Syndicated columnist Leonard Pitts, Jr. wrote, "as perversely entertaining as it is to watch someone work out his private psychodrama in the public space...there is a moral crime here."[28] Rekers condemned and punished people for behaviors he evidently engaged in himself.

Another well-publicized example is Reverend Ted Haggard, who resigned from his mega-church in Colorado Springs after admitting to having homosexual relations with a professional masseur named Mike Jones.[29] Haggard's behavior was patently hypocritical because he had condemned homosexuality so frequently and vigorously. In a documentary, *Jesus Camp*, he proclaimed with conviction that "we don't have to debate about what we should think about homosexual activity. It's written in the Bible."[30] Among his authored books, one had the title *From This Day Forward: Making Your Vows Last a Lifetime*.[31] Jones, for his part, wanted to reveal their relationship because he learned that Haggard (who went by the name of "Art" when he visited Jones) supported a Colorado ballot amendment that would ban same-sex marriage in that state. When Jones realized how much Haggard's influence might lead to passage of the amendment, he grew increasingly angry:

> I remember screaming at his picture on the computer. "You son of a bitch! How dare you!" Art and every straight-acting couple in America could get married and divorced as many times as they liked, yet two men or two women cannot get married even once, much less enjoy the legal benefit of marriage....I was becoming angrier by the minute.[32]...You goddamn hypocrite![33]

Haggard at first denied the allegations of sexual contact,[34] but evidence against this denial mounted quickly, as did the cascading waves of *schadenfreude*. His behavior was satirized in various forms from late-night comedy to a book-length treatment on sex scandals (*The Brotherhood of the Disappearing Pants: A Field Guide to Conservative Sex Scandals*).[35] One response from a pleased blogger summed up the tenor of most reactions: "I love the smell of hypocrisy in the morning."[36]

As for Mike Jones, he claimed to get no pleasure out of exposing Haggard's hypocrisy. Friends even commented that he should have been more lively when interviewed about his relationship with Haggard. But Jones wrote that he "was not happy about anything that had happened."[37] Perhaps he worried that being "lighthearted" would make his motives suspect. In any event, he recognized the glaring inconsistency between Haggard's public denouncements and his private behavior. Wrote Jones, "You must not speak out against something that you do in secret. You must practice what you preach. Let us not forget that the ultimate word in this story is *hypocrisy*."[38]

Preachers are easy targets. Their job requires that they encourage moral behavior in others—even though they are surely flawed themselves, just like their congregations. And, just like the rest of us, for that matter. It is an occupational hazard made worse by a greater need to keep up appearances and maintain at least a higher standing of moral behavior than those around them. But their professional activities may expose them to many powerful temptations as they counsel their flock. Sometimes, to quote Oscar Wilde, "The only way to get rid of a temptation is to yield to it."[39] Swaggart and Haggard both have redeeming qualities, obscured by the exposure of their hypocrisy. I, for one, enjoy Swaggart's preaching and his gospel singing. I am quite taken by the life story of someone who is, as one biographer of Swaggart, Ann Rowe Seaman, put it, so "full of sauce"[40] and so uniquely "poor and gifted and determined."[41] I admire how Haggard and his wife have handled life since his fall from grace. Haggard has been forgiving in his comments about Rekers (e.g., "we are all sinners"),[42] but even he noted that his own actions were not as hypocritical as Rekers's.[43] As I stressed in Chapters 1 and 2, the social science evidence makes clear the self-esteem benefits of seeing oneself as superior to others. When is it not open season for a downward comparison?

Take someone like Bill Bennett, the well-known and accomplished conservative thinker and author of books such as *Moral Compass: Stories for a Life's Journey* and *The Book of Virtues*. Bennett has a reputation in some circles for wagging the moral finger at others for their misbehavior.[44] In 2003, a story circulated that he had been gambling at casinos for years, losing as much as $8 million. Bennett had his defenders.[45] His books on virtues are effective tools for instilling moral values in kids. But many writers seized on this story, notably Michael Kinsley of *Slate Magazine*, who awarded Bennett a "Pulitzer Prize for *schadenfreude*." Kinsley guessed that many sinners had long fantasized that Bennett was a secret member of their club. And so he wrote that "[a]s the joyous word spread, ... cynics everywhere thought, for just a moment: Maybe there is a God after all."[46]

Preachers and others who make a living telling others how to live get top billing in the roll call of fallen hypocrites. But hypocrisy plays no real favorites. Politicians often feel the need to both aggrandize themselves and criticize their opponents in order to get elected. Thus, in scandals and the media attention that surrounds them, they come in at least a close second. Like preachers, who need to impress congregants, politicians have to position themselves to voters and constituents as beyond reproach.

WHY IS IT SUCH FUN TO WATCH HYPOCRITES SUFFER?

Yes, witnessing the suffering of hypocrites is felicitous fun. What is behind this distinctive pleasure? Hypocritical behavior reveals a breakdown between words and deeds, usually having to do with moral behavior. Hypocrites claim virtue but practice sin. According to one gospel account, hypocrisy among the religious leaders even made Jesus angry:

> Woe unto you, scribes and Pharisees, hypocrites! For ye make clean the out-side of the cup and of the platter, but within they are full of extortion and excess....Woe unto you, scribes and Pharisees, hypocrites! For ye are like unto whited sepulchres, which indeed appear beautiful outward, but are within full of dead *men's* bones, and of all uncleanness.[47]

Throughout history and across cultures, people find inconsistent behavior unappealing. "The person whose beliefs, words, and deeds don't match is seen as confused, two-faced, even mentally ill," notes social psychologist Robert Cialdini in his book *Influence: Science and Practice*, also referenced in Chapter 4.[48] Cialdini speculates that being inconsistent may even be worse than being wrong. It smacks of deception and is a violation of trust.

It is more than contempt from the sidelines that leads us to condemn hypocrites. Hypocrites often set themselves up as morally superior, forcing imperfect people around them to ponder their relative moral inferiority. Thus, even before their hypocritical behavior comes to light, hypocrites can be an irritating, disagreeable presence. Their "holier than thou" manner is annoying.[49] For example, Stanford University social psychologist Benoit Monin has found that the presence of a vegetarian can make an omnivore self-conscious. He showed that meat-eaters can feel morally inferior around vegetarians, who they anticipate will show them moral reproach.[50] Vegetarians need not say a word; their very existence, from a meat-eater's point of view, is a moral irritant. And so imagine the pleasure felt by a meat-eater when catching an avowed vegetarian snacking on a rack of ribs. Discovery of this deceptive, hypocritical behavior is a buoyant event. We are not as inferior as we were led to believe; now, we can assume the contrasting position of moral superiority. Naturally, this turn-around feels good.

There is another reason why misfortunes befalling hypocrites should be so satisfying. Often, these misfortunes amount to their being caught doing the *very thing* that they point the finger at others for doing. The precise matching of their moral rebukes and the behavior that lands them in trouble heightens the suitable feel of their downfall. Such reversals have extra special aesthetic appeal.[51] Justice rises up to meet poetry. This helps make the exposure of hypocrisy feel like such a satisfying tale.

I collaborated on an experiment with social psychologist Caitlin Powell in which we showed how pleasing it is to see hypocrites get caught for the precise thing they have criticized others for doing.[52] Our undergraduate participants read what appeared to be an article containing an interview with a fellow student. Half the time, the student interviewed mentioned being an avid member of a campus organization aimed at curtailing as well as punishing plagiarism. The student said in the interview, "It really gets me mad when I see people cheating or plagiarizing. That's just lazy. Our actions have helped in the punishment of three recent cases of cheating." For other participants, the student was simply mentioned as being a member of a university club. In a second, follow-up article, the same student was charged with one of two possible moral lapses: he had been caught and suspended either for plagiarizing or for stealing. We also gave our participants questionnaires after each article to gauge what they thought and felt about the student, his misconduct, and his subsequent punishment. As we expected, the student was seen as more hypocritical when he had been a member of the organization focused on academic misconduct and was subsequently caught plagiarizing compared to when he had just been a member of the club. In this case, our participants also thought his punishment more deserved *and* more pleasing.

What was more interesting was a comparison of reactions to the two kinds of misbehaviors, depending on whether the student had been a member of the organization focused on academic misconduct or the club. When the student had been a member of the club, his misfortune was viewed as *equally* deserved

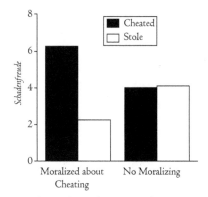

Figure 5.1. The effect of prior moralizing about cheating on the intensity of *schadenfreude.* Prior moralizing about cheating resulted in markedly greater *schadenfreude* in response to a person caught cheating compared to stealing.

and experienced as equally pleasing, regardless of whether he was caught stealing or plagiarizing. After all, both behaviors were morally wrong. How about when the student had been a member of the organization that aimed to combat plagiarism? (See Figure 5.1.) Participants now felt much more pleased when the student got caught for the precise behavior he criticized others for doing, that is, when he was caught plagiarizing. And this is the important part: they felt this way *even though the misbehaviors were equally immoral.* Why? Knowledge that the student had criticized others for plagiarizing transformed how participants felt about the student getting caught. The matching of misconduct and prior statements enhanced the perception of hypocrisy and the deservingness of the misfortune.

There is little doubt about it. Deserved misfortunes are a joy to witness, whether due to hypocrisy, as was the case in this experiment, or to other factors that make misfortunes seem deserved. We can understand why John Portmann, after his wide-ranging scholarly examination of the nature of *schadenfreude*, concluded that deservingness is the main explanation for why we can take pleasure in the misfortunes of others. Indeed, much more can be said about this frequent cause of *schadenfreude*, and the next chapter will take up some of these points.

CHAPTER 6

Justice Gets Personal

O what a brilliant day it is for vengeance!
—Aeschylus[1]

When I heard on the news they finally got him, I was filled with joy.
—Saundra Woolen, mother of an Army sergeant killed in the Pentagon on 9/11, on hearing the news of Osama bin Laden's death[2]

I am not a vengeful man, but I do enjoy a touch of retribution now and then.
—New Yorker cartoon caption by Ed Koren[3]

One appeal of witnessing deserved misfortunes is that any joy we feel can seem free of malice. As I highlighted in the previous chapter, this is especially true when our judgments of deservingness follow from clear, culturally shared standards. Our thinking then has the stamp of impartiality, and we gain the license to feel *righteous* pleasure.[4] But it is important to recognize that there is a strong motivational component to judgments of deservingness that can heighten this pleasure, sometimes in a subjective, biased way. This is a process well worth exploring.

BELIEF IN A JUST WORLD

One way that this subjectivity happens is because we are often motivated to construe the world as a just place. We need to believe in a "just world" in which people generally get what they deserve and deserve what they get.[5] Believing in a just world allows us to go about our lives as if events are guided by predictable, orderly forces. The alternative belief, that the world operates in a random fashion in which deservingness is absent, undermines the value of planful actions. The chaos it implies causes anxiety. These are existential conclusions that most of us resist.

This motive to believe in a just world, originally proposed by psychologist Melvin Lerner, seems innocent enough, but research by Lerner and others shows that it can lead to the ironic effect of blaming innocent people when they suffer. Lerner and his colleague Carolyn Simmons did a series of now-classic studies in the late 1960s and early 1970s that supports this idea. In their first study,[6] observers witnessed another person who appeared to be receiving electric shocks. The reason for these shocks was designed to seem unfair, and, indeed, knowledge that this innocent person was receiving these shocks produced compassion in the observers. When given the opportunity in one condition, they chose to rescue and compensate the person. But an additional condition gave observers the expectation that this person would continue to receive the shocks. Surprisingly, observers tended to derogate the character of the victim. Lerner and Simmons suggested that reactions in *both* conditions could be explained by concerns over justice. If people need to believe that the world is a just place in which people get what they deserve, then they will construe all events as confirming this belief. In the first condition, the easy recognition that the victim was undeserving of the shock led to compassion. In the second condition, the disturbing sense that an innocent victim would continue to receive undeserved shock led to a more *rationalized* view that she must deserve it. Lerner and Simmons argued that the just world motive provides a substantial filter through which we interpret and react to both good and bad things happening to others.

BLAMING THE VICTIM AND ENJOYING IT TOO

The idea that people need to believe in a just world might explain reactions to events that are otherwise perplexing. Consider the memorable case in the late

1980s of a young woman who was raped at knife-point after she had been kidnapped from a Fort Lauderdale restaurant parking lot. The perpetrator was captured and put on trial, but the jurors acquitted him. The jury foreman commented, "We all feel she asked for it [by] the way she was dressed."[7] The victim had been wearing a white lace miniskirt, a tank top, and no underwear. This may have been a provocative, attention-getting ensemble, but did she deserve her assault? It seems the jurors thought as much. Otherwise, how could they have found the perpetrator innocent? A need to believe in a just world may offer one clue.

In his 1980 book, *The Belief in a Just World: A Fundamental Delusion*, Lerner explained how he came up with this idea. His first thoughts about the just world motive were prompted by noticing *schadenfreude* in others. Early in his career, when he worked among doctors and nurses who cared for psychiatric patients, he saw many instances of these professionals joking about their patients behind their backs, sometimes to their faces. These reactions jarred him because, generally, these patients were unlucky souls and had little control over their psychological problems. But he did not view his colleagues as callous. Rather, he concluded that their reactions were coping responses to the unpleasant reality they confronted in these patients. Eventually, he developed the notion of a need to believe in a just world as a prime motive for such reactions. If these patients largely seemed to "deserve" their troubles, one could feel comfortable joking about them.[8]

Lerner's core idea is far-reaching in its implications. Believing in a world with no semblance of justice may indeed lead to an unsettling existential uncertainty. Perhaps even the most world-weary and cynical individual may believe, superstitiously, in a kind of karma. On the outside chance that there is some cosmic principle that will even the balance and correct injustice, they avoid dismissing the fates entirely. A bad deed will be punished—somehow, in some way, at some time.

The possibility that people have a need to believe in a just world connects concerns over justice more strongly with *schadenfreude* for at least two reasons. For one, when there are good, "objective" reasons to blame people for their misfortunes, we will be all the more eager to do so. After all, these valid reasons will go along with the motivational grain. And so, when people appear responsible for their misfortunes (e.g., the driver has an accident while texting or the investment banker goes broke because of risky loan practices), we will zero in on their role in the outcome all the more. We will seize on this information, even embellish it. The objective details of deservingness nicely satisfy the just world motive. The second reason is that the range of unfortunate events that can be construed as "just" increases. This is because our perceptions of causality are likely to be distorted by a need to perceive a just basis for the misfortune when none exists in the first place—which may be why victims are at risk for receiving blame.

That just world motivations might bias our judgments of deservingness raises the general problem of human biases and how they might distort judgments in ways that create *schadenfreude*. Research by social psychologist Mark Alicke demonstrates that we tend to see others as having more control over bad outcomes than they actually have. As a consequence, this perception of "culpable control" means that others will be seen as more blameworthy—which should enhance pleased reactions to their suffering. Generally, we show what Alicke labels an outcome bias. Especially when we want to evaluate someone negatively, we work backward from negative events and perceive more intentionality and foresight than is warranted by the facts.[9] *Schadenfreude* itself may encourage this process: if we find people's suffering amusing, we may conclude that they must be blameworthy.

JUSTICE AND SELF-INTEREST

I noted in Chapter 5 that many were pleased when Bernie Madoff was punished for his Ponzi scheme—but his victims were the ones who cheered the loudest. Likewise, of the many happy at news of Osama Bin Laden's death, relatives of those who died from the terrorist attack master-minded by Bin Laden were most gratified. Saundra Woolen, whose son died in the attack on the Pentagon on September 11, 2001, said, "I wish they could have gotten him alive and given him a slow death....Either way, he's gone and I'm glad."[10] People responsible for treating *us* poorly will seem to deserve their suffering more surely than those who have offended others. And their suffering will create especially satisfying *schadenfreude*. We will delight in it.

In the Aesop fable, the ant felt good to see the grasshopper suffer from hunger. After all, the grasshopper had danced, sung, and taunted the ant during the summer while the ant had worked and stored food for the winter.

We easily develop grievances against people and come to dislike them, sometimes hate them, because they have mistreated us. These can seem petty sentiments, and so they often remain private. But they nonetheless set us up for feeling *schadenfreude* if these people suffer. And we probably feel that even their severe suffering is deserved. I am persuaded on this point by the example of Sir Kenneth Dover, the late distinguished scholar of Greek life, literature, and language.[11] Dover was a prolific scholar who wrote pioneering books on the Greek Classical Age. His writings overturned many assumptions about this period in history. Remarkably, despite his impressive scholarly record earned at Oxford and St. Andrews universities, he may be best known for a few admissions made in a memoir that he wrote at the end of his career.[12] The book includes frank observations about many aspects of his life.[13] The admissions attracting the most attention concerned his intense dislike of another colleague at Oxford, Trevor Aston. This man's exasperatingly manipulative personality, drunken behavior, and chronic threats of suicide caused Dover, who was then the administrator charged with dealing with Aston's behavior, to contemplate ways of furthering these suicidal intentions. Dover wrote: "My problem was one which I feel compelled to define with brutal candour: How to kill him without getting into trouble."[14] Dover had found Aston such a maddening burden that he considered that through an "act of omission" on his own part Aston might act on his suicide threats.[15] Only the legal implications seemed to cause Dover to balk at following through on such plans. When Aston did take his own life, Dover described his own reaction the following morning: "I can't say for sure that the sun was shining, but I certainly felt it was. I said to myself, slowly, 'Day One of the Year One of the Post-Astonian Era.'"[16]

Was Dover lacking in normal human compassion, or was he simply being refreshingly candid in confessing to emotions that others were privately feeling as well?[17] Some, such as James Howard-Johnston, a lecturer in Byzantine studies at Oxford, thought the former, arguing that Dover was "cold, clinical and ahuman."[18] Others, such as Brian Harrison, a history fellow and tutor, disagreed: "I'm 100 percent behind Kenneth. It's astonishing he bore it all those years."[19] Dover was sensitive to this question, and, in his memoir, he related that on hearing the news of Aston's death, two of his colleagues confessed to nothing but relief.[20] He noted that all the proper things were said at Aston's funeral and at his memorial service, but he also believed the general sentiment was probably not far different from his own.

Should readers have been shocked by what Dover wrote about himself? I am inclined to agree with Stephen Halliwell, a professor of Greek at St. Andrews University, who wrote the *Guardian* obituary on Dover. He suggested that Dover was unfairly criticized for honestly exploring his life. Dover embraced the task of giving a frank and full accounting of his emotions and desires; that some parts of life seemed unbecoming obscured the broader story of a remarkably accomplished and admirable person.[21] Putting aside Dover's lethal thoughts, it seems natural to find pleasure when misfortunes happened to people we despise,[22] especially if the reason why we despise them is because they have badly treated us. These misfortunes are likely to "feel" just—and pleasing.

A few years ago, a friend of mine told me about the firing of a manager at a big company. For a time, they had worked at the same company. My friend, as well as many of his co-workers, felt that this man treated them poorly. He had been unkind to many of them, often humiliating and bullying them. But finally, he went too far, and the company president decided to fire him. My friend was decidedly excited about the news—as were many others. My friend said to me, "I finally get it. You know that emotion you study, what is it 'farfegnugen'?"[23] Well, guess what, I'm feeling it." He went on to describe the details with unashamed excitement and delight. He had a smile on his face as wide as the Cheshire Cat in *Alice's Adventures in Wonderland*. It took really disliking (if not hating) someone for him to recognize his own capacity for *schadenfreude*.

In Chapter 4, I noted the memoir written by Albert Haas, the French physician who had survived the German extermination camps.[24] One of the last camps suffered a typhus epidemic. Haas found consolation in the "apolitical nature of the lice that spread the disease."[25] Although many of the SS guards who caught it were healthy enough to recover, some did not. Haas and his friends were "especially pleased when one of the sharpshooters stationed in the watchtower died of the disease."[26]

The life of Malcolm X also provides examples in which the experience of mistreatment from others can cause pleasure if they suffer. As a Muslim minister in the Nation of Islam, Malcolm X used his remarkable rhetorical skills and unique charisma to unsettle the status quo of the 1950s and early 1960s. Perhaps more than anything, he held whites accountable for their abominable treatment of African Americans. One way he achieved this was by suggesting that most slaves would have been happy if their masters suffered. In a speech at Michigan State University in 1962, he contrasted the "house Negro" with the "field Negro." The house Negro, because he lived comparatively better than the field Negro (although he wore the master's secondhand clothes and ate leftovers), identified with the master. The identification was so strong that when the master got sick, he would say, "What's the matter boss, we sick?" But the "house Negro" was the minority. The "field Negroes" made up far greater numbers. How did they feel when the master got sick? Well, as Malcolm X put it: "[T]hey prayed that he'd die. If the house caught on fire, they'd pray for the wind to come along and fan the breeze."[27] The implied *schadenfreude* hit its mark and may have unsettled many listeners. Is there much doubt that misfortunes happening to these slave masters would have seemed well deserved to those suffering slavery in the fields? The resulting *schadenfreude* must have been keen.

REVENGE AND ITS DELIGHTS

When justice is personal, the righting of the wrong can merge most clearly with the powerful motive of revenge and its resulting gratifications. The pleasure derived from revenge is complicated, however, by factors creating ambivalence over this pleasure, at least in the context of present-day Western culture. An example is the experience of Simon Wiesenthal, survivor of multiple Nazi concentration camps, who made it his life's work after World War II to track down and capture Nazis war criminals.[28] His most celebrated case was the capture of Adolf Eichmann, now infamously remembered as one of the main planners of the Holocaust. Eichmann had been hiding in Argentina until a group of Israeli agents snared him as he was coming home from work in a Buenos Aires suburb, thanks in part to Wiesenthal's information gathering. Wiesenthal was associated with other triumphs as well, including exposing the man who had been responsible for arresting Anne Frank and her family. Even though he had exceptional just cause for hunting these men down, he was careful to avoid characterizing his motive as vengeful. Wiesenthal's motto, often repeated, was "Justice, not vengeance."[29]

Wiesenthal denied being motivated by revenge. Rather, he wanted to ensure that people didn't forget the horrors of the Holocaust.[30] He had good reason for this concern. Not long after the war, much of the world largely lost interest in pursuing Nazis. As the Cold War struggle took center stage and became the priority for powerful governments, it became better to use ex-Nazis for various purposes, such as scientific and espionage work, than to investigate whether they had committed war crimes.[31] There was also the problem of some people refusing to believe what had happened. Wiesenthal faced a postwar generation that could conclude that *The Diary of Anne Frank* was a fabrication and the death camps were propaganda. Hunting down Nazis, then, was a way for Wiesenthal to restore and permanently settle the record by bringing those responsible to justice. He may have prudently avoided letting it seem as if his motives were personal, to stay clear of seeming biased, even though he once conceded that he had wanted revenge, "perhaps...for a short time in the very beginning."[32]

Psychologically, however, it is strange to separate justice from revenge. We feel the urge to take revenge when someone has wronged us.[33] We want the person who has wronged us to suffer "just" as we were made to suffer. This is the main point of revenge. We feel that the harm was unfair and unjust. Although though the grievance may sometimes be subjectively derived through self-serving thinking, the experience of it is saturated with a sense of injustice even so. Also, regardless of this potential for self-serving construals, the urge to take revenge, because of its close link with justice, is made up of a mix of related emotions, including anger, hate, indignation, and outrage, all focused on the wrongdoer.

Of course, some instances of personal revenge are uncluttered by ambivalence. Once again, I am reminded of the memoir by French physician Albert Haas, who managed to survive the circles of hell that was the system of German death camps. His last camp was Gusen I (the name itself gives one chills). When word came that the Americans would soon arrive to liberate the camp, the order was given to destroy the whole camp with explosives. This was to hide evidence and prevent testimonies. But a resistance group in the camp had been planning an uprising using stolen weapons and was ready when the SS officers made their move. Despite their weakened state, the prisoners had strength in numbers. Haas was barely lucid from a worsening fever, but with a "gun in his hands" he "found the strength."[34] He joined the fight. Near the camp gates, he confronted a frightened SS man who raised his arms, begged not to be shot, and said, "I didn't do anything!"[35] This was too much for Haas, for, as he candidly described his own reaction, the SS man's "blanket denial of any guilt violently liberated all of the anger I had been storing for so long. I emptied my gun into him."[36]

Evolutionary psychologists conclude that vengeful urges are instinctual. Acting vengefully in response to harm would have served as a powerful, adaptive deterrence against future harm.[37] Legal scholars like Jeffrie Murphy agree. Murphy suggests in his book, *Getting Even: Forgiveness and its Limits*, that vengeful feelings and the actions that they inspire should have helped our ancestors defend both themselves and the moral order.[38] He argues that a moral person must have both an intellectual and emotional reaction to a wrong. It is probably the emotional commitment to insisting on one's rights that leads to corrective action. If we feel no outrage over injustice, we will fail to redress a wrong.[39]

Murphy also reflects on why revenge has such a bad reputation—and so can seem decoupled from justice. He notes that in both literature and films, revenge is so often portrayed in extreme and pathological ways. He gives the example of the early 19th-century novella *Michael Kohlhaas*.[40] In it, a man, angered by mistreatment from an official and by the death of his wife from a beating, goes wild. Before he is through, he sets fire to part of two towns in efforts to find out where the official is hiding, thereby harming many innocent people. Murphy points out that this man's response is "insanely over the top, and if all revenge was like that then nothing could be said for it."[41]

Examples of excessive vengeance in films come easily to mind, such as the ending of *The Fury*, mentioned in Chapter 5. How about *Commando*, one of Arnold Schwarzenegger's early films with a revenge theme? Schwarzenegger's daughter in the film is kidnapped by a group of lowlife criminals, and, in the process of rescuing her, he leaves a path of surplus mayhem and death. In a hyperbolic moment, he skewers a man with an exhaust pipe and says, "let off some steam."[42] The inflated features of these stories are probably part of their appeal. Would they be remembered if the avenging heroes had been less over the top and more proportional in their reactions? Revenge need not be out of proportion. But the trouble is that personal revenge is more likely to be disproportionate to the initial harm. The poet W. H. Auden summed it up in a definition he gave for justice:

> Justice: permission to peck
> a wee bit harder
> than we have been pecked.[43]

And so, as the reaction to being wronged loses a sense of proportionality and seems more rationalized than rational, it is difficult to conclude that "justice" is being served.

Nonetheless, that the nature of the vengeful motivations *can* have a rationalized component does not alter the subjective feel of the related emotions. Misfortunes suffered by others, when *perceived* to be deserved, are pleasing to behold—especially from the vantage point of the person who feels wronged.

When we look behind extreme acts of violence, vengeful motives are a frequent cause.[44] A desire for revenge can be so powerful that it supplants any other concerns, even self-preservation. There is unlikely to be a more powerful human passion than vengeance. The satisfaction of taking revenge is often correspondingly sweet. In a well-known passage, Geronimo describes the moment when he and his fellow Apache warriors exulted over their defeat of the Mexican soldiers who had killed many beloved relatives.

> Still covered with the blood of my enemies, still holding my conquering weapon, still hot with the joy of battle, victory, and vengeance, I was surrounded by the Apache braves and made war chief of all the Apaches. Then I gave orders for scalping the slain. I could not call back my loved ones, I could not bring back the dead Apaches, but I could rejoice in this revenge.[45]

Geronimo and his people had suffered greatly, and so we interpret his actions as revenge, not sadism. But it is likely that in cultures in which revenge is frowned on, enacting it may bring a mixture of both joy and regret. For example, in Western culture today, as much as we enjoy themes of revenge in movies and novels, we are admonished against actually taking revenge ourselves. Legal systems assert their dominion over punishment, making it illegal to take the law into one's own hands. In Judeo-Christian traditions, God reserves the right to take revenge.[46] Phrases from the Bible, such as "Vengeance is mine; I will repay, says the Lord," are lodged in our thinking.[47]

An experiment by Kevin Carlsmith, Tim Wilson, and Dan Gilbert supports this view about our attitudes toward revenge.[48] Undergraduate participants, in groups of four, thought that they were playing a multiround computer game with each other. Players were given some initial money that they could decide to invest in the group or keep for themselves. The instructions made it clear that investing in the group (cooperating) would ultimately lead to the greatest overall amount of money, which would be distributed equally at the end of the game. To stimulate investing, a 40 percent dividend was promised to the group total, to be distributed at the end of the game. But there was also a temptation to "free ride." If a single player decided not to invest in the group, he or she would earn the *most* money, and the other players earn less. What was best for the group was for *all* participants to invest their money—but there was also a temptation to act selfishly by keeping one's money and also receiving a quarter of the final distribution (which was also made larger by investments from others). The experimenters programmed the apparent behavior of the others so that it appeared that one participant ended the game with a series of selfish choices, *even though this participant had urged the other players to cooperate at first.* There was a "punisher" condition in which participants were allowed to financially penalize any or all of the other players (literally, "payback") and then report how they felt. There was also a "forecaster" condition in which participants completed the game and were asked how they *would* feel if they punished this free-rider.

The researchers found that forecasters predicted that retaliation would be *more* satisfying than what was actually reported by punishers. This effect seemed to be explained in part by a measure of how much participants ruminated over their actions. The measure came 10 minutes after the end of the game, suggesting that punishers continued to brood over the experience more than did others. Thus, it appears that people often overestimate how satisfying revenge will be because they are unaware that their vengeful actions can cause them "to continue to think about (rather than forget) those whom they have punished."[49] And so, does revenge work? Because of rumination, there may be at least one downside. If we go by these researchers' results, after people have taken revenge, rumination may cause increased regret over their vengeful behavior.[50]

Social psychologist Sung Hee Kim argues that one function of revenge is to restore self-esteem, diminished by the fact that another person has so little respect for us that they are willing to harm us. Revenge restores the balance.[51] But by stooping to the wrongdoer's level, one's moral superiority can seem diminished, at least in most modern cultures. And so, unless the initial harm is extreme or the harmdoer is especially despicable, internalized norms against taking revenge, guided by culture, may sap the pleasure out of the vengeful act. No wonder countless Hollywood films show heroes who hold back from vengeful behavior until so goaded that few viewers will think less of them. We want our heroes to take revenge, but we want them to do so from an unimpeachable moral high ground.

The research by Carlsmith and his colleagues nicely highlights our complex attitudes toward revenge. It also helps us appreciate another important point about how *schadenfreude* arises. The strong impress of cultural norms against revenge means that indirect revenge, the act of bearing witness, might in fact bring greater pleasure to an individual than direct revenge. There is a lot to be said, in terms of psychological gain, for this indirect, "passive" form of outcome. Although one might temper the outward expression of joy, there is no danger of being browbeaten over having acted in an uncivilized way. At the same time, the misfortune should go a long way toward appeasing vengeful feelings. The experiment by Carlsmith and his colleagues partially supports this idea as well. In an additional condition, participants witnessed the punishment rather than enacting it. This produced significantly greater positive feelings than the "punisher" condition, comparable to another "forecaster" condition in which participants predicted reactions to witnessing the punishment. Participants in the "witness" condition also ruminated less. Yes, witnessing the suffering of someone who has wronged us has a lot going for it over inflicting the suffering ourselves. It is *schadenfreude*, guilt-free (and avoids counter revenge too!).

As I have already noted, some scholars claim that we feel *schadenfreude* only when we witness another person's suffering, not when we bring it about ourselves.[52] *Schadenfreude* is passive, not active. I think this demarcation is too neat. A friend of mine grew up in Eastern Kentucky near the area famous for the feud between the Hatfields and the McCoys. His grandfather was a Golden Gloves winner as a teen and, even in his late eighties, is still ornery and ready for a fight. He was just 16 when Pearl Harbor was attacked, but he lied about his age and enlisted on the spot. Unluckily, he was one of the many American soldiers captured by the Japanese in the Philippines when U.S. forces were overrun and defeated there at the start of the war. He suffered through the Bataan Death March, so rivetingly chronicled in the book *Ghost Soldiers* by Hampton Sides.[53] During the march, a buddy was decapitated by a Japanese soldier simply because he was too big and tall, so it seemed. My friend's grandfather also endured years of appalling hardship in a POW camp until he and the other surviving soldiers were rescued toward the war's end. My friend told me that his grandfather avoided talking about this experience, but there was one incident that he didn't seem to mind telling. He and the other men suffered backbreaking labor in rock quarries. They were overseen by guards who treated them cruelly and who were indifferent when a man died from the labor. The soldiers hated these guards and would find ways to have them suffer "accidental" deaths themselves. Once, his grandfather was carrying a large rock and found himself looking over a ledge where a guard was standing below. He took aim and let the rock fall. It found its target and crushed the guard's head, killing him instantly. He would tell the story with the glee and satisfaction of justice served. It was an invigorating memory of an event now over 60 years past. I confess that when my friend told it to me, I smiled a little as I imagined the incident too.

Were my friend and I the only ones feeling *schadenfreude*, not his grandfather, because he dropped the rock, and we did not? The distinction is far from hard and fast. In any event, I found it difficult to fault my friend's grandfather for taking pleasure in the guard's death. It was not sadistic—he was not someone who ordinarily found joy in hurting others, nor did he seek such pleasures.[54] The conditions were extraordinary. Going by the calculus of fairness created by the war, "justice" was served. In my mind's eye, as my friend recreated the event for me, and as I saw the big grin on his face, I seemed to live vicariously his grandfather's happy satisfaction. I also felt a whiff of something similar when Albert Haas described how he dealt with the SS man, noted earlier in this chapter. There seems no question that misfortunes happening to others who have severely wronged us appeal to our deep-rooted sense of justice.

In *Hamlet*, Shakespeare's timeless revenge drama, Rosencrantz and Guildenstern are to be the instruments of Hamlet's death because they carry sealed instructions for the King of England to have him killed. But Hamlet intercepts the document, changes the instructions, and directs that the English King have them killed instead. He feels little compunction because these two school friends are toadies to his treacherous uncle and are to be trusted like "adders fang'd." He anticipates being pleased over the outcome, "For 'tis the sport to have the engineer hoist with his own petard."[55] Certainly, we expect the playgoer to sense the sport in it too.

CHAPTER 7

Humilitainment

I feel the producers really exploited my lack of talent at this time. I looked like an idiot up there.
I want to be good, not something that people will laugh at.
     —William Hung[1]

It has always been a mystery to me how men can feel themselves honored by the humiliation
of their fellow beings.
     —Mahatma Gandhi[2]

The boys who pull out grasshoppers' legs and butterflies' wings, and disembowel every frog they
catch, have no thought *at all about the matter.*
     —William James[3]

In the fall of 2003, William Hung was an obscure college student at the University of California at Berkeley. Nothing about him foretold the celebrity status he would achieve by mid-January 2004 as the last auditioner for the third season of the hugely popular reality TV program *American Idol*. He wasn't much of a singer. He performed his audition song, "She Bangs," with an awkwardness that was the furthest contrast to the sexy original rendition by Ricky Martin. He had a nerdy, toothy look evoking Mickey Rooney's regrettable portrayal of a Chinese houseboy in *Breakfast at Tiffany's*—complete with an accent left over from having spent the first 11 years of his life in Hong Kong.[4,5] Hung turned out to have an endearing, good-natured authenticity to him that transcended the entertainment aims of the show, leading to a wacky run of post-series celebrity fame. But he was no *American Idol.*

Although Hung had no shot at winning the competition, the producers of the show must have suspected, *must have known*, that they had in their hands the kind of comically bad performance that many viewers of the show would enjoy. Thousands auditioned for the final 12 spots in the *Idol* competition. During the preliminary weeks, when the highlights of these auditions are broadcast, the producers could choose to air only the cream of this very large crop. But part of the formula for the success of *Idol* has been that bad performances and the judges' sometimes withering critiques are highlighted as frequently as the talented contestants and the high praise that they receive. With Hung, the best of the worst was saved for last. His humiliation, anticipated with teaser clips, was a ratings bonanza.

THE APPEAL OF HUMILIATING THE NAIVE AND UNTALENTED

Since its first season in 2002, *American Idol* has been one of the most highly viewed shows on television. There are many reasons for its popularity. Without the opportunity to see talented performers emerge from obscurity and mature over the weeks and to enjoy the guest appearances from music legends, it would lack the cocktail of ingredients that has made it so popular. But without the balance of viewing the humiliating as well as the uplifting, the extraordinary appeal of the show would diminish.

Humiliation might be one of the worst things to experience.[6] It renders a person's public self in tatters, defective and inferior. People in such situations are like marks who are socially dead and who, as sociologist Erving Goffman wrote, "are sorted but not segregated, and continue to walk among the living."[7]

How could it be pleasing to witness such social pain? One explanation may be in the social comparison implications for the viewer. As I underlined in Chapters 1 and 2, any downward comparison, which is partly what another person's humiliation implies, can mix pleasure with sympathy. Certainly, for most people, watching William Hung performing so poorly on the screen created no danger of experiencing a deflating "upward comparison" with someone superior to them. On any visible dimension of comparison, even the most ordinary viewers would have felt no threat to their own relative judgment of themselves. On the contrary, most people could conclude that they were better looking, more talented, more self-aware—more cool—than Hung. Some non-Asians might have found satisfaction in having certain stereotypes of Asians supported, especially if they had felt their own self-worth threatened by this successful minority group. Over time, Hung showed many admirable qualities. His authenticity was beguiling. But, at his audition, just about anyone could have felt superior by contemplating the absurd idea that someone of Hung's appearance and talents could imagine advancing to the next level of competition, much less winning.

Why aren't the pleasures of feeling superior supplanted by the pain of witnessing humiliation? While Hung performed, viewers saw sequences of the judges' mockery. One judge, Randy Jackson, placed a handkerchief over his face to hide his reaction. Paula Abdul, usually soft-hearted, was unable to suppress her outward amusement; she laughed uncontrollably. The third judge, Simon Cowell, characteristically felt no need to hide his ridicule and soon stopped the performance before Hung had finished the song. "You can't sing, you can't dance, so what do you want me to say?"[8] Painful for Hung, clearly, but not for many viewers. In fact, the judges' mockery was a large part of the fun. Their reactions seemed irrepressible—a natural response to the performance. Here were three experts clearly enjoying themselves—approving similar pleasure in viewers.

Other features of *Idol* also help promote amusement over empathy. Auditioners perform *voluntarily*. No one forces them to audition. If someone has the naive boldness to think he could be the next *American Idol*, why should he receive our pity if his performance is embarrassing and receives ridicule? And when contestants become hostile in response to pretty accurate feedback, as many do, they deserve their humiliation all the more. As I underscored in Chapters 5 and 6, the deservingness of a misfortune is a sure path to creating *schadenfreude*. The modest and lovable manner of William Hung was atypical of poor performers selected to be aired. Hung's response to Simon Cowell's critique was, "Um, I already gave my best, and I have no regrets at all."[9] This response, so humble and uncoached, was surely one reason why Hung was eventually embraced by viewers and why he enjoyed more than his 15 minutes of fame. Indeed, he benefited financially from his anti-*Idol* persona. More typical was the behavior of another contestant from the preliminary rounds, Alexis Cohen, who delivered a barrage of vulgar expletives and gestures in response to Simon Cowell's critique of her performance. Cameras followed her progress out of the audition room and building as she continued her crude outbursts. At some level, this was also "fun" to watch. It added to the perception of her "inferiority" and upheld the deservingness of her humiliation.

American Idol is just one example of a prominent theme in reality TV in which humiliation is the marquee ingredient. According to analysis by media scholar Amber Watts, there has been an increase in the number of programs (such as *Survivor, Big Brother, America's Next Top Model, Jersey Shore*) that use real-life formats to exploit the many ways that people can be humiliated as a lure for pleasing viewers.[10] They are on tap 24/7, as is obvious to anyone who watches a small sample of television fare. A content analysis conducted by other media scholars, Sara Booker and Brad Waite, revealed that the most popular reality TV shows contained more humiliation than scripted dramas did. They coined the term "humilitainment" to label the trend.[11]

When it comes to exploiting the entertainment value of humiliation, *American Idol* is actually tame. It has counternarratives of success attributed to hard work and sometimes goosebumps-raising performances. Moreover, some auditioners seem eager to trade public humiliation for short-lived fame. Other programs use especially intense humiliation as their main hook.

I caught a memorable episode of the short-lived show called *Howie Do It*.[12] Hosted by comedian Howie Mandel, it was a kind of amplified *Candid Camera*, as its core element was to show people humiliating themselves in an array of extreme situations. The show's Web site unashamedly summarized the goals of the show:

> During each episode, the unsuspecting "marks" will think they are the stars of a new game show or reality show, or that they are auditioning for a big Hollywood movie or television role. What they don't realize is, they ARE the stars, but in the most unexpected and entertaining way, in front of millions of people on TV.[13]

One segment of the episode involved a young man taking part in a campy Japanese-style game show. The game required that he shock a fellow teammate at doubling levels each time he, himself, missed a general knowledge question. His teammate was actually hired by the show and was instructed to pretend to feel the shocks. The producers rigged things so that at the third missed question, the teammate screamed in pain as the electrical current hissed, smoked, and crackled. He then appeared to lose consciousness and stop breathing. Quick CPR by two paramedics got him breathing again but not before the young man concluded for a brief moment that he had killed his teammate.

Viewers see this replayed on a large screen to a live audience who know what was actually going on and laugh along. Mandel provided a running commentary designed to heighten the laughs. Adding to the humiliation, "contestants" wore skintight suits resembling long underwear and silly red caps. Of course, the young man was extremely upset to think that he had almost killed his teammate, but the studio audience howled with laughter and clapped their approval.

The young man was soon told that his teammate was actually just fine and that he had been part of a big joke. This knowledge hardly soothed him. This "mark" was not easily cooled. He yelled, "You cruel sons of bitches!!!!" How did Mandel respond to this outburst? He looked at the viewing audience and admitted, "We're cruel, but we're funny."[14] We can admire Mandel's honesty, but, to paraphrase George Orwell as he recalled the humiliations he suffered as a boy in a British boarding school—such, such are the joys.[15]

HUMILITAINMENT FINDS A HOME ON THE SEAMY SIDE: *TO CATCH A PREDATOR*

Perhaps the most extreme example of popular programs using intense humiliation as their main draw is *To Catch a Predator*. It ceased to produce new episodes in 2008 but lives on as of this writing in reruns and specials, such as *Predator Raw*. Each episode involves a sting operation designed to catch a series of men who appear intent on having sexual relations with a minor, leading up to an ignominious turnaround in every case when each man is told that his recorded exposure will be aired on national TV. This show, its value in alerting the public to the problem of online predators notwithstanding, may just be the consummate example of how far television can go to use humiliation as the key attraction. Its features provide insights into why this type of show can also supply opportunities for *schadenfreude*. It is worth a full look.

The producers of *Predator* work with a private watchdog organization to pull off these stings. Staff members create fake, underage decoys who post their identities on chat lines. Early in the chats, the decoys use photos to suggest that they are underage and make false statements that their ages range from 12 to 15. The decoys refrain from initiating sexual content, but once this line has been crossed by a man, they vigorously begin exploring sexual themes in any direction that can seem credible. The decoy will encourage a meeting. If the man agrees to meet, a site is selected, usually a suburban house, arranged by a phone call with the decoy. These men turn out to be easy marks. "The result? Fish in a barrel, every time," as Jesse Wegman of the *Huffington Post* summed it up.[16]

The site for the meeting has been rigged inside and out with as many as 17 hidden cameras and microphones. A young-looking actress, made to look like the girl or boy the man is expecting to meet, greets the man and invites him into a patio area or inside the house, typically the kitchen. After a brief conversation that ends with the decoy stepping out of the room for a moment, the man is surprised by the host of the show, Chris Hansen—who enters usually through the door that the decoy has just exited. Often, Hansen begins his conversation in an ironic way, as if his surprise presence is part of an *expected* flow of events. "What's going on?" he might say. Or, if the man has brought some food and drink for the anticipated meeting, Hansen might say, "Going to have some fun?" Hansen asks the man to take a seat, a request that is usually obeyed instantly, and then he begins questioning the man's reasons for being in the house. Viewers already know some basic details of the online conversation, and when the man almost invariably lies about his intentions, viewers follow along as Hansen confronts the lies. Hansen typically holds a copy of what appears to be the full transcript of the online chat the man has had with the decoy. He will read passages from the transcript that seem to contradict the man's claims while viewers watch the man hesitating and squirming as he tries to reconcile the transcript statements with his current claims. Once Hansen seems satisfied the conversation has run its course, he announces who he is and why he's there, using variants of this phrase:

> "I have to tell you that I am Chris Hansen with *Dateline NBC* and we are doing a story about computer predators/adults who try to meet teens online for sex."[17]

As Hansen reveals his identity, two *Dateline* employees with large, shoulder-held TV cameras and others holding long boom mikes emerge through entryways and angle for close views of how these men react. Of course, these men have already grasped that things are not going according to plan. Most realize that they are in big trouble. Some even recognize Hansen from earlier episodes of the show. But it is when Hansen makes his announcement and the cameras appear that the full enormity of what is coming down usually hits them. Some men immediately try to exit the room, covering their faces with their hands or by pulling up their shirts. Some collapse to the floor. When a man makes it outside, he finds himself surrounded by a group of police officers with guns raised, shrieking commands, who usually shove the man to the ground, handcuff him from the back, and then lead him away to certain arrest and arraignment. These men—instant pariahs—are surely near the bottom of fortune's wheel. With their reputations obliterated, they have, to borrow from Shakespeare, lost the immortal part of themselves, and what remains is bestial.[18]

While it aired new episodes, the show was a dependable sweeps-week draw for NBC. The reruns, some in more elaborated and less edited formats, continue to attract audiences. Chris Hansen has become an icon and a go-to expert on online predatory behavior—even testifying before Congress on the issue. The show is so well known that some of its repeated features have become part of popular culture, most notably the point in each exchange when the men realize they are to be humiliated on national TV, their lives wrecked in the most public of ways. The phrase, "I am Chris Hansen" is now recognized to the point of frequent parody, appearing in some form in shows ranging from *The Simpsons* to *30 Rock*.[19]

WHY IS *PREDATOR* SO ENTERTAINING?

As Steven Winn of *Slate Magazine* put it so aptly, the show has a "queasily transfixing" appeal.[20] There are a number of reasons why. Clearly, some viewers enjoy learning about the dirty secrets of others. On the grand stage of the 21st-century public square, the show is gossip writ large. There is certainly a pornographic element in the details of the online chats between the men and the decoys.[21] Little is left to the imagination. And because this material is presented in the context of what appears to be a highly *deserved* sting, many viewers can obscure their awareness of any voyeuristic and pornographic gratifications by being distracted by righteous disgust. Again, as I stressed in Chapters 5 and 6, deserved misfortunes create a direct route to *schadenfreude*. But, as with the appeal of watching William Hung and the other less talented *American Idol* contestants, we also know that a big part of the *comic* pleasure likely results from the satisfaction of downward comparisons, spiked with humiliation. And *Predator* seems to take this satisfaction to another level. How else could Jimmy Kimmel say this when introducing Chris Hansen as a guest for his late night TV show?

> Our next guest is host of the funniest comedy on television. It's called *To Catch a Predator*....If you've never seen it, it's like *Punk'd* for pedophiles. It's a great show....Please say hello to Chris Hansen.[22]

Predator may help us feel better about ourselves, but this is through another person's extreme humiliation. How is it that the producers of *Predator* are able to get away with humiliating someone so mercilessly on national TV, let alone serving up almost wall-to-wall opportunities for raw voyeuristic and pornographic fulfillment? How is it that they can trust that most people will find it agreeable to see these men brought down so low and exposed in such a vulgar, grubby glare—without being troubled by guilt?

THE LOWEST OF THE LOW

The title of the show tells us a lot. Viewers watch with the operating assumption that the men who appear are "predators"—classified into a squalid category of humanity from the start. There are few labels held with deeper disgust, fear, and contempt than a "sexual predator" or "pedophile," even though the actual category of behavior is broad and ranges in degree and in cure.[23] Taking sexual advantage of a child ranks at or near the top of most cultures' lists of immoral behaviors. It is not only repugnant, but it also suggests an unalterable defect, a moral leprosy, a placing of the person outside the circle of humanity. Even among criminals, molesting a child is usually regarded with a singular disgust and probably boosts the self-esteem of the average inmate—"Yes, I killed a man, but I'm no pedophile."[24] Sex offenders are at special risk for physical assault in prison as a result. Unlike even felons convicted of violent crimes, those convicted of child molestation are put on criminal registries and Web sites. Letters are sent out to neighbors when they move into a neighborhood, and they are often unable to live within 1,000 feet of schools.

Predator does nothing to alter these perceptions. Douglas McCollam, an attorney and contributing writer for *Columbia Journalism Review*, argues that the label "predator" alone creates immediate images in many viewers' minds of a "drooling, trench-coated sex fiend hanging out at the local playground with a bag full of candy."[25] Because of high-profile examples of child abductions, such as the Polly Klaas case, people's fears are easily roused.[26] These under-standable worries grant the show considerable leeway. There seems little need to treat such people with the basic respect owed to human beings. Not only do they deserve humiliation, but they *must* be caught and then humiliated as a way of *deterring* this vile behavior. This must help explain why viewers find the humiliation of these men so pleasing—and entertaining. After all, these men, these *predators*, showed up with the clear intent to have sexual contact with young girls or boys. Where is the defense for this? Humiliation is a just start of their punishment, a fitting prelude to a jail sentence.

Gone are the days of public hangings, stocks, and pillories. Modern sensibilities lead us to resist the idea that we could deliberately take pleasure in seeing others humiliated—as least as official policy.[27] Yet these sensibilities seem to remain inert in the case of people who molest children. This means that the producers of *Predator* have an effective firewall against easy criticism when the show humiliates these men, clearing all involved from guilty feelings for participating in this process. The crystalline sense of deservingness creates a clear path to *schadenfreude* free of moral clutter.

It is hard to overstate the contempt most people have for those who molest children. It is so deep and reflexive that showing any sympathy for these men risks contaminating the defender with a nasty stench. I feel this risk keenly. I have read many commentaries on *Predator*, and no writer fails to include a phrase emphasizing disgust over the category of behavior linked with these men, lest even implied criticism of those involved with the show be miscon-strued. McCollam raises credible concerns about the ethics of the show, but even he notes, "Let's concede up front that this is an unsympathetic bunch of would-be perverts."[28] Truly, "predators" are a reviled category of humanity—the idea of viewing them in less than damning terms has potentially tainting effects on one who would do so.

AN EASY STACKING OF THE DECK

Even if viewers are inclined to doubt the full deservingness of the humiliations, the show does little to further these inclinations. Although it may seem that the evidence against these men is being provided in a fair and objective fashion, in fact, viewers get only an edited version of the online chat and of the interaction between Hansen and the men. The average episode contains about 10 interactions. Some of the chats extended for days; others for less than an hour. At best, viewers learn only a few exchanged lines of dialogue, and many of those selected are sexually charged. *Dateline* claims that the men always initiate the sexual material and suggest the initial meeting, but the development of this stage is rarely laid out in full. There is little room for fine distinctions here, and viewers have to trust the producers in these and other matters. And there is little in how the program evolves that disrupts this structure and causes one to distrust the narrative themes. The chat conversations, when they are described, are often typed on the screen as if they are happening live. These recreations may exaggerate the implications of the written content and heighten their effects on viewers. The material selected is usually so disgusting (and "titillating") and incriminating on the face of it that anything else that might have been said that might allow viewers to see the men in a more positive light seems beside the point. Furthermore, Hansen always has a big ace up his sleeve: No matter what the apparent extenuating circumstances might be, no matter what excuses the men might have, the plain fact is that they showed up at a place expecting to have some sort of sexual contact with an underage person. There seems no cause to be distracted by trivial details that suggest a more nuanced view of the "predator's" intentions, responsibility, and blameworthiness.

Hansen has a huge advantage over these men as he steps into the room. Hansen knows what their apparent intentions are, as do viewers, and these men *do not know* that he knows (and they surely do not know that a national audience will also know). Hansen uses this advantage to make these men look foolish, ridiculous, or worse—dialing up the humiliation and the *schadenfreude.*

There are many deft touches enhanced by the editing process that add to the potential for *schadenfreude*. One case involved a prominent doctor who carried himself in a refined way compared with most of the other men. The sting in this case was situated in the backyard patio of a house in a suburban neighborhood. The decoy appeared to have made a pitcher of crushed ice lemonade, and she suggested that he pour her a drink while she went to change clothes. As he slanted the pitcher, the ice held for a moment and then avalanched down, overloading the glass and splattering. The man tried to maintain his cool. This small comic moment at the doctor's expense added entertainment value to the bigger drama that began when the doctor looked around for a towel, only to spot *Dateline*'s camera crew. He immediately turned, put on his sunglasses in a feckless instinctive move to hide his identity, and raced out of the patio. When he got to the driveway of the house, three police officers swarmed, guns drawn in his direction, directing him to the ground. He was pushed to the cement pavement and handcuffed behind his back.[29]

It was an extraordinary sequence with few unrecorded moments. In addition to the police officers, other people also came into view. One man held a large TV camera over his shoulder and moved within a few feet to the doctor's right. A second man moved in from the right. Why these extra cameras? After all, there were fixed, hidden cameras already covering every square inch of space (as the editing shows). Might not these added cameras cause viewers to start wondering whether law enforcement is getting too cozy with the entertainment goals of *Dateline*? However, if the point of the show and secret of its appeal are to humiliate for entertainment purposes, the host of cameras amplifies the sense of excruciating humiliation. With the next edited shot, there was a close-up of the doctor's reactions (some moments after he had been allowed to get back on his feet). This shot showed him protesting, "I wasn't doing anything…oh man, I wasn't doing anything!" From about two feet away, there was a shot of his face as he seems to be half crying. Then, there was a series of edited moments taking viewers through the process of the doctor being questioned by police. Hansen's voice provided steady commentary, at once clinically detached ("The police ask routine, personal questions but the doctor appears distracted"), sometimes expressing disbelief ("It's hard to believe that someone of his stature would show up to meet a girl who said she was 13"), always with an air of moral superiority free of qualms about the tactics being used.[30]

Hansen appears well insulated from doubts about the appropriateness of the tactics employed by the show. In an informative 2007 book he wrote about *Predator*, he described many of his interactions with these men. He stated that it was important not to go "overboard" but granted the "prosecutorial" tone that he sometimes used. Although there were "some sad cases that come knocking on our door,"[31] he emphasized the manipulative features of the men's actions, the offensive aspects of their chats, the fact that they made the initial contact, the intent of their actions, and the overall threat they pose for society. With these and other arguments in mind, he admitted that none of the many exchanges inspired in him any strong sympathy.[32]

THE GRATIFICATIONS OF HIGH STATUS AND REVENGE

Social science research on why people watch reality TV generally fits with why certain content appears in programs such as *American Idol* and *Predator*. Media researchers Steven Reiss and James Wiltz argue that people will watch TV, or any stimulus, to satisfy basic motives and desires. In one study, Reiss and Wiltz examined the free-time activities of a large group of people. Participants indicated how much they enjoyed different types of travel, sports, and music, as well as various popular reality TV programs. They also completed a personality measure tapping 16 basic desires and their associated joys when these desires are fulfilled. Two motives were most clearly associated with reality TV viewing. The strongest of these two was *status*, or, as Reiss and Wiltz define it, a "desire for prestige" with the associated joy of "self-importance." The next strongest was vengeance, a "desire to get even" with the associated joy of "vindication." The greater the number of reality TV shows viewed and liked, the more important these two desires.[33]

Both *American Idol* and *Predator* invite viewers to feel good about their relative status and hence their sense of importance. With *Idol*, William Hung was given screen time more because of his inferiority rather than his talent. With *Predator*, the men profiled are already near the lowest of the low, but the show is structured to bring them down further still. As Dan Snierson and Josh Wolk of

Entertainment Weekly commented bluntly, "Do we watch reality television for precious insight into the human condition? Please. We watch for those awkward scenes that make us feel a smidge better about our own little unfilmed lives."[34]

What about vengeance? In both programs, and more so with *Predator*, participants "deserve" their humiliations. With *Idol*, these humiliated contestants are considered fools to think they could win. No one is forcing them to audition. With *Predator*, what else do these perverted men deserve but crushing humiliation—and, of course, jail time? They receive what they deserve.

In some ways, shows like *Predator* really do harken back to times when humiliation was a more general punishment of choice for many cultures.[35] Nathaniel Hawthorne's *The Scarlet Letter* is a work of fiction, but it captures the spirit of the Puritans who believed that punishment *should* be humiliating.[36] Until the 19th century, stocks and pillories served as a public punishment instead of imprisonment. The convicted were sentenced to stand in public sites, such as village greens, that people frequented. It was common for people to make fun of victims and throw all manner of things at them, from rotten food to dead animals. The pillory was a favorite because the victim's face was immobilized, along with his or her hands. Sometimes the ears were nailed to the wood to prevent the face from moving. For many onlookers, it must have been a feasting time for *schadenfreude*.[37]

Are some segments of television programming today serving a similar role? *Predator* educates viewers about a potential societal threat, but compelling entertainment seems to drive many of the choices that the producers make. The gratifications of humiliation and resulting guilt-free *schadenfreude* are a potent draw. Deserved humiliation and anticipated *schadenfreude* seem to be the formula for the show's success, and the decisions appear made to swell the gratifying effects of this pairing.

The producers of *Predator* (as well as *American Idol* and so many other reality TV shows) know there is a line that they must avoid crossing. They may test the limits of humiliation, but they surely wish to avoid the chance that *schadenfreude* is replaced by outrage over the treatment of these men, a decline in viewing, and the withdrawal of advertising dollars. The continued reruns of *Predator* suggest that this line has not been crossed, even though no new shows have been produced since the 2008 episode in which a Texas man committed suicide rather than face arrest and public humiliation. Hansen has achieved cool celebrity status and is respected enough to testify before Congress on the problems of online sexual predators, despite using humiliation as a catapult to these achievements. This suggests that it is these men who have been effectively demonized rather than the show itself.

I admit, however, that watching Hansen orchestrate the humiliations on *Predator* is disturbing—even as I will also admit that he and his production team have created a show that captivates irresistibly. I find myself at once entertained, spellbound, and more than a little sullied. I am reminded of the ratings-hungry reporter, Richard "Dick" Thornburg, in the *Die Hard* films. He's the one who gets punched in the nose by Detective John McClane's wife, Holly, in the first movie and tasered toward the end of the second. The reporter, played perfectly by the actor William Atherton, is a caricature of the type, and yet he seems hardly exaggerated. In the first movie, when part of an office building explodes, Thornburg witnesses the explosion but doesn't know yet whether his camera man had his camera running:

THORNBURG: My God, tell me you got that.
CAMERAMAN: I got it, I got it!!
THORNBURG: Eat your heart out, Channel Five![38]

For Thornburg, it is all about getting the sensational story. He claims that he is a crusader for the public's "right to know," but he will do just about anything to get the salacious scoop. If this means humiliating people on TV, so be it. Ironically, after Holly hits him on the nose, he gets a restraining order against her—because "that woman assaulted me and she humiliated me in public."[39] This was a brilliant touch.

The cut-throat demand for high TV ratings in the increasingly complex, competitive world of TV programming probably creates strong pressure to go for the entertainment jugular rather than for sensation-free edification. The gratifications of witnessing seemingly deserved humiliation—and the resulting *schadenfreude*—must be hard to resist exploiting under these intensely competitive conditions. At the same time, should we encourage programs such as *Predator*? The exposing of a societal problem and its prevention are the ostensible goals of the show, although Hansen also admits his desire to produce absorbing television. It is not at all clear that the show uncovers a behavior that is as much a problem as the episodes suggest.[40] Many experts claim that most sexual abuse of children occurs in the family or among people who know each other.[41] How likely is it that the majority of men who show up at the sites would have done so without the ambitious tactics of the decoys? How much do we learn about the nature of online sexual deviancy from this show? Does *Predator* create a false impression of the problem, stirring unwarranted fears, creating events rather than reporting on them, and inappropriately demonizing some individuals rather than helping the public understand the general problem of deviant sexual behavior?

Most of all, should a civilized society sanction the humiliation of people—regardless of what they appear to have done? Should we encourage shows that rely so much on the gratifications of this form of guilt-free *schadenfreude*? Make no mistake about it: Hansen inflicts extreme humiliation on these men. Although it is easy to conclude that they deserve it, there is huge collateral damage done to the families of these men, innocent people who must deal with the shame and embarrassment of the aftermath long after *Predator* moves on. Whether Hansen and the show's producers (and viewers) should feel sympathy for these men is a complex moral question. Is *Predator* a bold, groundbreaking work of investigative television or, to use Jesse Wegman's words again, a "theater of cheap morality, wrapped in an orgy of self-righteousness"?[42] You be the judge.

CHAPTER 8

THERE'S SOMETHING ABOUT ENVY

The man who is delighted by others' misfortunes is identical with the man who envies others' prosperity. For anyone who is pained by the occurrence or existence of a given thing must be pleased by that thing's non-existence or destruction.
—ARISTOTLE[1]

Envy… is hatred in so far as it affects a man so that he is sad at the good fortune of another person and is glad when any evil happens to him.
—BARUCH SPINOZA[2]

Homer: Oh, come on, Lisa. I'm just glad to see him fall flat on his butt! He's usually all happy and comfortable, and surrounded by loved ones, and it makes me feel… what's the opposite of that shameful joy thing of yours?
Lisa: Sour grapes.
Homer: Boy, those Germans have a word for everything!
—THE SIMPSONS[3]

Koreans have a phrase, "When my cousin buys a rice paddy, my stomach twists." This captures well the pain of envy and helps explain why a misfortune that brings an envied person down can yield emotional pay dirt in the form of *schadenfreude*. Envy is the familiar blend of painful discontent, ill will, and resentment that can result from noticing another person enjoying something that you desire but seem unable to obtain. But when a misfortune befalls the envied person, the negative comparison drops away, bringing relief and joy. Contemplating it "untwists" the stomach. The misfortune may even provide hope for the future by hobbling the competition.

Envy is a universal human emotion. It is natural to feel envy when we lose out to someone else and must continue to gaze on the envied person now enjoying the desired thing.[4] As I underscored in Chapters 1 and 2, social comparisons matter, and envy is a special testimony to this fact. It matters when a person you love chooses someone else who is better looking and more talented than you. It matters when you aspire to compose great music but fail—in contrast to a friend who receives high praise for his recent composition. Most people can identify with the character of Salieri in the film *Amadeus*. Salieri, although accomplished in his own right, is rendered mediocre by Mozart's effortless genius. Perhaps there is no better capturing of envy than the scene in the film where F. Murray Abraham (as Salieri) looks up in pain while sight-reading the miraculous notes on the originals of Mozart's sheet music.[5]

Social psychologist and neuroscientist Susan Fiske, whose book, *Envy Up, Scorn Down: How Status Divides Us*, I referred to in Chapter 1, summarizes the neuroscientific evidence on envy and suggests a consistent pattern of brain activation when people feel envy.[6] People responding to envied targets show brain activation in the amygdala, an area of the brain associated with reactions to something emotionally important to us, whether good or bad.[7] The amygdala appears necessary for the instant evaluation of another person who is superior to us in an important way. Another part of the brain linked with envy is the anterior cingulate cortex (ACC). Fiske suggests that the ACC is important for envy as a "discrepancy detector."[8] In a sense, we cannot feel envy unless we detect a *difference* between ourselves and another (superior) person. A third part of the brain associated with envy is the medial prefrontal cortex (mPFC), an area that activates when we try to understand what another person is thinking and feeling.[9] This seems especially important to do when confronted with an envied person who may control things we desire and whose presence matters to us more than does the presence of people with lower status.[10] In sum, as one would expect with a blended emotion such as envy, brain activation is complex. But there seems to be a signature pattern of brain activation in envy that reflects our recognition that someone has something important that we do not have and that requires our keen attention if we are to do something about it.

Throughout this book, I have highlighted the personal benefits that result from downward comparisons. I have argued that just about any misfortune befalling another person, from a social comparison perspective, is a potential boost to self-esteem. Where such misfortunes reside, opportunity knocks. If any misfortune suffered by another person has the potential to yield benefit, a misfortune befalling an envied person is a windfall.[11] Since envy thrives best in competitive circumstances, the gain from the misfortune will often be direct and palpable. Also, if we envy someone, by definition, the dimension of comparison is important to us, thus adding greater value to what the misfortune brings. An extra bonus is that the misfortune eliminates the painful feeling of envy—no small thing. It is transformational: inferiority and its unpleasantness become superiority and its joys. A painful upward comparison, in an instant, becomes a pleasing downward comparison. What a turnaround! The late American novelist and curmudgeon Gore Vidal famously confessed, "Every time a friend succeeds, I die a little."[12] If this can be true, then the reverse can also be true: "Every time a friend fails, I am more alive."

Mark Twain, in his autobiography *Life on the Mississippi*, describes a boyhood event in Hannibal, Missouri, that illustrates the joys of seeing an envied person fall. In his retelling, Twain notes that *every* boy in Hannibal, Twain heading the list, wanted to be a riverboat pilot and wanted it badly. One boy had the job that they craved. He also knew more than they did about everything that mattered, and he pulled it off with the kind of style that had the girls riveted. Twain's and his friends' hostile envy was about as intense as one sees it—and great was the *schadenfreude* when the boy suffered a misfortune on his riverboat. Twain described the feeling: "When his boat blew up at last, it diffused a tranquil contentment among us such as we had not known for months."[13]

Novelist Walker Percy also captures the easy path from envy to *schadenfreude* in his eccentric self-help book, *Lost in the Cosmos*:[14]

> Your neighbor comes out to get his paper. You look at him sympathetically. You know he has been having severe chest pains and is facing coronary bypass surgery. But he is not acting like a cardiac patient this morning. Over he jogs in his sweat pants, all smiles. He has triple good news. His chest ailment turns out to be hiatal hernia, not serious. He's got a promotion and is moving to Greenwich [CT], where he can keep his boat in the water rather than on a trailer.
>
> "Great, Charlie! I'm really happy for you."
>
> Are you happy for him?[15]

No, Percy argues. For the "envious self," this kind of news is hardly cheering. He asks the question, "how much good news about Charlie can you tolerate without compensatory catastrophes...?"[16] It is as if something unfortunate happening to Charlie is the only possible cure for the envy and unease that his good news is actually causing in you. What are the chances that your own fortunes will change? Also, is there a morally acceptable or doable way to bring Charlie down? Percy bets that if you find out later that the promotion failed to come through, this would not be bad news at all—although you may try to deny, suppress, or hide the joy the news brings.

WHAT IS THE EMPIRICAL EVIDENCE LINKING
ENVY WITH *SCHADENFREUDE*?

Cognitive psychologist Terry Turner and I were part of a group of researchers who collaborated on an experiment testing a connection between envy and *schadenfreude*.[17] We first evoked envy in our undergraduate participants by showing them a videotaped interview with a student who had plans to attend medical school. We hired an actor to play the role of either a superior (enviable) student or an average (unenviable) student (eventually, we let the participants in on our deception). As he discussed his academic and extracurricular activities, we added scenes in which he was engaging in these activities. In the envy version, we showed him working away on his organic chemistry homework, peering through a microscope in a cutting-edge biology lab, and walking across Harvard Yard on his way to a summer class that should help him get into Harvard Medical School. We also included a scene showing him entering an expensive condo that his father had bought for him while he was in school, driving a BMW, and cooking a meal with an attractive girlfriend. In the average version, we showed him struggling with his homework and washing test tubes in a biology lab. We also showed him entering an unappealing high-rise dorm, riding crowded public transportation, and eating pizza with an average-looking female acquaintance. Toward the end of each version, we paused the tape for a minute and asked participants to complete a mood questionnaire. Some of the items measured envy. Then, an epilogue appeared on the screen to update the participants about what had happened to the student since the interview. This was where we inserted a misfortune. The epilogue noted that the student had been arrested for stealing amphetamines from the lab where he worked and thus had been forced to delay plans for medical school. A second questionnaire contained items tapping pleased reactions (such as "happy over what happened to the student since the interview"), camouflaged by other items designed to distract the participants from our actual focus.

As we expected, participants felt more *schadenfreude* when the enviable student suffered than when the average student suffered. Even more telling, any envy reported after the initial pause in the video "explained" much of this effect. Participants who actually reported feeling envy while watching the first part of the interview were most likely to find the later misfortune pleasing.

Also, participants who reported higher scores on a personality measure of envy completed before viewing the interview (i.e., "envious types") were more likely to find the misfortune pleasing.

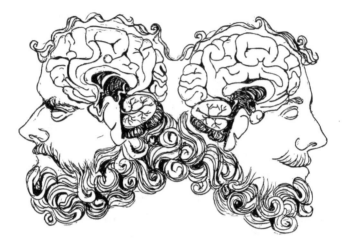

Research using brain-scan technology also supports the links between envy and pleasure—if the envied person suffers.[18] A Japanese team of researchers monitored the brain activity of people as they imagined themselves in scenarios in which another person was of either higher or lower status. Imagining envy activated the anterior cingulate cortex (ACC), an area of the brain also associated with experiencing physical pain. The participants were then asked to picture this other person suffering various forms of misfortune, from financial trouble to physical illness. This produced greater brain activity in a different brain region, the striatum, a pleasure or reward center. This pattern of activation was particularly true for those participants who had reported the most envy at first. The lead researcher, Hidehiko Takahashi, summed up the results using the Japanese phrase translated as: "The misfortunes of others are the taste of honey."[19] A Korean might add: Especially if the stomach has been twisting because of envy.

ENVY AND HOSTILITY

Envy is a blend of ingredients, each of which helps explain why it should be so closely connected to *schadenfreude*. Twain's account highlighted the envied boy's superiority, and envy indeed contains feelings of inferiority. But without accompanying hostility, the *schadenfreude* produced by the boat exploding would hardly have been so gratifying. People do not feel warmly toward those whom they envy. In fact, hostility may just be the feature of envy that distinguishes it from other unpleasant reactions to another person's superiority, such as discontent alone.[20] One can readily see this in Twain's account. The envy that he and his friends felt is far from benign. The hostility in their envy clearly contributed to why the explosion caused such contentment.[21]

There is something distinctive about envious hostility. People feeling envy are willing to take a loss themselves, as long as it also means that the envied person will suffer *to the same or greater relative degree.*[22] This can seem self-defeating, unless one realizes that, to the envious, the pleasure of gaining in an absolute sense is often insufficient compensation for the pain produced by witnessing the envied person's relative advantage.

It is no surprise that envy is usually a hostile emotion. Envy is triggered by noticing a desired attribute enjoyed by another person, but it is largely a frustrated desire.[23] Imagine the experience of noticing and wanting another person's advantage, all the while knowing that one could easily obtain the advantage eventually. Perhaps there would be a brief feeling of discontent, but this would go away quickly when the path to acquiring the advantage was clear. This is a type of envy, but it is benign in nature.[24] The experience would also be quite different if the prospect of obtaining the advantage were naught. The comparison itself may seem irrelevant. We envy people who are *similar* to ourselves, *except* that they have something that we dearly want but lack. The similarity allows us to imagine the possibility of our having the longed for thing, even if we know that our desires are likely to be frustrated. When we envy in a hostile way, we have the tantalizing sense of what it might be like to obtain what we want—we can almost taste it—but we feel unable to realize this desire. The frustration of any keen desire, the blocking of an important goal, is a dependable recipe for anger and hostility—and will often trigger *schadenfreude* if the person causing the frustration suffers.

THE TABLOIDS AND THEIR APPEAL

The editors of popular tabloid magazines such as *The National Enquirer* would appreciate the observations of Edmund Burke, the 18th-century philosopher and statesman. He suggested that theatergoers anticipating a tragic performance on the stage would quickly lose interest and empty themselves from the theater if they heard that a criminal was just about to be executed *outside* in a nearby square.[25] Burke believed that people have "a degree of delight, and that no small one, in the real misfortunes and pains of others."[26] Moreover, in his view, real misfortune probably trumps the "imitative arts" every time.

Some have taken this way of thinking even further. In their recent biography of Mao Tse-tung, *Mao: The Unknown Story*, Jung Chang and Jon Halliday make a persuasive case that Mao was someone who took a special joy "in upheaval and destruction."[27] But Mao also believed that he was not alone in this preference. For instance, he claimed that *most* people would choose war over perpetual harmony:

> Long-lasting peace is unendurable to human beings, and tidal waves of disturbance have to be created in this state of peace....When we look at history, we adore the times of [war] when dramas happened one after another...which make reading about them great fun. When we get to the periods of peace and prosperity, we are bored.[28]

Still others, such as Walker Percy, referred to earlier, have also claimed that people have a pleasure-linked fascination with disasters and calamity, at least when these things are happening to *other* people. The appeal of the tabloid press and the heavy coverage of crime, accidents, and natural disasters in the media testify to the validity of such claims.

In addition to its reliance on real misfortunes, another consistent feature of the tabloid press is its focus on troubles happening to celebrities. A study of *The National Enquirer* that I conducted with psychologist Katie Boucher confirmed this feature.[29] We examined approximately 10 weeks of the magazine. For each story, we rated the status of the person who was the main focus of the story and how much the story detailed a misfortune happening to that person (e.g., divorce, scandal, weight gain, health problem, etc.). As the status of the person in the story increased, so did the likelihood that the story would also focus on misfortune. Although the rich and famous fascinate us, most of us feel infinitely less successful than they and probably a little envious. The chance to read about celebrities' setbacks can be irresistible—which explains much of the success of these tabloid magazines.

MARTHA STEWART'S MISFORTUNES

Let's examine the case of Martha Stewart,[30] whose indictment and ultimate conviction for insider trading was made to order for the tabloids. Stewart is a remarkable American success story.[31] But, as Michael Kinsley noted in an article for *Slate*, her period of troubles represent "a landmark in the history of *schadenfreude*."[32] Following an early career as a model and then as a successful stockbroker, she began using her long-time interests in cooking, decorating, and gardening to develop a series of hugely successful business ventures. After releasing her first book, *Entertaining*, which was a *New York Times* best seller, she published an almost yearly series of other books on topics ranging from pies, hors d'oeuvres, and weddings to pulling off a good Christmas celebration. Along the way, she wrote many magazine articles and newspaper columns and was a frequent guest on national television programs. By the time of her indictment for insider trading in 2002, she had created a media empire, Martha Stewart Living Omnimedia. It included her own magazine, *Martha Stewart Living*, a daily television program, a catalogue business (Martha by Mail), and a floral business (marthastewartflowers.com), among other ventures. When the company went public on the New York Stock Exchange, she became a billionaire by the end of the first day.

Before her indictment, as the information about her alleged stock dealings emerged, Martha Stewart allowed Jeffrey Toobin, legal analyst for *The New Yorker*, to interview her at her Connecticut home. He sensed that the ridicule that she was receiving (such as the mock magazine cover, *Martha Stewart Living Behind Bars*, ubiquitous on the internet) was probably taking its toll on her, and perhaps this seemed an opportunity to right the balance. His observations about this interview were telling.

Stewart positioned herself as just about perfect, free of flaws. When Toobin was served Hunan chicken for lunch, Stewart emphasized that it was done in the best way possible. She gave Toobin the recipe so that he could replicate it later. The kitchen was a marvel, with every kind of copper pot and cooking utensil. From Toobin's description, everything about her home, about what she served him, about the way she talked and acted, seemed aimed at perfection. Martha Stewart was bound to inspire envy in many people.[33]

One senses a point of diminishing returns for Stewart as she revealed more about her marvelous lifestyle to Toobin, and comments Stewart made suggest that she was aware of the social price that could come with advantage. Toobin noticed that the utensils for lunch were thin silver chopsticks. Stewart explained that the Chinese associate thinner chopsticks with higher status, which was why she "got the thinnest I could find. That's why people hate me."[34] She also seemed well aware of the *schadenfreude* that her troubles were creating for her and even used the word to capture the tabloid tenor of most reactions in the media. However, she expressed puzzlement over this because she saw her main business as helping women become better homemakers, and "to be maligned for that is kind of weird."[35]

Stewart must have suffered emotionally from the negative treatment she received from much of the media. Toobin noted that the unattractive photos of her in many publications irritated her. She was peeved that *Newsweek* suggested that people would have treated her better if she had been nicer to them during her rise to fame and fortune. Her response in each case added to the sense that she thought pretty highly of herself. About the photos, she said, "I'm a pretty photogenic person, I mean, and they manage to find the doozies." About *Newsweek's* claim, she said, "I've never not been nice to anybody."[36]

Stewart's unrelenting pursuit of flawless living, however close it may be to realization, created a big target for envy. I am reminded of an often-cited experiment done in the mid-sixties by Elliot Aronson and colleagues, not long after the Kennedy administration's bungling of the U.S. invasion of Cuba.[37] These social psychologists had been struck by the rise in Kennedy's popularity following this botched attempt to overthrow Fidel Castro. Why would a blunder enhance the president's appeal? They reasoned that before this incident, the handsome, talented, and charismatic Kennedy had cut so impressive a figure that people might have found it hard to identify with him and thus harder to like him. Perhaps this mistake "humanized" him and made him more likeable. In the experiment, participants listened to an audio tape that showed another student either performing very well or poorly on a College Bowl quiz team. Following the performance, in some cases, participants then heard the student clumsily spill a cup of coffee. Ordinarily, one might think that clumsy behavior would reduce the appeal of both the superior and the average performing student. But, consistent with the researchers' intuitions, the superior performing student actually became more attractive and likeable after he made the spill. If there were any negative effects from the pratfall, the average performer was perceived as less appealing.

There is an obvious lesson in this for Stewart. As much as people might admire competence in other people, when it comes to actually liking them, too much competence becomes a handicap. We might select the highly able person to be our neurosurgeon or lawyer, but we avoid their company for lunch. A touch of weakness and vulnerability goes a long way toward taking the edge off the negative effects of superiority. A little less of "I'm Chevy Chase, and you're not" tempers the evil eye of envy.[38]

I remember watching a *Tonight Show* episode around the time of the first season of *Survivor*, the TV show that helped ignite the ascent of reality TV. The basic premise of the show is that members of a group are placed in a remote location and are voted off until a single "survivor" remains. Jay Leno, the host of the *Tonight Show*, chose about five people from his audience and placed them on a traffic "island" somewhere in Burbank. In a parody of the *Survivor* show, every 10 minutes or so, the audience voted off one from the group. Before they headed off for the island, however, Leno introduced the group to the studio audience by letting each say a few things about him- or herself. I recall being a little put off by the first person. He introduced himself as student at Stanford University and then went on to list a number of impressive things he was doing with his life. My initial, uncharitable thought was that I hoped he was the first to go. And I was not surprised when he was indeed the first one booted off. The other contestants were just average folks and certainly were more humble. I detected an emphatic quality in the audience's first decision—and a burst of laughter-spiked *schadenfreude* accompanied the verdict.

Jay Leno would appreciate as much as anyone why his audience laughed. In a 2012 interview for *Parade Magazine*, he was asked whether the digital age influenced his approach to comedy. His view was that humor really does not change much across generations. If one looks at the trappings, there may appear to be shifts in content, but the underlying process remains the same. Leno summed it up well: "[T]he fat rich man stepping out of the Cadillac and into the mud puddle" will always be funny.[39]

Leno's use of an expensive car in his example is a good one because cars are often the source of envy. According to consumer psychologist Jill Sundie, the flaunting of luxury items has been a common theme in most cultures from Egyptian pharaohs and their golden thrones to present-day Lamborghini owners.[40] In one study, she and her colleagues asked student participants to respond to one of two articles about another student. The student in the article noted that he owned either a $65,000 Mercedes or a $16,080 Ford Focus. Next, participants were shown a photo ostensibly taken of the car, along with a verbal description of how it had broken down at a shopping center, stranding the owner and some friends. The car had its hood up in the photo. Students reading about the Mercedes were much more likely to admit feeling happy when learning of the car's mechanical failure than were those who read about the Ford, especially if they also reported envy. As one would expect when envy is involved, it was the hostility linked with their envy that was most closely related to their pleasure.

An analogue to this study occurred in May 2012, and a video of it produced many approving hits.[41] A bright yellow, $250,000 Lamborghini spun out of control when the driver oversteered while making a turn in a Chicago neighborhood. No one was hurt, but the car ended up sandwiched between two other cars. Passengers in another car recorded it all. The video shows these passengers making invidious comments about the Lamborghini before the accident and their keen delight after it happened. They even turned around to take a closer look. The video collected 3.8 million views in about 24 hours based on YouTube statistics. The unfortunate driver took quite a ribbing. Echoing SpiderMan, one viewer wrote, "With great horsepower comes great responsibility."[42] Many were dripping with envious ill will, with comments such as "stupid rich person trying to show off."[43]

ENVY IMPOSES ITS WILL

Would hostile envy directed at highly competent people be dulled if they are likeable? One would think so. Naturally, the suffering of a liked person produces less *schadenfreude* than the suffering of a disliked person, as studies led by Israeli psychologist Shlomo Hareli confirm.[44] And yet envy may not be so easily defeated. In our study that I described earlier, where we showed envy leading to *schadenfreude*, we were careful to make the interviewed students likeable, and equally so, in both the high- (superior student) and low-envy (average student) conditions. Nonetheless, in the high-envy condition compared with the low-envy condition, greater *schadenfreude* followed the misfortune.

I have collected many accounts of people's experiences of envy. It is not unusual for the target of the envy to be described as friendly and nice, in addition to having desirable talents or possessions. But the effect of these likeable qualities on the envying person can sometimes worsen the frustration of not having what is desired. Typically, people feeling envy find reasons to dislike the target of their envy so as to rationalize their invidious ill will. The envied person might be unfairly seen as "arrogant" or "obnoxious," for example. Likeable qualities in the envied person short circuit the easy route to rationalizing one's ill will—these qualities make it difficult to find plausible reasons to justify it. But because the frustrating disadvantage cannot be willed away, the envy does not necessarily cease. One participant wrote: "I envied and hated Sarah because she was smarter and more beautiful than me, and what made it worse, she was also a nice person. I had no good reason to hate her." Likability, therefore, may be no sure antidote for defusing another person's envy. Even though the nice envied person suffers less hostility from others than the obnoxious envied person, niceness does not solve the fundamental problem that envied people represent—they are advantaged and superior. No wonder Jonathan Swift, who had imagined both small Lilliputians and large Brobdingnagians in *Gulliver's Travels*, could write about the possible hostile consequences of an envy-causing contrast with a fellow writer in this way:

> In Pope I cannot read a line,
> But with a sigh I wish it mine;
> When he can in one couplet fix
> More sense than I can do in six;
> It gives me such a jealous fit,
> I cry, "Pox take him and his wit!"[45]

Toobin had many good things to say about Martha Stewart. Although she lives a life of privilege, she was not born into wealth. She lives her well-earned life of luxury with gusto and a good measure of authenticity. As he put it, "[the] Martha Stewart persona is no act."[46] And she has plenty of friends who can testify to her good character and good deeds. Toobin noted that she generally declined to criticize her tormentors; she had no complaint with the late-night comedians.[47]

But envy has a logic all its own. Homer Simpson's envy of his neighbor Ned Flanders is a case in point. In the episode of *The Simpsons*, "Dead Putting Society," Ned invites Homer to tour his recreation room. It has all the bells and whistles, including a bar with exotic, foreign beers on tap. Ned's son skips into the room, kisses him on the cheek, and thanks him for the help his father gave him on his science project. "Kids can be a trial, sometimes," Ned says, as if this was the worst of his son's behavior. Then, Ned's attractive wife appears with a tray of tasty-looking sandwiches for them to enjoy. Homer soon brims over with envious ill will toward Ned, despite the fact that Ned gives him no just cause for it. Homer accuses the bewildered Ned of deliberately flaunting his advantages, and he leaves after hurling a flurry of insults.

Homer hates Ned but without being able to articulate a credible reason for doing so. That evening, Homer unloads his envy-caused hostility on Ned as he lies in bed with his wife Marge. She is puzzled because, despite her probing questions, Homer is unable to come up with a legitimate reason for his hostility. The exchange ends in this way:[48]

MARGE: Was he angry?

HOMER: No.

MARGE: Was he rude?

HOMER: Okay, okay, it wasn't how he said it either. But the message was loud and clear: Our family stinks![49]

Ned Flanders is a painful irritant to Homer simply because he is a frequent presence and because he is superior. Homer lacks the self-awareness to label his pain as envy, but he is able to appreciate why having Ned as a neighbor can be more of a curse than a blessing. This is why Homer finds it so delightful when Ned's business does so poorly. Likewise, Martha Stewart, who is so attractive, so very cultured, so astonishingly accomplished—and rich—is just about perfect. Too much so. The average person probably needed relief from the impossible standard that she represents and the envy her success creates, as the *schadenfreude* over her legal troubles showed.

CHAPTER 9

ENVY TRANSMUTED

I do know envy! Yes, Salieri envies.
Deeply, in anguish envies——O ye Heavens!
Where, where is justice, when the sacred gift,
When deathless genius come not to reward
Perfervid love and utter denial,
And toils and strivings and beseeching prayers,
But puts a halo round a lack-wit's skull,
A frivolous idler's brow?... O Mozart, Mozart!
—PUSHKIN[1]

And this man
Is now become a god, and Cassius is
A wretched creature and must bend his body
If Caesar carelessly but nod on him.
—SHAKESPEARE[2]

Hatred is active displeasure, envy passive. We need not wonder
that envy turns so soon to hatred.
—JOHANN WOLFGANG VON GOETHE[3]

There is much more to be said about envy and its link with *schadenfreude*. I have given little attention to one feature of the emotion that has huge implications for how it works within the psyche of the average person suffering it. This concerns what most scholars assume is the largely suppressed or subterranean way that envy operates in everyday life. Generally, we deny feeling it. We keep our distance from the emotion, especially in how we present ourselves to others and often even in our private, internal owning up to it.[4] My aim in this chapter is to show that this feature of envy actually makes *schadenfreude* much more likely if the envied person suffers, and it facilitates actions that bring about a misfortune.[5]

WHY DO WE DENY FEELING ENVY?

Admitting envy, even in our private thoughts, is to concede inferiority, as I stressed in the previous chapter. Most of us work hard to maintain the opposite view. Even if the evidence of our inferiority is obvious, we are quick to repair the narcissistic wound. We are well equipped and well practiced with defenses against such assaults to our self-image. When one defense fails, another seems to erect itself, and then another. As I emphasized in Chapter 2, this is why most of us can believe that we are better than average despite this being a mathematical impossibility—everyone cannot be better than average. When we weigh our strengths and weaknesses, we are usually guided by the preferred image of a superior self. This is the self who, despite demonstrable failings in the actual world, can still view itself as an important if not heroic figure, battling slights and injustices. This self, a kind of god unto itself, plays out fantasy roles of victory and revenge over those who seem to thwart its interests. This self is rarely inclined to envy, or so we convince ourselves. Admitting to envy would be demeaning and unbecoming. Other people may be plagued by this petty emotion, but we are not.[6]

Most of us also resist acknowledging our envy because of its hostile and thus repellent nature. It is unlikely that we feel at ease knowing we dislike, perhaps hate, people and might even enjoy seeing them hurt *simply* because they have advantages over us. What have they actually done to deserve such hostility? This is hostility directed toward a blameless target; this is an unjustified, even pathetic thing to feel. It smacks of meanness and spite, a conspicuous defect in moral fiber and another threat to the high opinion we like to have of ourselves.[7]

Adding to this private resistance to admitting our envy is the concern for our public image. Recognizing the inferiority revealed by our envy is painful enough in our private thoughts, but confessing it to others piles on the pain of humiliation. Few people have the patience to listen to the petty whining of the envious. They have contempt for the nasty ill will underlying the envy as well. Understandably, most cultures develop strong norms against feeling envy or expressing it, or, more surely, acting on the feeling. Therefore, expressing envy almost certainly receives censure from others. The hostile nature of envy, together with the embarrassment of inferiority, means that when people reveal their envy, they will probably feel further diminished and ashamed.[8]

Is there a religion that approves of envy? Not likely. Judeo-Christian traditions warn against it. Consider the familiar 10th commandment from the Old Testament of the Hebrew Bible:

> Thou shall not covet thy neighbor's house, thou shall not covet thy neighbor's wife, nor his manservant, nor his maidservant, nor his ox, nor his ass, nor any thing that *is* thy neighbor's.[9]

Some of its details sound almost quaint, but the point is broad and anyone can comprehend the core command: don't envy what another has. Even feeling it is a crime of thought.

Anyone with a passing familiarity with the Bible knows that the theme of envy is part of its narrative fabric. This helps explain why the text can read like a pot boiler.[10] Envy is likely the main reason that Cain killed his brother Abel. Both Cain and Abel brought offerings to the Lord. The Lord frowned on Cain's "fruit of the ground" and accepted with warmth and respect Abel's "firstlings of his flock and of the fat thereof." And so, Cain "rose up against Abel his brother, and slew him" causing the Lord to send Cain away, cursed, to wander in the Land of Nod, to never again have the luxuries of tilling rich soil.[11] In this fashion, envy caused the first murder, leaving us with an early and clear moral lesson: don't envy. If your brother has it better than you, address your own failings—the solution is not to respond by killing him.

Christian conceptions of envy, sometimes personified in Satan, link envy to evil, as in John Milton's magnificent poetic creation:

> Satan—so call him now; his former name
> Is heard no more in Heaven. He, of the first,
> If not the first Archangel, great in power,
> In favour, and pre-eminence, yet fraught
> With envy against the Son of God, that day
> Honoured by his great Father, and proclaimed
> Messiah, King Anointed, could not bear,
> Through pride, that sight, and thought himself impaired.
> Deep malice thence conceiving and disdain,
> Soon as midnight brought on the dusky hour
> Friendliest to sleep and silence, he resolved
> With all his legions to dislodge, and leave
> Unworshiped, unobeyed, the Throne supreme.[12]

Satan, although powerful in his own right, is overloaded with envy of Jesus, who has God's greater favor. Weakened by this, his pride wounded and his malice aroused, he plots revenge and releases evil into the world. Is there a more alarming vision of what envy, unleashed, can do? It is hard to read this and think about envy in a benign, cheerful way.

Christian traditions also include envy in the cast of the deadly sins. Although the pain of envy is its own kind of punishment, the consequences of the sin of envy are singularly unpleasant. In Dante's vision of Purgatory, the envious have their eyes sewn shut with wire.[13] This seems fitting, for the root of the word envy derives from *in-* "upon" + *videre* "to see."[14] People feeling envy look at advantaged others with malice, casting an "evil eye" upon them—*and look with pleasure when misfortune strikes.* Envy may also be a sin that catalyzes others. Christian philosopher George Aquaro makes the case for envy being the core emotion driving most sinful behaviors, the one that creates the necessity for other commandments.[15] Without envy, Cain may not have murdered Abel. Alas, because the commandment to avoid envy may be impossible to follow, we must also have "thou shalt not kill."

It doesn't take a scholar of religions to see that envy is likely to be a troublesome problem for any faith, and so religious beliefs must provide a palliative for those less fortunate. According to the Bible, Jesus said, "Again I say to you, it is easier for a camel to go through the eye of a needle, than for a rich man to enter into the kingdom of God."[16] It is the meek rather than the wicked, powerful, and arrogant who will inherit the earth. This is good news for the disadvantaged person because it gives moral worth to inferiority and promises rewards for it in the long run. And yet the gnawing, immediate fact of disadvantage is hard to ignore in the moment. Inequality—and the envy that can result, regardless of commandments against the feeling—probably eats away at the foundations of a particular religion's explanation and justification for such inequalities. Envy signals a destabilizing discontent with one's lot that can place religious beliefs under suspicion and on shaky ground. The supreme being and creator of all things is implicated when envious discontent arises in response to his or her handiwork. Envy may initiate a questioning of the wisdom of the plan itself.[17]

LAYERS OF SELF-DECEPTION

The effect of envy's link with an inferior self and with a repellent reputation is that envy produces multiple levels of self-deception and public posturing.

Again, most certainly, people will avoid confessing their envy. Scholars, such as anthropologist George Foster, give examples of how envy is detected in its opposite, so much do the envious try to hide their true feelings. "Against whom is that eulogy directed?" is the line Foster cites from a novel by Migel de Unamuno to capture this jolting idea.[18] People can concede their envy in private, of course. They can come clean *both* in private and in public. But envy is frequently, as social and political theorist Jon Elster writes, "suppressed, preempted, or transmuted into some other emotion"[19] because there are "strong psychic pressures to get rid of the feeling."[20] This means that many people are feeling envy, perhaps acting out of envy, but are *unaware* of it—even though *others* may label them as envious and motivated by the emotion.[21]

ENVY, INJUSTICE, AND *SCHADENFREUDE*

There is another important element to throw into the blend: envy often comes mixed with a sense of injustice. When we feel envy, we are also likely to think that the advantage enjoyed by the envied person is undeserved, or at least that our own *disadvantage* is undeserved.[22] We *resent* the envied person's advantage. Why is this? The pioneering social psychologist Fritz Heider saw envy as emerging from a strong tendency toward the "equalization" of lots.[23] We believe that others who are similar to ourselves in background characteristics *ought* also to have similar rewards. Otherwise, a core sense of balance and rightness seems violated. Because envy is most likely to arise between people similar to each other[24]—except for what triggers the envy—the advantage will seem to violate this sense of what ought to be. Thus, envy often comes flavored with resentment.

In a similar vein, Freud claimed that the very origins of justice feelings come from the child's envy over inequality. Claims of unfairness might serve as a way of appearing to legitimately cry foul over unequal treatment. An element of our reactions to inequality, even as adults, may therefore have roots in how we reacted to inequality when we were children. According to Freud, the preoccupations of our younger self leave a strong residue. In this sense, the child is father to the man because we never quite rid ourselves of this early childish insistence on equality.[25]

I suspect another factor contributing to a sense of injustice in envy is that so many of the things creating envy are beyond the average person's ability to change.[26] One can only do so much to adjust one's physical beauty, intelligence, athletic ability, and musical talent—the list of attributes goes on and on. Even things such as wealth and family background are often insurmountable differences that separate people permanently at the starting gate of life. Such inequalities are undeniably important contributors to success in life, both in work and in attracting romantic partners. Hence, they are raw ingredients for envy. To this extent, people feeling envy cannot be blamed for their inferiority and therefore do not "deserve" it. Neither, to this extent, do envied people "deserve" their advantage. Even so—and this is an important point—*these differences are not considered an unfair basis for meting out rewards*, at least in most cultures. On the contrary, they are sources of merit. If Anna is less gifted at math than Susan, she will have no cause to cry foul if Susan is the one selected for the quiz bowl. If Mary attracts Paul's attention because of her physical beauty, plain Jane cannot take Mary to court over this advantage, "unfair" though it may be. From the subjective view of people feeling envy, these advantages can seem unfair, but this unfairness must be suffered without redress. If the emotion driving the sense of injustice is envy, most cultures insist on the grievance remaining a private one. These lines from Edward Fitzgerald's translation of *The Rubáiyát of Omar Khayyám* capture the frustration that fate can bring:

> The Moving Finger writes; and, having writ,
> Moves on: not all your Piety nor Wit
> Shall lure it back to cancel half a Line,
> Nor all your Tears wash out a Word of it.[27]

Envy can imprison us in a paradox because we feel both a sense of injustice and a sense of shame. In Heider's words, "Envy is fraught with conflict, conflict over the fact that these feelings should not be entertained though at the same time one may have just cause for them."[28] Envy, by this logic, is a hostile feeling that seems justified and yet damnable. It comes with an aggressive urge having a subjectively righteous character, and yet, acting on this hostility in a way that reveals one's envy is a repugnant move. A private part of oneself wishes to assert one's rights, because, as I outlined in Chapters 5 and 6, a desire for justice is a powerful motive. Furthermore, to a degree, a self-assertive impulse seems adaptive for succeeding in life. But cultural norms against envy create hesitation. In fact, you're damned if you do and damned if you don't.

Evolutionary psychologists Sarah Hill and David Buss give another reason to think that envy joins itself with resentment. From an evolutionary psychology perspective, envy serves an important adaptive function. It alerts us to conditions in which we rank lower than others in domains important for survival and reproductive success. The unpleasant nature of envy does not diminish its adaptive value but rather enhances it. In the competitive arenas of life, envy should lead to actions that increase resources compared to rivals and that upgrade social status and the benefits that follow from higher social status. Envy, by this logic, is both an alarm and a call to action. Hill and Buss suggest that envy may have evolved as a way of construing oneself as more deserving of scarce resources compared to rivals. They also argue that it is adaptive to find even the deserved advantages of other people as undeserved, at least to a degree; for example, by finding reasons to view the envied person as morally corrupt. The anger, hostility, and resentment created by perceiving the envied person's advantage as undeserved will make it more likely that people feeling envy will compete vigorously for the valuable resource. The process of natural selection is, as Hill and Buss phrased the point, "inherently competitive, selecting for individual phenotypes—and the genes that code for them—based on their ability to outperform existing alternate forms in domains that affect fitness."[29] The fusing of resentment with envy is an adaptive blend.

Max Scheler, guided in part by ideas originated by fellow German philosopher Friedrich Nietzsche, wrote about a chronic state of mind that he argued originated in envy and other, related painful states of frustration. Like Nietzsche, he borrowed the term *ressentiment* to give the phenomenon a label. One way this state can emerge, he argued, is when prolonged experiences of envy produce a sense of impotence so debilitating that one begins to suppress the emotion, despite its potency. This, in turn, produces a grudging, rancorous, embittered attitude toward life. In this psychologically poisoned state, envied things become reduced in value. This is no fun, but at least we need no longer accuse ourselves of envy. The things we once desired no longer seem worth having. However, because *ressentiment* is born of repressed envy and the *actual* valuing of these things, it is a conflicted, unhealthy brew. And, among other toxic effects, it creates particularly ugly emotions when advantaged people suffer. In the end, aggression, even cruelty, may result—as I will explore in the next chapter.

Although these ideas inspired by Nietzsche and Scheler are hard to test empirically, a series of studies done with Dutch participants by social psychologists Colin Leach and Russell Spears provides some support. These researchers' main goal was to show that feelings of inferiority would prime people to take out their frustration and anger on successful others, which would emerge as *schadenfreude* if successful others fail. In one study, undergraduate participants were told that their own university had done poorly in their league on a quiz competition called "IQ." Their feelings of inferiority and shame were measured immediately afterward. Then they learned about the winner of another league and reported how this success made them feel. Finally, they found out that this successful university had lost to the winner of their own league, and they again reported their feelings over this outcome. Indeed, these students were likely to find the loss of this other university pleasing. The students' pleasure was related to their prior feelings of inferiority and shame, as well as to the anger they felt over the other group's initial success. Specifically, students who felt inferior and ashamed over their own group's failure tended to be the ones who also felt angry over the other group's success. And this anger was closely linked to *schadenfreude* when this group suffered a defeat. Leach and Spears evoke Nietzsche's notion of the "vengefulness of the impotent" to capture this process.[30]

Another empirical contribution comes from work by Zlatan Krizan and Omesh Johar, who have examined the role of vulnerable narcissism in envy and *schadenfreude*.[31] Vulnerable narcissists have a complex jumble of features. Like all narcissists, they are usually self-absorbed and interpersonally tone-deaf. They are also apt to fancy themselves superior to others and to expect that the world concurs with this assessment. As a result, they typically feel entitled to special treatment and are taken aback if they don't receive it. But vulnerable narcissists, compared to "grandiose" narcissists, are less confident about their superiority and less confident in how others see them. Their narcissism may mask a core low self-esteem, and their behavior tends to reflect defensive efforts to convince themselves of their own superiority. Vulnerable narcissists should be especially susceptible to envy and *schadenfreude* because of their low self-esteem.

Studying how narcissism might combine with envy to cause *schadenfreude* is a particular challenge. Narcissists are especially unlikely to reveal their envy because, as social worker and psychotherapist Hotchkiss notes in her book, *Why Is It Always About You?: The Seven Deadly Sins of Narcissism* "to admit envy would be to acknowledge inferiority, which no good narcissist would ever do."[32] But Krizan and Johar employed a clever procedure that minimized the likelihood that participants would know that the study's focus was on envy and *schadenfreude*. Undergraduate participants thought they were simply giving their reactions to the format of news stories. They expected to see two related stories, one on a computer screen and the second on paper, and then give their reactions to the different formatting. They also completed a personality measure of vulnerable narcissism, but this was done in a mass screening at the beginning of the semester. There was little chance that participants would detect the researchers' interest in narcissism or envy. The first article contained an interview with another student who was either of high status and enviable *or* of low status and unlikely to be envied. Then, participants were taken to a different room and given a memory test (to distract them from the true purpose of the study). Finally, they were given the second story, which detailed how the same student from the first story had been found guilty of plagiarism and received a one-year academic probation.

As in other studies mentioned earlier, participants found the student's downfall more pleasing when it happened to the high-status person than the low-status person. And envy, reported just after the first article, was a big factor in explaining why. Moreover, vulnerable narcissists were even more likely to feel envy, and this envy resulted in more intense feelings of *schadenfreude* at the envied individual's misfortune. These results provide convincing evidence that our private self-views, when they are threatened by another person's superiority, set us up for feeling envy—and *schadenfreude* if the envied person suffers. And some of us, if we possess a shaky self-esteem joined with narcissism, are even more likely to follow this pattern.

SALIERI'S PRIVATE GRIEVANCE AND THE REVENGE THAT FOLLOWS

The film *Amadeus*, as I noted earlier, contains a good example of this tension between the sense of injustice, which is often part of envy, and the social censure also linked to the emotion.[33] Salieri, the respected court composer, envies the young and miraculously talented Mozart. But he avoids fully admitting to envy, construing Mozart's talent as an *injustice* committed by God. Salieri views Mozart as immature, indecent, and undeserving of his musical gifts. He resents Mozart's talents and is outraged at the injustice that he, Salieri, has only the capacity to appreciate Mozart's talent, rather than to duplicate it. He is a frustrated prisoner of mediocre abilities. Can he cry out against this injustice? No, because differences in ability are not considered an injustice by the standards of his culture. Ability and talent are sources of merit. Therefore, Salieri blames God, whom he deems to be responsible for awarding ability and talent among people. He knows that he will get no sympathy from others, however, if he makes any open efforts to right this wrong. Furthermore, he would not want others to think that he is envious because this would add public shame to his frustrations.

Salieri, mediocre by his own and others' verdicts, suffers many humiliations as Mozart outperforms him at every opportunity, usually in front of others, who laugh along with Mozart. In one scene, Mozart is performing impromptu at a lavish costume party and imitates the style of well-known composers. Salieri, disguised and incognito behind a mask, is in the crowd and calls out for Mozart to do "Salieri." Mozart proceeds to mock Salieri to the howling delight of the rest of the crowd. Salieri's mortification shows through his mask when Mozart takes on the look of a Neanderthal and with slow deliberateness plods his way through a Salieri melody. He literally apes Salieri.

The now-vengeful Salieri vows to undermine Mozart's career and plan his death. The success of both efforts brings him intense *schadenfreude*. He decides to feign a liking for Mozart and becomes his apparent friend and supporter. His actual feelings are hostile and vengeful, fed by a sense of injustice that we, the viewers, can easily recognize as envy. He encourages Mozart to include a section of ballet in his opera, *The Marriage of Figaro*, despite his knowing that the Emperor Joseph II will object when he views its initial performance. He watches Joseph's reaction as he views a rehearsal and anticipates with pleasure Joseph's disapproval. This fails to happen because Joseph enjoys the piece, and Salieri's hopes are dashed. But later, when the full production debuts, he receives a "miracle." Although Salieri realizes that the opera is path-breaking in quality, he also knows that Joseph's attention span is short. In the final number, Joseph yawns once, a signal that the opera will only have a few performances. This failure is a triumph for Salieri, and he smiles the smile of satisfying *schadenfreude*. Later, when Mozart's magnificent *Don Giovanni* also suffers a short run, Salieri once again silently exults.

Eventually, he pivots toward murder. "Before I leave this earth I will laugh at you," he vows in secret, his whole being now fully poisoned by envy and a desire for revenge. Mozart is already physically weakened by overwork, made necessary by financial woes. Concealed by a mask, Salieri visits Mozart and offers him extra work composing an opera, hoping that this will direct Mozart to an early grave through physical exhaustion and illness. Mozart accepts the offer, and, as he works, Salieri watches for hopeful, *happy* signs of Mozart's weakening physical condition. He is pleased to see Mozart almost delirious as he conducts an inaugural production of *The Magic Flute*. He is elated when Mozart collapses at the keyboard. He supervises bringing Mozart home and arranges a way to keep Mozart working by offering to record the notes as Mozart composes. He is gratified to see Mozart's strength fade while he works to meet the deadline for the commission. Mozart does indeed die of exhaustion and illness—again, much to Salieri's pleasure.

The experience of Salieri may be unusual in certain respects. He is actually more aware of his envy than others who might reach a vengeful state propelled by fully repressed envy.[34] Also, his anger is egged on by intentional humiliation from Mozart. Such deliberate humiliations enacted by the envied person may be rare in everyday experiences of envy; nonetheless, the film dramatizes the point that envy can lead to an extreme endpoint created by powerful tensions stirred up within the envying person. Invidious comparisons register in our emotional solar plexus. Usually, altering the pecking order is unrealistic—a reason why the emotion is so painful. The disadvantage remains a stubborn fixture, creating a persistent need to cope with inferiority, repugnant feelings of hostility—and frustrating resentment over being unfairly treated. This is mainly why the emotion can transmute itself into a private grievance no longer having the label of envy.[35] Once transmuted, events can more easily trend toward a justified pleasure if the envied person suffers and even justify vengeful actions that bring about the suffering, also resulting in pleasure.

This way of thinking about envy crosses over from the commonplace to something sinister. Common envy is often disturbing enough in its consequences, but the example of Salieri suggests that it can slope toward something uglier—toward a *schadenfreude* laced with malice and aggressive intent.

It is important to keep the hostile, potentially violent endpoint in mind. It is the difference between laughing over the seemingly benign joke and the willingness to stand happily by while another person suffers—or worse, to be responsible for perpetrating the harm. Generally, social norms keep hostile actions at bay. But because envy can be such an ugly, yet also a righteous feeling, and because owning up to it threatens the self-esteem of the envying person, its transmutation into a more palatable emotion, such as pure indignation and resentment, is a frequent outcome. Again, once transmuted and relabeled, the envying person need no longer wait in frustrated anticipation for a misfortune. Transmuted, this passivity can take a holiday, even a permanent vacation. A more certain virtuousness replaces shame and provides a license for something more active. Now, the envying person might take action to bring the misfortune about.

The progression from finding a bad thing amusing to wishing that it happens, and from anticipating it to engineering the deed, is difficult to unpack given the complicated motives that drive the change. Envy, I think, motivates in ways that deceive both the self and others, creating its own opportunities, manufacturing its own clever justifications, energized by the pain of the emotion and masked by its relabeling. This is the evil eye of envy, so feared in most cultures. The envied person is now the voodoo doll, vulnerable to attack. And so, Salieri is more easily able to take action against Mozart because he largely sees his decision as revenge against injustice.

In Richard Russo's novel *Bridge of Sighs*,[36] the narrator, currently in his 60s, looks back with improved understanding and describes a boyhood event in which he caused the injury of a friend, Bobby, whom he both liked and envied. On Saturday mornings during one summer, they would go with the narrator's dad when he delivered milk in his truck. They would play at "surfing" in the back of a truck, a game that meant balancing on milk crates as the truck navigated through the streets. The trick was to stay balanced on the crate even as the truck took turns. Bobby was better at the game, as he was at most things, and this created mixed feelings and desires in the narrator. Although he liked Bobby, even loved him in a way, this did not prevent envy and its attending hostile leanings from taking hold. I think Russo captures perfectly how envy-triggered aggression can happen, and it is well worth quoting in full:

> [A]s the summer wore on I became troubled by the knowledge that part of me was waiting for, indeed looking forward to, my friend getting hurt. It had, of course, nothing to do with him and everything to do with my own cowardice and jealousy. The jealous part had to do, I think, with my understanding that Bobby's bravery meant he was having more fun, something that my own cowardly bailing out had robbed me of. Each week I told myself I'd be braver, that this Saturday I wouldn't reach out and hold on for safety. I'd surrender control and be flung about, laughing and full of joyous abandon. But every outing was the same as the last, and when the moment came, I grabbed on. Gradually, since wishing for courage didn't work, I began wishing for something else entirely. I never wanted Bobby to be seriously injured, of course. That would have meant the end of everything. But I did wish that just once he'd be hurt bad enough to cry, which would lessen the gulf I perceived between him and me.

> And so our milk-truck surfing ended the only way it could. I didn't actually see Bobby break his wrist when he was flung against the side of the truck. I heard the bone snap, though. What saved me from suffering the same fate was

my cowardice. I'd seen the curve coming and at the last second reached out and grabbed one of the tied-off milk crates. Bobby, taken by surprise, went flying.[37]

For a few minutes after the event occurred, they sat quietly beside each other in the back of the truck while the narrator's father drove them home. Bobby broke the silence and said, "You didn't call the turn."[38] These words clarified the initial ambiguity of what had happened and why it had happened. His failure to warn of the curve was by hidden inclination, needing a sober accusation to let the motive break the surface. He wanted the accident to happen because of his envy, and, when it happened, part of him was happy over it. This was the essential truth of the matter, made clear once the narrator matured.

There is a sense that *schadenfreude*, when linked with envy, often exists in a kind of fantasy world of frustrated anticipation and privately articulated *hopes* for misfortune. During moments allowing for reflection, the wished-for misfortune, perhaps in fine detail, takes shape. Primed by mere imagination, the real thing, if it ever happens, is an extraordinary bolt out of the blue. When we have taken no role in the misfortune, if luck grants us this outcome, it is a thing of beauty. We can be free of any guilt that might arise.

As pleasing as a misfortune might be to witness when the envied suffer, the sad rub (for the rest of us) is that people who are envied tend *not* to suffer. They have it better. We are the ones who suffer. Whatever our dreams may be, *they* are living them.[39] But as envy goes underground, feelings of injustice and outrage can overtake envy in its manifest form, providing a foundation for unimpeachable, justified action—in the form of a kind of revenge and its dark thrills.

This is not a process to trifle with. In the next chapter, I take this transmutation of envy into righteous revenge to its furthest extreme and ask whether it might help explain the extreme, brutish treatment of the Jews by the Nazis.

CHAPTER 10

DARK PLEASURES UNLEASHED

There were many Jews who did not show the necessary restraint and who stood out more and more in public life, so that they actually invited certain comparisons because of their numbers and the position they controlled in contrast to the German people.
—HERMANN GÖRING[1]

One does not have to speculate about this link between envy and anti-Semitism in the Nazi mind; it can be confirmed and documented empirically by reading Hitler's many envious comments about Jews.
—JAMES GILLIGAN[2]

[T]he Jew is a money-getter; and in getting his money he is a very serious obstruction to less capable neighbors who are on the same quest. I think that that is the trouble.
—MARK TWAIN[3]

Perhaps most instances of *schadenfreude* are harmless, on a par with the pleasures of light gossip. Even when the feeling is linked with envy, there's little need to wag the finger. Envy and *schadenfreude* are also such natural emotions that alarm about their mingled frequency is unrealistic. And yet we must be mindful that envy can motivate, without full awareness, the engineering of misfortune— and its anticipated pleasures. This takes us into troubling moral territory. In this chapter, I chart a dark example of this, a kind of outer moral limit: the Nazi persecution and murder of the Jews. How was it that so many Germans were able to engage in the systematic, pitiless, *often pleasing to observe* mistreatment and ultimate killing of over six million Jews? Of course, the answer to the question is complex and multilayered, and the scholarship on this question is correspondingly vast.[4] Addressing the question can seem to raise even more questions, taking one further away from understanding. Almost any attempt to explain the horrors of the Holocaust can seem inadequate to the task, oversimplified, and futile—like looking into a hideous kaleidoscope that changes and mutates with each viewing. With these far from trivial caveats in mind, in this chapter, I explore the role that envy may have played in these horrors.

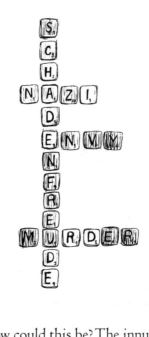

Envy of the Jews—how could this be? The innumerable instances of prejudice and harm occurring before the period of the Holocaust in Germany, when it reached a heretofore unimaginable crest in the Nazi atrocities, suggest a group to be pitied rather than envied. Only a group held in vicious contempt could cause such brutish treatment. How could Jews be the spur for strong envy if they are also linked with negative stereotypes suggesting inferiority, another common theme in their history? Coinciding with these stereotypes were the contrasting beliefs of Aryan racial superiority that the Nazis promulgated. To explain these seeming contradictions, let's first take a close look at the evolution of anti-Semitism in the obsessed spearhead of the Holocaust, Adolf Hitler. Did Hitler envy the Jews and, if so, did this envy contribute to his hatred—and pleasure at their systematic persecution and elimination?

ADOLF HITLER AND THE EVOLUTION
OF A LETHAL ANTI-SEMITE

Mein Kampf, the autobiographical screed and political manifesto Hitler wrote in the early 1920s, is a good place to start when looking for clues about the role of envy in Hitler's hatred of the Jews.[5] Some of the details of his account undoubtedly misrepresent how his ideas actually evolved, but the book still provides a revealing vantage point for understanding his thinking.

On its face, Hitler's narrative is not about his envy. He tries to convince readers that he came to believe that the Jews were a depraved race of people and that his lasting feelings were a blend of disgust and intense contempt—seemingly devoid of envy. Hitler claimed to be drawn toward this anti-Semitism *against his will.* His inner struggle (his "*kampf*") was long and disturbing, and, as he stated, "only after months of battle between my reason and my sentiments did my reason begin to emerge victorious."[6] Initially, he had been horrified by accounts of religious persecution of Jews in prior centuries. Even when he first moved to Vienna, he rejected the "sharp" tone of the Viennese anti-Semitic press. He thought it "unworthy of the cultural tradition of a great nation" and he "was oppressed by the memory of certain occurrences in the Middle Ages."[7] In fact, he noted that envy may have partly explained these reactions *in others.*[8] Other people might have been motivated out of envy but surely not himself—or so he would want us to conclude. Did he protest too much and so reveal the opposite?

His early descriptions of his learning about Jews provide illuminating evidence of his envy. What is it about Jews that would make one envy them? For starters, one would have to *notice* them, and, interestingly, as a young man in Linz, Hitler claimed to be barely aware of their presence. The small number of Jews in Linz were so "Europeanized" and "human" that he "even took them for Germans."[9] However, after moving to Vienna, he did start noticing Jews. He began seeing Jews *everywhere*, and this disturbed him. And it was not only that they seemed to be everywhere; Hitler also perceived their having a powerful influence. From these twin perceptions, his envy may have been pricked.

In his book *Envy: The Seven Deadly Sins*, Joseph Epstein suggests the strong links between envy and Nazi anti-Semitism, and, as an example, he gives a characterization of the Vienna close to Hitler's day:

> Consider these rough statistics from Vienna of 1936, a city that was 90 percent Catholic and 9 percent Jewish: Jews accounted for 60 percent of the city's lawyers, more than half its physicians, more than 90 percent of its advertising executives, and 123 of its 174 newspaper editors. And this is not to mention the prominent places Jews held in banking, retailing, and intellectual and artistic life.[10]

Wouldn't these kinds of statistics in Vienna and other cities in Austria and Germany make hollow the claims of Jewish inferiority and Aryan superiority? These facts would have likely had invidious effects on anyone craving beliefs in Aryan superiority. Indeed, Hitler became preoccupied with the pervasive influence Jews appeared to have *despite their small number.*

> I now began to examine carefully the names of all the creators of unclean products in public artistic life....The fact that nine tenths of all literary filth, artistic trash, and theatrical idiocy can be set to the account of a people, constituting hardly one hundredth all the country's inhabitants, could simply not be talked away; it was the plain truth.[11]

As he perceived their disproportional influence, he also transformed his view of Jews from one based on religious distinctions to one of race and, furthermore, a race having vile and pernicious characteristics. He encountered Jews in their distinctive caftans and side locks and began sensing something foreign rather than native. He would wonder: "Is this a German?" He still claimed to be troubled by the anti-Semitic pamphlets and their atrocious accusations. They seemed so unscientific and shameful, and he feared that he would be committing an injustice to believe them. But the Jews' essential and degenerate separateness took complete hold on his perceptions:

> Wherever I went, I began to see Jews, and the more I saw, the more sharply they became distinguished in my eyes from the rest of humanity.[12]

Having separated Jews from other people, Germans most importantly, he bristled at the notion that Jews could label themselves the "Chosen People." He recognized their powerful influence, a fact incompatible with inferiority and likely to spur envy. However, he focused on those perceived attributes of Jews that inspired his contempt and would have clouded recognition of his envy. Jews were parasitic, immoral Zionists. Any outward condemning of Zionism by a Jew was a back-stabbing smoke screen for a favoring of Jewish rather than German interests. All their activities, whether "in the press, art, literature, and the theatre" exuded an outward and inward repulsiveness; they were "germ-carriers of the worse sort."[13] And there was no aspect of cultural life without the degenerate influence of Jews.[14]

The transformation into a committed anti-Semite completed itself when Hitler linked Jews with political causes having Marxist elements. Here as well, he perceived their *disproportionate* influence. But, once again, he seemed to blunt the invidious effects implicit in this perception by focusing on the seditious threat these Jews posed to Germany. This threat was especially true in the press, which he saw as dominated by disloyal, treacherous Jews. Here is a characteristic sample of Hitler's thinking:

> I gradually became aware that the Social Democratic press was directed predominantly by Jews...there was not one paper with Jews working on it which could have been regarded as truly national, according to my education and way of thinking.

> ...I took all the Social Democratic pamphlets I could lay my hands on and sought the names of their authors: Jews. I noted the names of the leaders: by far the greatest part were likewise members of the "chosen people," whether they were representatives of the Reichsrat or trade-union secretaries, the heads of organizations or street agitators. It was always the same gruesome picture. The names of the Austerlitzses, Davids, Adlers, Ellenbogens, etc. will remain forever graven in my memory. One thing had grown clear to me: The party with whose petty representatives I had been carrying on the most violent struggle for months was, as to leadership, almost exclusively in the hands of a foreign people; for, to my deep and joyful satisfaction, I had at last come to the conclusion that the Jew was no German.[15]

Hitler detailed his futile attempts to persuade the Jewish members of the party of the "madness of their doctrine."[16] But he eventually concluded that they had no interest in whether their beliefs were good for the future of Germany. And just when he thought he had them persuaded, they would turn around and spout the "same old nonsense as though nothing at all had happened, and, if indignantly challenged, affected amazement."[17] Hitler was intensely frustrated by these interactions with Jews, marveling at the "agility" of their persuasive language and the "virtuosity" of their deceit.[18] There was a clear, invidious residue produced by his being outwitted, but the plain result was that he hated Jews with a ferocious passion.

Decades later, when Albert Speer, Hitler's top architect, was asked why Hitler was anti-Semitic, he gave three reasons. One was Hitler's pathological desire to destroy. Another was that he blamed the Jews for Germany's defeat in World War I, thus denying him the opportunity to achieve his dream of becoming an architect. But a third reason, probably related to his frustrated dreams as well as to a desire to destroy, was that he "secretly admired and envied the Jews."[19]

Speer knew Hitler about as well as anyone, and I think that Speer was right on the mark. It is likely that a part of Hitler's "struggle" was with his envy. Initially, he had claimed to be appalled by the way Jews had been treated in previous centuries and was concerned that hating Jews would be an injustice. He had seen envy as an explanation for the anti-Semitic pamphlets, *and so he could see this motive in others.* But it may be that as his own envy grew, his subsequent "struggle" was to find a way to hate the Jews without attributing his motives to the ugly, humiliating emotion of envy. He may have envied and hated the Jews earlier than he claimed, as his friend during his late teens, August Kubizek, believed. Once they walked past a synagogue in Linz, and Hitler said to him, "This shouldn't be here."[20] Even Kubizek admitted, however, that Hitler's experiences in Vienna "might have deepened" his anti-Semitism.[21] Arguably, envy found a way to transmute itself into disgust, and then into righteous, justified, "deserved" hatred. As clever as these so-called chosen people might be, they were morally corrupt and traitorous in their motives. Perhaps at some earlier point, the idea of the Jews as the chosen people would have accentuated only the invidious implications of their disproportionate influence for Hitler.[22]

However, now, he seized on it as evidence for Jewish arrogance, adding further justification for his disgust and hatred.

Historian John Toland, in his biography of Hitler, notes a revealing statement made by Hitler in 1941 to Walther Hewel, an early member of the Nazi Party and one of Hitler's few friends. It was a few weeks before the invasion of the Soviet Union and during a period in which Hitler set in motion preparations for the liquidation of the Jews. By Hewel's account, Hitler likened himself to a medical scientist who had "found the bacillus" and had therefore discovered a way to deal with the problem of the Jews. And in words suggesting the invidious roots of his hatred, he said, "one thing I have proven is that a state can live without Jews: that economy, art, culture, etc., can exist even better without Jews, which is the worst blow I could give the Jews."[23] This statement fits with the envious mind set, although Hitler would not have acknowledged it, of course. By the time he wrote his memoirs, he had long convinced himself that by achieving the annihilation of the Jews he would be an avenger for God, so justified did he believe his hatred.[24] Hitler probably envied the Jews, but this seemed fully hidden from his awareness.

SCAPEGOATING THE ENVIED JEWS

Does Hitler's path to hating the Jews generalize in some respects to other Germans who also hated the Jews? Could envy help explain not only the Holocaust, but anti-Semitism going back centuries? Many respected thinkers have argued so, from Mark Twain to Friedrich Nietzsche.[25] More recently, Dennis Prager and Joseph Telushkin, in their analysis of anti-Semitism, *Why the Jews? The Reasons for Antisemitism*, make the more general point this way:

> In nearly every society in which the Jews have lived for the past two thousand years, they have been better educated, more sober, more charitable with one another, committed far fewer violent crimes, and have had a more stable family life than their non-Jewish neighbors. *These characteristics of Jewish life have been independent of Jews' affluence or poverty.*... Of course, it is impossible to measure precisely to what extent the higher quality of Jews' lives has been a major cause of antisemitism. Few antisemites list the Jews' good qualities as reasons for

attacking them. But it is human nature for individuals and groups perceived as living better lives, however that may be understood, to elicit jealousy and resentment.[26]

Prager and Telushkin's analysis is especially useful because they suggest that it is not just the obvious markers of wealth, power, and influence that may have created envy. The more subtle but evident cultural strengths usually present in Jewish communities could also be a trigger.[27]

Social psychologist Peter Glick has addressed the question of envy and Nazi anti-Semitism within the Stereotype Content Model, an innovative theory of prejudice proposed by him and fellow psychologists Susan Fiske and Amy Cuddy.[28] Traditional theories cast prejudice as a generic negative feeling toward another group. Glick, Fiske, and Cuddy argue that this way of thinking about prejudice is too general, and, for example, overlooks that groups vary in terms of their perceived status or competence. Prejudice against poor Hispanics is very different from prejudice against successful Jews (or, Asians, etc.). Both feelings can be "negative," but only one is likely to also contain envy—namely, toward groups enjoying stereotypically high status and competence. Traditional views of prejudice also tend to neglect another important dimension in which other groups differ: whether or not they are perceived as a threat. This is the "warmth" dimension of the Stereotype Content Model. Members of highly competent groups might simply be admired (a high warm feeling) rather than envied (a low warm feeling) if, for example, there is no concern that they will take away jobs from one's own group. These two fundamental dimensions inherent in our perceptions of other groups (warmth and competence) are crucial to take into account. They address two adaptive questions we should ask about members of other groups: first, are they friends or foes? And, second, are they weak or powerful? Will they like us, and will they hurt us if they can? Not surprisingly, groups with stereotypically higher status (e.g., economic advantages) are perceived as more competent and, if they are perceived to be in competition with us, are also seen as low in warmth and therefore threatening. And this combination of high status and low warmth in another group encourages in us feelings of envious prejudice, as empirical work has confirmed.[29]

Glick stresses that the remarkable successes of Jews would have been of little consequence, psychologically, for those inclined to dislike the Jews—if it were not for Jews also being perceived as a competitive threat. The Nazis, capitalizing especially on the willingness of people to believe bogus anti-Semitic documents, such as *The Protocols of the Elders of Zion*, claimed that Jews represented a kind of conspiracy aimed at accruing power and favoring only their own interests.[30] As we have seen, a constant theme in Hitler's statements, as well as in propaganda spewed out by other Nazi leaders, was that this sense of threat was reinforced by the belief that many Jews were in leadership positions in the communist movement and its spread. And as we have also seen pulse through Hitler's own writings, many Germans—and most Nazis—blamed Jews for Germany's humiliation in World War I and its economic problems following the war and believed the Jews were in bed with the Communists.

In relating his theories of stereotyping and prejudice to anti-Semitism, Glick applies the idea of *scapegoating* to this type of prejudice. In scapegoating, we see ingroup members, particularly when feeling threatened by, for example, economic circumstances, lash out against a vulnerable outgroup, usually one that is perceived as inferior.[31] But Glick points out that this partially fits the history of anti-Semitism. True, stereotypes about Jews had long included negative features suggesting the kind of "inferiority" (e.g., dirty, greedy) so persistently claimed in Hitler's writings. Indeed, the Nazis did their best to promulgate these beliefs.[32] However, other stereotypes of Jews imply a kind of power and superiority (e.g., clever, cunning). Glick argues that viewing the Jews as "inferior" *as well as* powerful created a particularly malicious form of scapegoating, an intense, envy-tinged blaming of Jews for Germany's economic woes.[33]

The wide assimilation of Jews into German culture might have worked to reduce this sense of separateness. But Glick notes that this blending was seen as false. The Nazis, entranced by ideas of race, saw group identity in blood rather than in beliefs. What's more, Jews' efforts to fit in could be taken as evidence of conspiratorial motives, as Hitler claimed. Again, as a distinct racial group, Jews were considered both powerful and threatening. Victims of their own success, they were held to be manipulative, powerful threats. The reward for being so perceived was to suffer even more surely from a particularly virulent, unrelenting form of envious prejudice.

The persistence of envious prejudice, particularly in the case of Nazi Germany, can be explained by a number of factors. Like Epstein and other scholars, Glick also emphasizes that Jews *were* overrepresented in many important aspects of professional and cultural life and that the talents and drive suggested by such success would have been hard to dismiss. The Nazis exaggerated and distorted the prevalence of Jews in powerful positions, claiming that these influential Jews represented a coordinated, monolithic entity bent on domination, but there was just enough surface evidence to justify the sense of power and threat. When economic conditions are poor, it is not surprising that people, in their collective frustration, will search for plausible causes for the hardships they are suffering. Blaming these hardships on another group—one perceived to be different, as well as competent, manipulative, and out for themselves—has a certain plausibility to it. Moreover, Jews who were able to lend money in tough economic times could be construed as making money off the misery of Germans.[34] Had economic and political conditions in Germany been different, Glick suggests that Jews might have been tolerated, even seen as useful. But stressful economic times call for explanations for why things are going so poorly. Ideological movements, such as the National Socialism endorsed by the Nazi Party, supplied plausible and well-packaged propaganda that could be used to blame the Jews. Explanations fueled by envious stereotypes took firm hold.

Glick points out that if hatred toward Jews was simply a function of their being a threatening outgroup, this alone would not explain the nature of the hostility directed at them. If it was a straightforward function of threat, then once the basic threat was dealt with, hostile action should cease. Hatred of the Jews was a thing apart, however. The Nazis wanted to eliminate Jews arguably because, in part, their very existence created painful envy. Envious hostility predicts a willingness to suffer in other respects, as long as the envied object can be neutralized or destroyed. The goal of elimination trumps many other concerns.

Consider the Nazis' treatment of Albert Einstein. Imagine if Einstein had not been a Jew. He would have been feted as the best example of Aryan superiority. But, inconveniently, he was a Jew and, as would be the pattern expected by envy-inspired hatred, the Nazis undermined their full potential by virtue of their treatment of the Jews. If the talents of Einstein and other Jewish scientists had been harnessed by the Nazis, the German war effort would likely have benefited greatly. Germany might have been the first to develop an atomic bomb. Instead, Einstein and other brilliant scientists were persecuted, forced to leave Germany, or delivered into the incomprehensible horrors of the extermination camps.[35] But again, people feeling envy get little enjoyment over contemplating the achievements and brilliance of those whom they envy, even when these achievements might lead to some form of personal gain. And so, envy provides a way of understanding why the Nazis would act in puzzling, counterproductive ways.

THE PLEASURES OF PERSECUTION IN ONE'S MIDST

Stereotypes alone can generate envious, prejudicial reactions—and one result is *schadenfreude*. A study done with Princeton University students by Mina Cikara and Susan Fiske assessed people's reactions to negative events happening to members of one of four kinds of stereotyped groups.[36] Each group fit one of the four categories of the Stereotype Content Model. Cikara and Fiske predicted that members of stereotypically envied groups (i.e., a high competence/high threat type of group) would create more positive reactions to the group member's suffering than any of the other three categories. A self-report measure and a physiological measure both confirmed this prediction. Compared to the other three groups, the suffering of envied groups generated less empathy and more smiling.

Can we extrapolate such findings to better understand the Nazis, whose stereotypes of Jews were at the far extreme? As the Nazis rose to power, humiliation, violence, and destruction against Jews increasingly became the sanctioned norm and, ultimately, government policy. Keenly aware of the wealth, property, possessions, and professional positions held by many Jews, the Nazis focused on taking these things away, often violently. Sometimes property was simply destroyed, as in the events of *Kristallnacht*, in which many Jewish shops were damaged and synagogues were burned. Most average Germans were probably shocked and disturbed by these extreme actions. They did not have the stomach for it, especially since scores of Jews were also killed in the process. Some, such as pastor Dietrich Bonhoeffer, resisted the Nazis from the start. He noted, "If you board the wrong train it is no use running along the corridor in the opposite direction."[37] But it may be that these increasingly brutal actions occurred in part because not enough people were expected to object, because many actually turned a blind eye—and because some displayed their appreciation and pleasure.

We can be confident that Hitler was pleased. Although Hitler disguised his role in *Kristallnacht* as well as his enthusiasm for it, there is evidence for both. Historian John Toland relates a credible account from Fritz Hesse, one of Hitler's press agents. It occurred on the very night of *Kristallnacht*, during a dinner at which Hitler, the Propaganda Minister Goebbels, and other Nazi leaders were present. Hesse was also there, and he overheard Goebbels telling Hitler that the attack against the Jewish businesses and synagogues was about to happen. Hitler's happy reaction to this information was unmistakable. Hesse remembered that "Hitler squealed with delight and slapped his thigh in his enthusiasm."[38]

Hitler also recognized that many Germans did not share in his exuberance, and so he pulled back from these violent tactics. Instead, a series of laws was passed and policies implemented that did the job in a "legal" manner more fitting the sensibilities of the average German. These actions may have pleased the mildly envious in a way that the violent approach could not. In any event, many Germans *benefited* directly or indirectly, whether it was the shopkeeper who was able to get rid of competition or the student who was able to take the position in a professional school that otherwise might have gone to a Jew.

There is ample evidence showing the common pleasure that some Germans took in the suffering of Jews, such as gathering to watch Jews scrubbing streets with toothbrushes or soldiers pulling the beards of old Jewish men. There was *schadenfreude* aplenty.[39] Historian Donald McKale gives an example of how the Nazi leadership responded to the horrific conditions created by herding many Jews, mostly in Poland, into ghettos. A Nazi "leisure" organization, *Kraft durch Freude* (literally meaning "Strength through Joy"!), supervised bus tours. German soldiers took these tours through the ghettos and laughed at suffering Jews as if they were visiting the "zoo to see animals."[40] Funerals were interrupted so that the soldiers could pose for photographs with rabbis and the grieving family members.

Of course, inferring the *actual* emotional amalgam associated with these and other actions is difficult. Nonetheless, envy provides one credible explanation for some of the behavior that emerged and the pleasure this behavior often produced in witnesses—and in perpetrators.

FROM ENVY TO *SCHADENFREUDE* TO ACTION

I suggested in the previous chapter that once *schadenfreude* becomes the normative response to the mistreatment of a group of people, worse behaviors, even genocide, might enter the imagination of the envious person. In this sense, as Russell Spears and Colin Leach note, *schadenfreude* can be a kind of deliberate passivity which provides encouragement for others willing to commit further and more extreme mistreatment.[41]

Schadenfreude may motivate action in the observer too. When envy is at the root of *schadenfreude*, I argue that the line between passive and active becomes quite blurred. Enjoying misfortune evolves into longing for misfortune and then the willingness to bring it about. Mina Cikara and Susan Fiske did another study testing the Stereotype Content Model. This one assessed *actions* associated with envious prejudice. They showed that members of stereotypically envied groups might also suffer more *harm* compared to the other three groups.[42] Participants in the study were asked to imagine that they were participating in a *Fear Factor*–type game show. They were further told that they had the power to choose various ways that other group members should receive punishment in the form of a painful (but not lethal) shock. Members of stereotypically envied groups were most often chosen.

I have stressed envy's habit of transforming itself. For one thing, envy begins to "feel" like resentment, and, if a misfortune occurs to the envied person or group, it will "feel" deserved. Also, when *schadenfreude* is rooted in envy, there arises yet another incentive toward action because the envying person will not want to admit to his or her envious motive. Such an admission would be to concede inferiority and unjustified hostility, which in most people would cause shame. These are powerful reasons for people to deny their envy. Who wants to admit inferiority, and who wants to admit this as a reason to hate others? The shame in this blend is a terrifying threat to one's self-worth and, as so many scholars have pointed out, leads to all sorts of *less than conscious* defensive strategies to avoid both the public *and* private owning up to these feelings. The late social theorist Leslie Farber put it well when he suggested that envy has a protean "talent for disguise" that may fool others as well as "the envious one himself, whose rational powers may lend almost unholy assistance to the need for self-deception."[43] Thus, if the envied target is harmed, the deservingness of this outcome is emphasized and justifications work backward, in part from the action to the reason for the action. The target will be vilified, dehumanized, and then seen deserving of this treatment. The invidious roots of this pattern are usually well buried or camouflaged. Disgust rather than sympathy prevails.[44] As Mina Cikara, Susan Fiske, and others also suggest, the addition of the intergroup element ("us" vs. "them") probably enhances these processes.[45] Now, one is acting for the group and against the enemy. Collective, group goals rather than personal "selfish" goals seem to be the motivation for Germany and the Reich, rather than a personal grudge.

In Hitler's case, as I argued earlier, once he could convince himself that the Jews *deserved* his hate, without attributing to himself an envious motive, he could vow to destroy them. And vow he did. In a speech to the Reichstag in January 1939, he foretold the fate of the Jews. He claimed that, during his long struggle, Jews laughed at his prophesies of gaining power and enacting a "solution of the Jewish problem." But he claimed that these same Jews were "now choking" on this laughter. As if he believed he would have the last laugh, he prophesied the "destruction of the Jewish Race in Europe."[46]

CIGARS AND COGNAC OVER
PROBLEM SOLVED

On January 20, 1942, in the Berlin suburb of Wannsee, the SS led a meeting of many leaders of the German bureaucracy whose cooperation would be needed in enacting the full-scale, systematic genocide of the Jews. The Wannsee Conference was chaired by Reinhard Heydrich, chief of the Nazi security agencies. Adolf Eichmann, who would later hold chief responsibility for planning the killing operation, also attended, along with various other SS officers and Nazi officials. The plans were not unanticipated by the representatives; many already knew of mass killings that had already been taking place as the German army advanced into Eastern Europe. A written record survived from this meeting, only slightly altered by euphemistic phrases to veil its full purpose. This record, along with retrospective accounts obtained later from, for example, Israeli interrogations of Eichmann, reveals the eager, accommodating attitude attendees had for the plans.[47] Given our understanding of *schadenfreude*, I suspect there was more eagerness over it than we can know.[48] But investigation by Donald McKale indicates that, after the meeting, cigars and cognac were shared merrily by Heydrich and other attendees. Eichmann, himself, later recalled how satisfying it was to know that the "Popes of the Third Reich" had put their seal of approval on the plan, thereby seeming to rid everyone of doubts. He said, "At that moment, I sensed a kind of Pontius Pilate feelings, for I felt free of guilt."[49]

In his book on the Wannsee Conference, historian Mark Roseman also infers that *schadenfreude* was part of how Heydrich and others Nazi leaders felt about the meeting.[50] It was probably true that almost all the attendees supported the goal of exterminating the Jews, but there were a few sticking points that might have created objections. One had to do with the many Jews of mixed parentage or Jews who were married to non-Jews. Heydrich probably expected that Wilhelm Stuckart of the Interior Ministry would advocate greater protection of Jews in these categories. Not so. Just about all of the officials voiced their desires to exterminate the Jews quickly and completely. Eichmann's recollections may reveal a desire to exaggerate the enthusiasm of the attendees so as to lessen his own accountability—nonetheless, this was his assessment:

> [N]ot only did everyone willingly indicate agreement, but there was something else, entirely unexpected, when they outdid and outbid each other, as regards the demand for a final solution to the Jewish question. The biggest surprise, as far as I can remember, was not only Bühler but above all Stuckart, who was always cautious and hesitant but who suddenly behaved there with unaccustomed enthusiasm.[51]

Roseman notes that the "galvanized" Heydrich sent copies of the protocol to the attendees.[52] In an accompanying message, he wrote that "happily the basic line" had now been "established as regards the practical execution of the final solution of the Jewish question."[53] It was now official. Genocide was the plan, and it was a cause for celebration.[54]

Schadenfreude in its most disturbing forms and guises was there to see, whether envy was part of the formula for its presence or not. Interestingly, the

2001 film *Conspiracy*, which attempted to recreate faithfully the actual Wannsee Conference, has *schadenfreude* as a dominant theme throughout—from the crude anti-Semitic jokes to the bursts of enthusiasm and rappings on the table generated by each step in the direction of finalizing the plans for the Jews' annihilation. There are hints of the role of envy, masked, as would be expected, by a transmuted righteous belief that the Jews deserved this fate. At first, Stuckart (played brilliantly by actor Colin Firth), as the historical record indicates, appears to have some resistance to the extreme measures being proposed. He reminds everyone that he was the primary author of the 1935 Nuremberg Laws establishing the legal definitions of various categories of Jews that were the basis for codifying their persecution. Indiscriminate deportation of Jews by the SS, in his view, would create legal chaos. He overhears one of the SS officers saying to another attendee that Stuckart must "love" the Jews. This triggers in him a vigorous defense of his "credentials" as a hater of Jews, and a more sophisticated one at that.

> [F]rom your uniform I can infer that you're shallow, ignorant, and naïve about the Jews. Your line that the party rants on about is…is…how…how inferior they are some…some…some species.…I keep saying how wrong that is. They are sublimely clever. And they are intelligent as well. My indictments of that race are stronger and heavier because they are real, not your uneducated ideology.…They are arrogant and self-obsessed and calculating and they reject the Christ and I'll not have them pollute German blood…he doesn't understand…deal with the reality of the Jew, and the world will applaud us. Treat them as…as imaginary fantasy evil, human fantasy, and the world will have justified contempt for us. To kill them casually without regard for the law martyrs them…it will be their victory…when you have my credentials, then we'll talk about who loves the Jew and who hates them.[55]

Stuckart, in this albeit *imagined* dialogue, breaks through the absurd logic of those in the room who use their distorted beliefs of the inferiority of the Jews to bolster their case for annihilation. He still wants them purged, with a passion unsurpassed by anyone in the room, however. He manages to justify this desire by embracing other negative stereotypes about Jews, as Glick's perspective on envious prejudice would predict. These attributes seem enough for even Stuckart to discount the role envy may play in his hatred toward these "sublimely clever" people.

SUFFERING *SCHADENFREUDE* FIRSTHAND

Through interviews and memoirs, survivors of the Holocaust leave no doubt about the pleasure many Nazis and some Germans displayed over the suffering of the Jews. It is more difficult to know the origins of this pleasure. By reading these accounts and applying to them what we know about human emotion and behavior, I think many clues can be uncovered.[56] In one account, *Soldiers and Slaves*, Roger Cohen, columnist for *The New York Times*, describes a series of events that played out toward the end of World War II.[57] Cohen follows the wretched experiences of a group of about 350 men who were sent to the small East German town of Berga to build an underground fuel-making factory. It was a preposterous plan that had no realistic prospects of succeeding, but Germany was in desperate need of gasoline for its war effort. Most of the men were American GIs who had been captured by the Germans during the Battle of the Bulge, Hitler's last-gasp counteroffensive that took the advancing American forces by surprise.[58] Most were selected because they had Jewish-sounding names, admitted to being Jews, or looked Jewish. None had the slightest notion that they were now enmeshed in the Nazi plan to exterminate the Jews, even as they were herded into cattle cars. Cohen relates their experiences, recalled by the small proportion of men who managed to survive the circumstances of their capture, their treatment as slave laborers, and the final death march away from Berga as advancing American troops closed in on the region. He parallels their experience with that of a Hungarian Jew named Mordecai Hauer, who had also been sent to Berga after he and his family, along with more than 500,000 largely unsuspecting Jewish citizens of Hungary, had been efficiently rounded up by the Germans during the last phase of the war.

There are a number of recurrent themes in the narrative. With some exceptions, the German soldiers generally showed a clear hatred and contempt for the prisoners. Any hint of insolence or disobedience was met with instant, violent retaliation and further contempt. Humor and *schadenfreude*—and sheer sadistic cruelty—were also common in the camp. The guards' responses to disobedience from the prisoner were often to beat or execute one or more of them. The dead were usually suspended from make-shift gallows as an example to the others, with the guards taunting the dead with mocking humor.[59] One survivor, Private William Shapiro, struggling to comprehend the human depravity all around him, recalled a time when a number of prisoners had suffered this fate. In Cohen's words:

> Shapiro would cast a furtive glance at the gallows, anxious not to draw the attention of the SS troopers whose cruelty was often on display. Growing up in the Bronx, he had been shown photographs of a lynching in the South and had wondered at the smiling faces of the white murderers. He had never seen a hanging.[60]

It is one thing to witness a lynching and to ponder its meaning, but when it is accompanied by smiling faces,[61] it creates disorientation:

> Shapiro was at a loss. He had plunged into some netherworld where hangings were public and terrified adolescents with yellow triangles on their sleeves were made to stand at attention in the frigid air before being beaten with batons and rifle butts, but he could not say what this hell was, how it had been constituted, why it existed.[62]

The experiences of Hauer, the Hungarian Jew, hint more directly at how envy may have sometimes played a role in the vicious treatment of the Jews and echoes many of the ways Germans had also treated Jews from Germany and other countries. The Hungarian Jews thought they were protected from the Nazis by an agreement made between the German and Hungarian governments. As the war appeared to be coming to an end, most Jews did not fear that this agreement would change. Eichmann himself showed up in the early stages of the roundup to give a speech laced with lies that would induce the Jews to be compliant, telling them that they were being taken to camps for their own protection. However, as the situation deteriorated, the more sober members of the community voiced "dire forecasts." Hauer intuited that many Hungarians resented and envied the Jews because of their successes. He observed that many Hungarians:

> [H]ated the Jews, hated them for saving money, for not drinking, for educating their children, for moving up in the world. Now, with the Nazis in

Hungary, every frustration could be vented; all that the Jews had patiently amassed would be taken.[63]

Similar to what occurred in Germany and other countries, one preoc-cupation of the round-ups involved inspecting possessions,[64] notably any valuable items. Hauer recalled his father saying that one Hungarian official claimed that the Jews had "large amounts of gold and diamonds," and he wanted them for himself because "the Jews are leeches that suck the blood of other people."[65] Cohen notes that Hauer felt "no amount of gold would have satisfied this bigot from Budapest with his conviction that Jews had plundered the wealth of Hungary."[66] It is hard to escape the view that many Hungarians, like many Germans, envied the Jews and that the disappearance of the Jews led to the benefit and satisfaction of many. Envy, camouflaged by rationalized indignation and resentment, would help explain why the Hungarians could do the things that they did to the Jews or stand aside while the Nazis pursued their murderous goals. Hauer never heard anyone say they envied the Jews, but it seemed in the air, no matter how made over or masked.[67]

One of the puzzles raised by Cohen's account is why the SS guards contin-ued to push the prisoners to their deaths and, further still, march them away from the advancing American lines when it was clear that doing so was fool-ish. It made their behavior more incriminating in the probable event of their capture by the Allied forces.[68] I have emphasized earlier that a key point is that envy changes the nature of what one is "interested in." Envy inspires a hatred in which the most important goal is to bring the envied person down, even if it is costly to the self in other ways. Arguably, because of a mix of factors—envy being one—the Jews were hated in this way. Here is Hauer's recollection of what a newly arrived SS commander said to the prisoners who were assembled for their march away from the Berga camp:

> The enemy is nearing this town…but you won't be left here. The war is not over yet. The Fuhrer has promised us victory, and I believe him. He has a secret weapon, more terrible than our enemies have ever known. This weapon will turn the tide in our favor! But even if we should lose, there is nothing in it for you. You should know that I volunteered to serve in the SS because I hate

you dirty Jews. We have enough machine guns and ammunition to execute a group ten times larger than you are.[69]

When the war was over and Hauer made the disheartening trip back to his hometown in Hungary to search for survivors and evidence of prior life preserved, he came to discover how much had been taken away. He went by the house owned by a Dr. Grossman. It was one of the nicer homes in Goncz, but Dr. Grossman, of course, no longer lived there, nor did any of his family. They had all likely perished. In a cruel twist, the man who opened the door was someone named Veres, a man reviled by Hauer and his family. He had been an especially open anti-Semite and was proud of it. But now, Veres was full of good cheer and claimed to be only watching over the house until Grossman's return. He also claimed to have tried to help Hauer's family when the Nazis overran the town. Hauer was invited to eat with him and his wife to celebrate his surprise return home, but Hauer left in disgust.

A few years later, Hauer ended up in the United States, where he would carve out a good life for himself as a family man and as a teacher. But the Auschwitz tattoo—A9092—would be forever on his arm. To a degree, he was able to step back from the horrors he experienced and become almost accepting. He could see, for example, the capacity for *schadenfreude* in everyone, *even himself*. Cohen powerfully captures Hauer's thoughts in this way:

> The dog was in every man, a beast that could be unleashed. That, at least, was Hauer's conclusion. Man was a divided being. In the right circumstances, with enough encouragement, the dogs would rampage. He recalled how in the camps, on a bright day, he might sit in the sun and feel happy for a moment as he crushed the lice that crawled all over him. Killing them was some measure of revenge on a living thing actually weaker than him. The pleasure was ephemeral. But in everyone there lurked some potential to find contentment in another's pain. In Germany, all constraint had been cast off, the beasts had run wild.[70]

Hauer also found comfort, perhaps a little *schadenfreude*, in realizing that Germans would have to live with the knowledge of what they had done. This would be a heavy burden, and it was comforting to make such a downward comparison. And Hauer was lucky, at least in the sense that he survived. He, like the few lucky Americans soldiers who also survived, picked up the pieces and had successful lives. GI William Shapiro returned home, earned a medical degree, and had a long career as an obstetrician. His sentence in the hell of the Holocaust perpetrated by the Nazis ended when, during the forced marched away from Berga, he and other fellow soldiers were resting in a barn and heard the close advance of American troops. Shapiro, emaciated and weakened, staggered out of the barn to see a white star imprinted on a Sherman tank approaching his way. The SS guards had scattered. An American jeep drove up, and Shapiro heard the friendly words spoken by an American soldier, words that were in such contrast to the barking commands he had heard from the guards: "Climb in, soldier." And with those three words, a better world welcomed him.[71]

CHAPTER 11

How Would Lincoln Feel?

No one who actually knew the president ever quite understood Chevy Chase's Saturday Night Live *impersonation of him as a genial dolt who stumbled over doorsteps....Even the slightest misstep was taken as more proof that this graceful and athletic man, who had played on two national championship football teams at the University of Michigan and turned down offers from the pros, was, in fact, a bumbler.*

—James A. Baker III[1]

"He that is without sin among you, let him cast a stone at her." And again he stooped down, and wrote on the ground. And they which heard it, being convicted by their own conscience, went out one by one, beginning at the eldest, even unto the last: And Jesus was left alone, and the woman standing in the midst.

—John 8:3–11[2]

I am still a little afraid of missing something if I forget that, as my father snobbishly suggested, and I snobbishly repeat, a sense of the fundamental decencies is parceled out unequally at birth.
—Nick Carraway, The Great Gatsby[3]

One of my first bosses left a lasting impression on me. I helped him manage a group of high school student employees at the movie theater I mentioned in Chapter 5. Much of these kids' banter was at each other's expense. Mistakes inspired ribbing, sometimes ridicule. This was mostly how they entertained themselves between shows and after the concession rush. But they did not behave this way around my boss. When he emerged from the manager's office to make his rounds, gather the cash, check the Coke syrup, examine the ice chests, they would rein it in. It was not because they feared him. They respected him, as did I.

The source of our respect was something indistinct at first. It was not his physical presence. He was slight of build and had a pallor that caused him to blend into the surroundings. But he made wise decisions under pressure. Movie theaters usually run smoothly, but they are also only one broken projector away from a frustrated public wanting its money back. And sometimes boorish customers cause problems. To paraphrase Rudyard Kipling, my boss kept his head when everyone about him was losing theirs, even accepting blame for problems if this resolved the issue nicely.[4] But what really set him apart—and produced a kind of awe in me—was that I never once saw him either criticize or make fun of another person. He liked listening to jokes and saw the humor in people's behavior, but he left criticism to others and recoiled from unkind laughter.

It took a while for me to appreciate these things about him. I would watch him closely, wondering if he would deviate from the pattern. He never did. I soon found myself trying to copy him, so impressed was I with his way of being. This proved impossible. My more judgmental nature usually triumphed over my will. Even if I avoided making a critical remark or suppressed a pleased reaction to someone's small failure, the internal judge in me failed to purge itself.

What enabled him to be this way? Partly, it was just the way he was. He owned a greater capacity for empathy than the average person. But the more I watched him, the more I realized that a big reason was that he understood people better than we did. He had a highly developed understanding of what caused people's behavior, and this made him resistant to blaming people for their failures. He had suffered his share of hard knocks. Only in his early 30s when I knew him, he was already losing his sight because of diabetes that had struck him in early childhood. He would sometimes grab a candy bar, throw some change in the cash drawer, and eat it quickly as he went back to his office. Through the crack in the manager's door, I had once seen him injecting himself with insulin. He had only a high school education, and I suspect that he missed an early opportunity to go college. For some people, hardships make them resentful; in his case, these setbacks made him alert to the circumstances that can hold people back. Many people make quick negative judgments when seeing those around them fail (making it easy to find humor in their failings). My boss' instinct was to look for those circumstances beyond their control that may have caused their failure. He seemed temperamentally inclined to wonder what in their lives may have constrained them to act as they did.

I reflect on my boss because, as I near the end of this book, it is worth considering how we might curb our natural leaning to feel *schadenfreude*. I hope it is clear from earlier chapters that *schadenfreude* often goes with the grain of human nature rather than against it. But I think there is a lot we can learn from my boss if we want to avoid making *schadenfreude* a habit. By focusing on the situational factors that are often overlooked, the major causes of other people's misfortunes, we will feel empathy rather than *schadenfreude*.

PERSONALITY IS THE DEFAULT EXPLANATION FOR OTHERS' ACTIONS

The consideration of situational factors is not so easily done, however—there is at least one countervailing psychological bias that we need to overcome, what social psychologists sometimes call the "fundamental attribution error." This bias refers to our dual tendencies to overattribute the causes of other people's behavior to their internal qualities along with *overlooking* the possible role of situational causes. This bias goes precisely in the opposite direction of what leads to empathy, producing *schadenfreude* instead when others suffer.

I once saw a man get angry with a nurse in a hospital waiting room. What a jerk, I thought. This was my quick, automatic reaction. But then I caught myself. Some years earlier, I had also lost my patience with a nurse in an emergency waiting room. My eldest daughter had hit her head while playing on a slide and needed immediate medical attention. After an hour of waiting, I had reached my limit with the triage system and had started protesting insistently to a nurse. Soon, a doctor examined my daughter, and, 20 stitches later, we left the hospital. With the surfacing of this strong memory, I questioned my initial reaction to the man's behavior. I wondered whether this man had a good reason for losing his cool, too.

We see a man get angry with a nurse and our quick inference is that he must be a hostile person. This "explains" his behavior. He may be under enormous emotional stress—but we usually settle for thinking "what a jerk!" Unless we can put ourselves in the man's shoes and discover the situation from his perspective, this attributional bias will often prevail.[5]

This attributional bias has a direct bearing on how we react to the misfortunes of others. If I perceive the misfortune of another to be the result of that person's internal disposition or moral failing, then I'll probably think he deserves what he gets and I may feel a rush of pleasure at his pain. If I perceive his misfortune to be the result of the situation, then I may conclude that he does not deserve it and I will feel empathy—not *schadenfreude*. Let's say I made the assumption that the man yelling at the nurse was belligerent and selfish. In the moment, I had good reason to think so and I might feel pleased if the nurse called a security guard. But what if, right before I walked into the waiting room, the man had calmly asked the nurse for an update on his wife's condition, and the nurse had replied, "I need to be honest with you. Your wife is not going to make it. I need to attend to other patients." Now we see the situation differently. The man's behavior is forgivable, even commendable. Anyone who witnessed the entire exchange is unlikely to pigeonhole this man as a jerk.

A LESSON FROM STANLEY MILGRAM'S RESEARCH ON OBEDIENCE TO AUTHORITY

Recognizing our strong tendency to make internal explanations for other people's behavior, and the accompanying tendency to ignore situational causes, helps us avoid these tendencies when appropriate. But this recognition is difficult to achieve. A good example to illustrate the point is the classic research done on obedience to authority by social psychologist Stanley Milgram. This research was conducted in the 1960s, but, even today, it has the capacity to amaze. Most of the participants in Milgram's studies behaved in ways that seemed sadistic, and it is tempting to damn them for it and to infer sadistic traits to explain how they acted. Indeed, when I show a film made from these original studies, many students laugh at the participants and set themselves above them—until they learn more about the research. The procedure merits a close examination.

The participants were ordinary, mostly middle-aged men who responded to an advertisement for paid participants in an experiment on learning on the Yale University campus where Milgram was a professor. They showed up, two at a time, or so it appeared, and were told that the experimenters were interested in the effects of punishment on learning. One participant, determined by drawing straws, was given the role of "teacher" and the other the role of "learner." In fact, the procedure was rigged so that the real participant would always be the teacher. The other man was a stooge pretending to be another participant. The "learner" was instructed to memorize a list of word pairs with the expectation that the teacher would call out the first word in each pair and ask him to complete the pair in successive order. Each correct pairing would get a "good" and each incorrect pairing would result in an increasingly intense shock delivered by the teacher.

As the teacher watched, the learner was led to an adjacent room and hooked up to what appeared to be electrodes. The teacher also received a sample mild shock of 45 volts to show that the "shocks" would hurt, even at a low level. The learner then revealed information that would have weighty implication later on. He noted that a medical exam had detected a slight heart condition and asked if the shocks were dangerous. The experimenter responded confidently that they would be "painful" but cause "no tissue damage." All communication with the learner from this point was through an intercom. Once in the control room, the teacher sat at a table facing an apparatus used for delivering the shocks. This apparatus had a series of 30 switches representing successively higher volts of electricity. The 10th level (150 volts) was labeled "Strong Shock"; the 17th level (255 volts) "Intense Shock"; the 25th level (375 volts) "Danger, Severe Shock." At the final levels (435 and 450 volts), the control panel was marked "XXX," suggesting especially intense danger.[6]

At first, the learner did well (using a programmed sequence), but he soon began making errors, requiring the teacher give him shocks by pressing down the switches, each giving a harsh buzzing sound. At 75 volts the learner responded with audible grunts, and at 120 volts, the learner shouted that the shocks were painful. Groans of pain began at 135 volts, and, at 150 volts, the learner cried out, "Ugh!!! Experimenter! That's all. Get me out of here! I told you I had heart trouble. My heart's starting to bother me now. Get me out of here, please. My heart's starting to bother me. I refuse to go on. Let me out."[7] However, the experimenter calmly told the teacher to continue, using a sequence of prods such as the "experiment requires that you continue" and "you have no other choice, you *must* go on." At 270 volts, the learner emitted an agonized scream as well as further emphatic demands to stop the experiment. At 330 volts, the screams were intense and prolonged, and the learner, sounding panicked, complained about his heart and screamed once again to be let out. At the next voltage level, the intercom went silent, implying the real possibility that the learner had suffered a fatal heart attack.

What would you do if you were the "teacher" in this study? Milgram addressed this question to three groups: psychiatrists, college students, and middle-class adults, using a detailed summary of the procedure, complete with a diagram of the control panel. All 110 respondents believed that they would have disobeyed the experimenter at some point. Only four said they would obey until the shocks reached 300 volts, the highest level that anyone said they would go. The most common predicted level, for all groups, was 150 volts, and a typical explanation was "I can't stand to see people suffer. If the learner wanted to get out, I would free him so as not to make him suffer pain."[8] Milgram worried these responses might reflect a degree of vanity. He then asked respondents to predict how 100 *other* Americans from diverse ages and occupations would respond. Figure 11.1 shows the predictions made by the 39 psychiatrists, whose views were essentially the same as the views of the other two groups. All who responded to the survey felt that the end of the shock board was reserved for, as Milgram called it, the "pathological fringe."[9] In fact, the group of psychiatrists predicted that most people would not go beyond 150 volts, the point in the procedure when the learner made his first demand to get out of the experiment.

I know of no more persuasive evidence for how easy it is to underestimate the powerful influence of situational forces on behavior—because all three of these groups were *wildly* inaccurate in their predictions. The average percentage of actual participants (top line) behaved very differently: 65 percent of

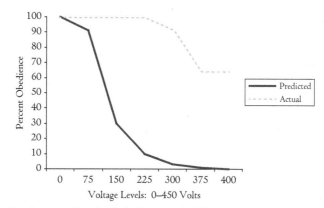

Figure 11.1. Predicted vs. actual levels of obedience in the Milgram study.

participants in Milgram's study not only went to the highest shock level, but *had to be asked* by the experimenter to stop giving the shocks. In summarizing the implications of the misaligned predictions made by the three groups, Milgram presaged the idea of the fundamental attribution error. He concluded that people assume that:[10]

> Unless coerced by physical force or threat, the individual is preeminently the source of his own behavior. A person acts in a particular way because he has decided to do so. Action takes place in a physical-social setting, but this is merely the stage for its occurrence. The behavior itself flows from an inner core of the person; within the core personal values are weighted, gratifications assessed, and resulting decisions are translated into action....Most people start with the presuppositions of this sort....They focus on the character of the autonomous individual rather than on the situation in which he finds himself.[11]

Again, the implications for understanding *schadenfreude* are important. Misfortunes often result from deliberate actions people have taken, making them appear responsible and deserving of their suffering. But Milgram's findings suggest that we are unlikely to recognize the situational factors that may have played a role in causing these actions. The situation "is merely the stage"[12] for their enactment. This means that internal qualities will seem to *explain* these actions. They will fill in the causal gaps, usually making the misfortunes seem more deserved—and *amusing* to this extent.

HOW MILGRAM'S RESULTS HELP UNDERSTAND
REACTIONS TO *PREDATOR*

Consider again *To Catch a Predator*, which I explored in Chapter 7, a reality TV program that I argued uses humiliation as a main hook to appeal to viewers. Each man who shows up with the apparent intentions of engaging in sexual relations with a minor is doing something that the vast majority of people assume that they themselves would not do. And so it is natural to see the man's behavior as an expression of a flawed, perverted inner core. In fact, this assumption will seem catalyzed by the perceived *absence* of countering situational factors. But might there be mitigating factors? Some of these men might have been abused themselves, some may have been more vigorously enticed than others, and some may have not believed the decoy to be minor. Some may have been particularly vulnerable to the clever, persuasive tactics used by the decoy. At the very least, there is wide variation in how we might judge these men—branded sexual predators—if we knew their stories. But the tendency to make the fundamental attribution error generally, together with the manifest abnormality and repulsiveness of the behavior, would discourage anyone from looking for a more complete picture. As a packager of *schadenfreude*, the show is not designed for situational analysis. It is improbable for these men to be perceived as anything but wholly perverted creatures, undeserving of our concern—even deserving of their humiliation, a punishment that civilized society normally disallows. The show allows, even encourages, viewers to delight in the downfall of these "predators."

It is so easy, perhaps automatic, to infer dispositional, internal causes for other people's behavior—so much so that it can require focus and effort to correct this initial, automatic inference even when situational factors warrant it. A series of studies by Dan Gilbert and his colleagues shows this. In one study, participants watched a video of a woman acting in a nervous and anxious way while conversing with a man. Viewers could not hear the conversation, but subtitles on the screen told them the topics being discussed: embarrassing topics (e.g., sexual fantasies) in one condition and mundane topics (e.g., hobbies) in another. As one would expect, subsequent ratings of "dispositional anxiousness" were greater in the hobbies condition than in the sexual fantasies condition. Highlighting this situational constraint affected judgments, as viewers inferred that being asked to discuss an embarrassing topic could make a person anxious. But if someone was anxious when discussing hobbies, then "personality" was the stronger cause of the anxious behavior. More interesting was what happened in two additional conditions. Viewers watched one of the two videos, but this time they were also asked to rehearse a set of word strings at the same time. Ratings of dispositional anxiousness in *both* conditions resembled the rating made in the 'hobbies' condition *without* the additional cognitive task. Evidently, viewers having the additional, distracting task failed to take into account the implications of the conversation topic on anxious behavior. The woman *acted* in an anxious way, and therefore she was *perceived* as dispositionally anxious.[13]

These and other experiments led to the conclusion that the causal attributions for behavior we observe in others start by automatically inferring a dispositional cause. The man gets angry with the nurse, he is a hostile person; the man continues to shock the learner, he is a sadistic person; the woman is behaving nervously, she is a nervous person, and so on. There is a straight and easy path from behavior to inferring disposition that requires little cognitive effort. We may then "correct" the dispositional inference if we are made aware of situational factors that counter our initial impression. The man is not a hostile person because his wife is severely injured; the man is not sadistic because he is only doing what most people would do in this situation; the woman is not an anxious person because she is discussing an embarrassing topic. The problem is that correcting our first impressions is much less automatic. And there are innumerable ways that this correction will be prevented from ever happening. Furthermore, we have a plentiful supply of seductive personality labels that are difficult to avoid using (such as "jerk," "sadist," and "neurotic") and fewer labels to describe circumstances (such as "it was a tough situation").[14]

Awareness of this attribution tendency provides at least an opportunity for a more complex explanation for someone's behavior, which might avert the instant flow of guilt-free *schadenfreude*. There is a clear lesson to be learned from our tendency to commit the fundamental attribution error: we would do well to make a conscious effort to learn more about the circumstances that might have caused a misfortune happening to another. Situational factors will compete on an even playing field with dispositional factors in our efforts to explain what happened. In the process, we might find ourselves less likely to laugh or smile.

WISDOM FAVORS AVOIDING THE FUNDAMENTAL ATTRIBUTION ERROR

It is certainly easy to find fun in the humiliation of people when we can enjoy self-righteous superiority over them or when they appear to richly deserve what they get. The strong tendency to make dispositional attributions for other people's actions is one reason this type of fun is so common. But some people succeed better than others in resisting the tendency. My boss was an example. I cannot think of a better way to sum it up than to say that he had wisdom. Perhaps he also had a greater natural empathy for others, but I think that life taught him to focus first on the circumstances that can shape people's behavior, especially if someone had failed or suffered from his actions. When those around my boss were quick to blame people for their failures, he bucked the instant consensus either by his silence or by offering an alternative, less condemning explanation. Did we ever catch him feeling *schadenfreude*? Of course. The emotion is part of everyone's DNA. But it was never malicious, and his wisdom moderated its prevalence.

ABRAHAM LINCOLN: WITH MALICE TOWARD NONE; CHARITY FOR ALL

There was a touch of Abraham Lincoln in my boss. Lincoln is admired by anyone who becomes familiar with the details of his life. Early in his political career in the Illinois state legislature, he made the mistake of making fun of a fellow legislator, James Shields, by publishing satirical letters about him. Lincoln had used a pseudonym, but Shields found out, felt his honor offended, and challenged Lincoln to a duel. Together with friends on both sides, Lincoln found a way to convince Shields to call off the duel, but not until it got close to happening. This experience taught Lincoln important lessons. Ashamed by the incident, he avoided harsh satire of others in print from then on. His stump speeches could be lively in their pointed humor aimed at his opponents, but even this habit disappeared over time.[15] He was so talented in mimicry and so perceptive about the human condition that these were hard habits to reverse completely, but when he lapsed, he felt chagrined and apologized.[16] He walked away from fights, laughed off insults, and rejected opportunities to mock and humiliate.[17]

Taking the perspective of others seemed to come naturally to Lincoln. He learned how to handle people effectively through tact, which he once defined as, "the ability to describe others as they see themselves."[18] Many accounts of Lincoln's life highlight the famous incident of his writing a critical letter to General George Meade after the battle of Gettysburg.[19] Lincoln had suffered many frustrations with his generals. There had been so many missed opportunities due to incompetence or the lack of initiative in these men, but the Union victory at Gettysburg could have been a fatal blow to the Confederacy. After many clashes with terrible losses on both sides, Meade had prevailed over the Confederate army under General Robert E. Lee, causing Lee to retreat across the Potomac to regroup and to prevent complete defeat. Retreat was slowed by flooding along the river, yet Meade failed to take this opportunity to crush Lee's army, despite explicit urgings from Lincoln by telegraph and special messenger. Thus, Lee had the time to build bridges that allowed his army's escape. Meade's failure to act exasperated Lincoln, and he penned a letter expressing his feelings. This is how part of it reads:

> My dear General...You fought and beat the enemy at Gettysburg; and, of course, to say the least, his loss was as great as yours. He retreated; and you did not, as it seemed to me, pressingly pursue him, but a flood in the river detained him, till, by slow degrees, you were again upon him. You had at least twenty thousand veteran troops directly with you, and as many more raw ones within supporting distance, all in addition to those who fought with you at Gettysburg; while it was not possible that he had received a single recruit; and yet you stood and let the flood run down, bridges be built, and the enemy move away at his leisure, without attacking him....I do not believe you appreciate the magnitude of the misfortune involved in Lee's escape. He was within our easy grasp, and to have closed upon him would, in connection with our other late successes, have ended the war. As it is, the war will be prolonged indefinitely. If you could not safely attack Lee last Monday, how can you possibly do so south of the river, when you can take with you very few—no

more than 2/3's of the force you then had in hand? It would be unreasonable to expect and I do not expect that you can now effect much. Your golden opportunity is gone, and I am distressed immeasurably because of it....[20]

Meade, sensitive to criticism, had already learned of Lincoln's frustration through other channels and had threatened to resign because he felt the criticism undeserved. But Meade never read the letter. It was found in Lincoln's materials after his death. On this letter, Lincoln wrote, "To Gen. Meade, never sent, or signed." According to historians, Lincoln saw no point in further upsetting General Meade, who had served the Union cause mightily. As distressed as Lincoln was by Meade's inaction, he was able to suppress the impulse to send the letter.

Lincoln did not care for alcohol, especially whiskey, because he disliked the effect it had on his thinking and on his self-control. But if others wanted to drink, this was fine. In his early days, he frequented the company of heavy drinkers and could enjoy their company even as he refused to drink. Mostly notably, he did not condemn alcoholics, unlike many others who did. In fact, he felt pity and compassion—because he recognized that alcohol could often have special hold on even the best of people—this "tyrant of spirits," as he called it.[21]

Lincoln's sensitivity to the situational factors affecting other people's behavior was not at the expense of a sense of humor. Lincoln delighted in jokes which, when he was present, were "plenty and blackberried,"[22] even bad puns. He was able to tell funny yarns about people so vividly that people's "sides were sore with laughing," according to President Van Buren.[23] But he was rarely unkind in his joking.[24] Lincoln used humor to put people at ease. If he did laugh at people's misfortunes, it was amusement that recognized human frailties that he himself shared.[25] Indeed, much of Lincoln's humor was directed at himself, especially at what he considered his "ugly" face.[26]

And so, Lincoln, for all his remarkable talents for seeing the humor in people's behavior, matured into someone whose instincts leaned more toward empathy than ridicule. Lincoln came to recognize the evils of slavery, but he did not condemn Southerners for owning slaves. When Southerners complained that slavery was a difficult system to eliminate, he could appreciate this point. "I surely will not blame them," he said, "for not doing what I should not know how to do myself. If all earthly powers were given me, I should not know what to do, as to the existing situation."[27] When he considered the matter carefully and imagined what kind of Southerners that Northerners would be if they grew up in the South, he thought, "They are just what we would be in their situation."[28] And yet, he knew slavery was wrong, in part because he could imagine what being a slave was like. To people who argued that slavery was "a very good thing," he noted that he had never come across someone eager to take advantage of the opportunity "by being a slave himself."[29]

Lincoln was a complex man, and I do not want to make a saint out of him. My aim here is to suggest that, to the extent that he displayed traits that we admire, he was also broad in his understanding of the causes of other people's behavior. His instincts, like those of my boss, led him to take into account the situational constraints that can play a major role in explaining people's actions—which is at least one reason why he said things such as, "I don't like that man. I must get to know him better."[30] He was also capable of seeing depravity in others when fitting, but in his tendency to avoid the "fundamental attribution error," he set a good example for us all.

The additional lesson here is that we are less likely to have *schadenfreude* dominate our reactions to another person's misfortune if we are able to focus on the situational factors causing the misfortune. Rather than *schaden-freude*, the prevailing emotion should be empathy, as it was for Lincoln, by all accounts. It is no accident that Lincoln was able to pen these immortal lines from his second inaugural address: "With malice toward none; with charity for all."[31]

CONCLUSION

The scandal? There was no need to be driven away by a little scandal. It would have been painful, grotesque, but a scandal was after all a sort of service to the community.
—SAUL BELLOW, HERZOG[1]

[A]n apostle of peace will feel a certain vicious thrill run through him, and enjoy a vicarious brutality, as he turns to the column in this newspaper at the top of which "Shocking Atrocity" stands printed in large capitals.

—WILLIAM JAMES[2]

Until the late fall of 2009, Tiger Woods seemed to live a life approaching perfection. After leaving Stanford University early to turn pro, he instantly became the ascendant golfer on the professional tour. During the more than a decade of dominance that followed, there were periods when he toyed with the competition. He hit shots impossible for mere mortals, maintained an astonishing level of focus, and carried himself with singular self-assurance and poise. Unlike so many other golfers, he actually looked like an athlete. "Tiger" was of a different breed of golfer, even a different breed of man, and, at the age of 34, was within easy striking distance of eclipsing the record of 18 major golf championships long held by "The Golden Bear," Jack Nicklaus. Woods became an international marketing phenomenon, transcending the world of golf, and the income from many lucrative endorsements propelled him into the near-billionaire class.[3] Woods enjoyed the kind of celebrity status that enabled him to double TV ratings with his participation in a tournament.[4] What was known about his well-guarded personal life also added to the luster. He married a stunningly beautiful Swedish woman who was a former fashion model. He had his own charity organization, the Tiger Woods Foundation, dedicated to helping children learn and achieve. His father, Earl Woods, had been able to say with confidence that his son "will do more than any other man in history to change the course of humanity."[5]

But his fall from grace was quick and cataclysmic. On December 9, 2009, he was taken to a hospital for injuries suffered when he reportedly crashed his Cadillac Escalade on his property in the early morning hours.[6] The details of how and why this happened are unclear, but much evidence suggested that there had been a domestic dispute caused by his wife's discovery of his apparently out-of-control infidelity. Within days, multiple women claimed to have had affairs with Woods,[7] and Woods himself, under the pressure of burgeoning evidence, admitted to betraying his marriage vows[8] and voluntarily took a leave of absence from golf to get his personal life in order. In a press conference, he apologized for selfishly hurting his wife, family, friends, and fans.[9]

This was no ordinary fall, and the tabloid media leapt on this story. As a milestone in the history of *schadenfreude*, the misfortunes of Tiger Woods surely surpass the troubles of Martha Stewart. Indeed, the *National Enquirer* was largely responsible for initially exposing Woods's infidelities,[10] but it was deemed fair game for just about every respected news outlet and internet venue.[11] The general interest in this story was broad and relentless, and *schadenfreude* was infused through many public reactions. Soon came the jokes.[12] "Tiger" was now the "Cheetah."[13] The late-night talk show writers took full advantage, and the blogosphere abandoned all constraint.[14]

Don Ohlmeyer, a longtime innovator in television sports and entertainment generally, was working at the time as an ombudsman for ESPN, the major sports network channel. His job was to provide independent analysis of the business of producing sports television at ESPN, and he found himself addressing how the network dealt with the indiscretions of athletes, with Tiger Woods heading the list. It was clear that viewers wanted to know everything about these indiscretions. Ohlmeyer struggled to think through the difficult balancing act of maintaining high journalistic standards while also feeding the monster that paid the bills. The tabloids and talk shows fired up their engines to serve a public that delights in the troubles of the rich, famous, and powerful, and then ESPN and other "mainstream media tag along."[15] Ohlmeyer noted that the bottom line of needing to serve the insatiable appetites of the public meant that ESPN had to keep its headlights on the story, just like pretty much everyone else. Coverage focusing on the misbehavior of Woods was what viewers wanted. Many ESPN.com articles about Woods attracted an enormous increase in viewer traffic compared to the average article. It seemed impossible to withhold reporting the details of Woods's story in light of this. Ohlmeyer, whose experience and role as ombudsman give him considerable credibility, concluded that *"Schadenfreude... seems to be a contagion afflicting many media outlets and their consumers."*[16]

One theme that I've carried through this book is that misfortunes befalling others can bring us pleasure because, sometimes, we benefit from these misfortunes—more than we are aware of or willing to admit. I argued in Chapter 3 that this is true most obviously in competitive situations when a rival suffers. We can easily infer that many other golfers on the professional tour might have been secretly pleased by Woods's troubles. It is hard enough to win a professional tournament, especially a coveted Major tournament, but the chances of winning were reduced to small odds indeed when Woods was playing. Some golfers may have cursed the fates to have their careers overlap with the reign of Tiger Woods. His fall from grace provided an opening.

As natural as it may be to feel *schadenfreude*, I have also emphasized that most of us are not quite sure that we ought to feel it, or at least disclose feeling it. I can only suspect that other golfers felt happy over Woods's troubles. I am unaware of any golfer, at least in interviews for the national press, who openly expressed *schadenfreude*. Most people are uncomfortable with admitting *schadenfreude*, generally, but particularly if it seems inspired by a selfish motive. It is *verboten*. Some on the pro tour acknowledged the obvious: that their own rankings might rise in the wake of Woods's troubles. British golfer Lee Westwood noted that Woods's situation made a higher ranking for himself more within reach.[17] At the time he made the comment, he was ranked number 3 in the world, behind Woods at number 1 and Phil Mickelson at number 2.

I have underscored throughout this book that the way we compare with others plays an important role in our self-esteem and in our emotional life. Competition itself is a kind of social comparison process. If we had no capacity to make social comparisons, then we would have no sense of what rivalry means. It is largely through social comparisons that we understand who has won and who has lost and through which we infer the levels of our abilities and talents. Social comparisons are important building blocks for self-assessments, self-evaluations, and the emotions enmeshed with these judgments.

Woods's remarkable success on the golf course and the way he seemed to realize perfection in almost every way a person can do so provided an acute contrast for most people, even if they were not interested in golf. Although some people might have been inspired by Woods, perhaps more felt diminished. Those plagued by envy surely found some measure of joy in his fall from grace. And, as inspiring as he might have been, many of us would have preferred to be him rather than be in awe of him. For golfers in particular, Woods probably changed the standards by which they judged themselves. This also fits with the role of social comparisons in how we judge our abilities and talents. Because of his physique alone, many on the pro tour would look at themselves in the mirror and conclude that they failed to measure up even before taking a swing. Often, it seemed as though, when Woods was playing, all the other golfers were playing for second. Ireland's Padraig Harrington, reminiscing about Woods's 15-stroke victory in the 2000 U.S. Open, said, "I was there...I was playing in the other tournament."[18] Ernie Els, paired with Woods in the final round and with two U.S. Open championships to his own credit at that juncture, noted, "It seems like we're not playing in the same ballpark right now....When he's on, you don't have much of a chance."[19]

The scandal around Woods's affairs reduced that contrast between him and other golfers. At the news conference where Woods, once such a colossus, apologized, he was reduced to humbler dimensions. The stunning personal and professional dimensions to this humbling undoubtedly registered with golfers and other people across the board. Some may have felt mostly pity and disappointment,[20] but others are likely to have felt to some degree boosted by the event.

As I have also stressed throughout this book, many instances of *schadenfreude* can be explained by envy. We are most likely to envy people who do better in areas important to us—those in the same line of work and with similar aspirations. Envy is more intense and more hostile when it represents a frustrated particular desire.

There is little doubt that envy of Tiger Woods could make some people feel *schadenfreude* over his misfortune. For many pro golfers, of course, Woods was no ordinary unflattering social comparison—he had all the features that would create strong, potentially hostile envy. No doubt Woods left a trail of frustrated, envious golfers in his wake as he racked up win after win, usually in dominating fashion, sometimes humiliating his competition—because they sometimes seemed to choke under pressure. Becoming a pro golfer is no easy process; golf is an extremely difficult game, and the competition to get on and to stay on tour is fierce. Nonetheless, I imagine that most felt like they were playing Salieri to Woods's Mozart.

I highlighted in Chapters 9 and 10 that people will rarely admit to envy, particularly the hostile kind. Because of his apparently sterling moral qualities, it was especially unacceptable to express hostile envy of Woods; it would have come across as mean and spiteful. Ironically, exactly because other pro golfers would be most primed for *schadenfreude*—because of their gain, because of a relief from a painful, envy-producing social comparison—I suspect that they were unwilling to express it openly. This was left to the tabloids, the late-night talk shows, the blogosphere, and other venues.

Another important factor in understanding public reaction to Woods's fall had to do with whether it seemed deserved. Deserved misfortunes produce more *schadenfreude* than undeserved misfortunes, another frequent theme in this book. We are pleased when a person gets his just desserts, even if it means that he'll suffer intensely as a result. The fact that Woods was solely responsible for his own downfall was a constant feature in many voiced reactions. Interestingly, a year before his extramarital affairs were revealed, Woods had taken a leave from the game because of a knee injury and the surgery it required. This may have pleased some, at least privately, for reasons we know well, but the general tenor of public reactions among golfers and fans was outwardly sympathetic. This dramatically changed following the revelations of infidelity, especially as the number and nature of his affairs quickly came to light.[21] His duplicity seemed extreme. After the birth of his son, he had placed a photo on his Web site with his baby and wife, suggesting perfect marital bliss. Woods had been extremely careful at crafting an image of a perfect life while apparently having affair after affair. The crafted image was clearly false. Did he begin to believe his father's prediction that he would "do more than any other man in history to change the course of humanity"?[22] When the information about the affairs surfaced, most people thought that he deserved the negative consequences—and were pleased.

It could have been worse for Woods. He was not someone to criticize others for their misbehaviors. His fault was in raising himself high rather than pointing out the failings of others. He was nonetheless faulted for maintaining an illusion of spotless living and for letting down those who believed in him. Other golfers spoke of Woods's deserving the negative publicity. The South African Ernie Els, who had been so completely humbled by Woods when they had been paired with each other in the 2000 U.S. Open, criticized the timing of the press conference at which Woods gave his apology. It overlapped with the start of a tournament in which Woods was no longer participating, thus hurting the sponsors. "It's selfish," said Ernie Els to *Golfweek Magazine*. "You can write that."[23] In Chapter 6, I argued that the perception of the deservingness of a misfortune is more acute when we have felt personally mistreated. Els, although highly accomplished in his own right and admired on and off the links,[24] may have felt a measure of personal humiliation over his U.S. Open drubbing, but there may have another reason. Although Woods rarely criticized other golfers, there was at least one exception. In September 2009, Woods was asked about how Els was responding to surgery to repair a torn anterior cruciate ligament (ACL). Woods, who had just gone through the same surgery, praised Els, but then noted: "Ernie is not a big worker physically and that's one of the things you have to do with an ACL injury. I feel pretty good with what I've done and I think Ernie could have worked a little bit harder."[25] Not only did he suggest Els was a bit lazy, he also contrasted Els's behavior with his own. For Els, the comparison must have hurt. In my opinion, it would be asking too much of Els not to feel a touch of *schadenfreude* when Woods's troubles emerged. I should *emphasize* Els's sterling qualities. When he was accepting the trophy for winning the 2012 British Open, he took time to thank former South African President Nelson Mandela (who had just turned 94) for what he had done for South Africa.[26] This was a stirring moment.

The comments of Jesper Parnevik, another pro golfer, also stand out. When Woods crashed his SUV, it was reported that Elin Nordegren, Woods's then-wife, used a golf club to break open a window so that she could extricate him from the car. Parnevik suggested that Nordegren "use a driver next time instead of a 3-iron." Why? In 2000, Parnevik and his wife had employed Nordegren as a nanny and had introduced her to Woods in 2001. Three years later, they were married. Parnevik, in some small way responsible for their marriage, felt sorry for her. He took Woods's betrayal of Elin personally. He said, "We probably thought he was a better guy than he is."[27]

STEPPING BACK FOR A MOMENT

Exploring the reasons why we feel *schadenfreude* over misfortunes such as what happened to Tiger Woods was the purpose of this book. However, as I have noted in earlier chapters, my focus on *schadenfreude* is not meant to overplay this reaction to another person's suffering—as natural and common a human emotion as I think it is.

Let's start with Homer Simpson, who is clearly prone to feeling *schadenfreude* when Ned Flanders fails. It is Homer's pleasure at seeing Ned's "Leftorium" do poorly that prompts Lisa to define the emotion for Homer. Toward the end of the episode, however, Homer has had his fill of feeling good when his friend is suffering, and he suddenly feels terrible for Ned who is about to lose all this property and savings "for a pig and poke."[28] Homer begins to cry over Ned's troubles and is weighed down with guilt over his earlier wishing for Ned's failure and over his pleasure when this did indeed happen. He leaps into action to save the business. He calls everyone he knows who is left-handed and urges them to go to the store to buy something. Soon it seems that all of Springfield are making their way to the store. In an ending echoing the final scene of Frank Capra's *It's a Wonderful Life*, when the townspeople of Bedford Falls come to the aid of George Bailey, the citizens of Springfield buy everything from can openers to accountant ledgers, all designed for the left-handed. Homer and Ned are now bosom buddies:

NED: Homer, affordable tract housing made us neighbors…you made us friends.

HOMER: To Ned Flanders, the richest left-handed man in town.[29]

The ended closes with Ned's son leading everyone in the song "Put on a Happy Face." It is a heartening ending without a trace of envy or *schadenfreude*. The inspired writers of this popular and long-lasting show surely knew that *schadenfreude* should neither be the whole story nor be the way to bring it to a close.

I ended Chapter 2 with the example of Bertie Wooster taking delicate pleasure in the knowledge that Constable Oates had to stand guard in the cold rain outside Bertie's window. No one had thought to tell Oates that Bertie was no longer a suspect in the theft of the cow creamer and no longer needed to be guarded. The thought of this caused Bertie to sigh contentedly and provided "a curiously mellow sense of happiness." Even so, few readers would accuse Bertie of being a sadist. Oates had treated Bertie abominably and, in the comic spirit of the novel, he richly deserved a few hours of discomfort. Until this point, Bertie had been imposed upon and mistreated by friends and foes alike and had suffered humiliations and physical injuries, all as he strove to satisfy the wishes of family and friends. Furthermore, he only experienced full contentment when he also knew that he had succeeded in actually helping them. He managed things so that his Aunt Dahlia could keep her cherished cook, his uncle could get a prized cow creamer, and a friend could acquire the permission to marry the girl of his dreams. The title of the novel, *The Code of the Woosters*, refers to the Woosters' credo to "never let a pal down"—largely the reason why Bertie gets enmeshed in these unpleasant situations. The end of a perfect day contains but a dusting of *schadenfreude*, adding a little spice to the knowledge that his friends and family have what they want.

And yet *schadenfreude* may almost always have a perverse feel to it, precisely because it is a feeling prompted by another's *suffering*. Our capacity to feel *schadenfreude* speaks to a side of human nature about which most of us are uneasy. For good reason, if we dwell for a moment on the appeal of humilitainment and on the insidious path from envy, to anti-Semitism, and then to pleasure in genocide. This is why the title of this book includes the word "dark."

While writing this book, I requested daily Google alerts signaling any story on the electronic media where the word *schadenfreude* was used. I averaged around two to three or so examples per day, and it was rare to find people admitting the feeling without an excuse. People would say, "I know I shouldn't have felt it but..." or "I have to admit that I couldn't help feeling..." Maybe this is one reason why there is no word for *schadenfreude* in English. It is a feeling that recoils from giving itself a label.[30]

But I agree with philosophers John Portmann and Aaron Ben-Ze'ev that the emotion need not be demonized.[31] I was struck by readers' reactions to a light-hearted column posted on the *Chronicle of Higher Education* Web site by a professor of English writing under the pseudonym "Alice Fenton." The column entitled "The Pleasures of Seeing the Deserving Fail" began by stating the delights of successful teaching, but then noted that, equally pleasurable although "much less discussed, are a series of what might be called negative victories."[32] Fenton described several variants, ranging from the irksome student who drops out to the student who fails but thoroughly deserves it. In other words, some students are simply hard to like.

She was wise not to give her real name. A passionate reaction quickly arose from many readers. Of the 101 comments I scanned, over half (52) were unambiguously critical and, of these, 32 were scathing.

- I want to take a shower after reading this piece. What's bad is that it's filled with pettiness and *schadenfreude*.

- What a horrid little essay.
- …to take pleasure in the ignorance, messed-up life, or dwindling life opportunities of a young person? That is a form of evil.
- She sounds like a bit of a sadist to me, taking pleasure in others' shortfalls. Shame on you, Alice…!
- Fenton's approach is simple-minded and hateful.
- What a sad, spiteful harpy.
- This essay is the product of a warped mind.

Fenton's honesty swiftly alienated her from over half of those responding—despite other passages in the article that emphasized the many joys she got from teaching, such as when the faltering student blossoms after much effort on both sides. There was no sense that the cases of *schadenfreude* were the prevalent part of her experience. Nor was she arguing that the emotion should be nourished. Rather, she was being unapologetically candid about the full range of emotions she felt as a college teacher, a profession that seems increasingly undervalued. For her troubles, many commenters, using rhetoric perhaps sharpened by the mostly unsigned nature of the postings, concluded that she was either a disturbed, hateful person or an embittered burn-out—and an incompetent teacher—or a blend of all of the above.

She had her strong supporters. This was my favorite:

Oh, for the love of Pete. Why is everyone so snippy? I thought this was a funny essay at a stressful time of term. I glory in the success of my students; I don't gloat or wish their failures, but I certainly recognize some of the scenarios "Alice" describes, and she's not asking us to let loose daily with our negative emotions, but simply allowing us a minute or two to sheepishly admit to one another that we do sometimes have petty feelings, and that it's perfectly natural.[33]

Fenton herself was unprepared for the responses she received, especially the hateful ones. After all, her experiences of *schadenfreude* were rare, and she was careful to start her comments by emphasizing the reasons to celebrate teaching. I saw no reason to disbelieve her. In fact, I thought that her admission of occasional *schadenfreude* gave her greater overall credibility. In another column in which she responded to the criticism, Fenton summed up her own defense well:

> To be human is to be unpleasant as well as pleasant.... Anger, dislike, weariness, *schadenfreude*: Those are all, for me, parts of human experience. That does not mean those emotions rule people, but it does mean they are there sometimes.[34]

Yes, *schadenfreude* is there—sometimes—and perhaps more in gray hues rather than in darkest black. In fact, most instances of *schadenfreude* may occur in quickly passing traces. These traces originate from the stories we choose to read as we surf the internet or from the gossip we overhear. If we are watching a golf match, *schadenfreude* will be part of the ebb and flow of the event, depending on whether we want a particular golfer to do well or poorly. Tiger Woods sends his ball into the water: *schadenfreude*—if we don't like him. A politician from an opposing party commits an embarrassing gaffe as election night approaches: *schadenfreude*. We see that a player for a rival basketball team that we detest gets injured: a mild rush of *schadenfreude* because the team will suffer—but sympathy for the player as well. A person whom we envy at work comes back from a vacation with an extra roll of fat around her middle or the hairline of a rival is receding surprisingly quickly: *schadenfreude*. Most of us, like Bertie Wooster, are basically good-natured and rarely wish severe problems on others, but we are not above taking pleasure in mild misfortunes when they are deserved. It is the rare person who acts on these fantasies, however. We rely on fate or acts of God. When the desired misfortunes fail to happen, we simply feel secret disappointment. A recently coined word for this feeling is *glückschmerz*—but that is another story.[35]

NOTES

Introduction

1. From http://www.snpp.com/episodes/7F23.html, retrieved April 5, 2010. I take this example from Powell, C. A. J., Smith, R. H., & Schurtz, D. R. (2008), Pleasure in an envied person's gain, in R. H. Smith (Ed.), *Envy: Theory and research* (pp. 148–164), New York: Oxford University Press.

2. From http://oxforddictionaries.com/definition/schadenfreude, retrieved May 24, 2012.

3. Howard, R. (Director) (1995), *Apollo 13* [film], Los Angeles: Image Entertainment. The film is an adaptation of real events. I do not claim actual knowledge of Jim Lovell's or Alan Shepard's behavior and feelings.

4. See http://www.miaminewtimes.com/2010-05-06/news/christian-right-leader-george-rekers-takes-vacation-with-rent-boy/, retrieved May 16, 2010.

5. See http://www.nytimes.com/2010/05/16/opinion/16rich.html, retrieved May 16, 2010.

6. Ibid.

7. See http://blogs.miaminewtimes.com/riptide/2010/05/rekers_on_the_record .php, retrieved May 16, 2010; http://www.miaminewtimes.com/2010-05-06/news/christian-right-leader-george-rekers-takes-vacation-with-rent-boy/1, retrieved May 28, 2010; http://blogs.miaminewtimes.com/riptide/2010/05/george_rekers_is_a_homo-sexual_says_escort.php, retrieved May 28, 2010; and http://blogs.villagevoice.com/run-ninscared/archives/2010/05/more_on_george.php, retrieved May 28, 2010.

8. See http://topics.blogs.nytimes.com/2009/01/13/the-age-of-schadenfreude/, retrieved December 17, 2011.

9. See http://www.psychologicalscience.org/index.php/publications/observer/2005/march-05/reality-check.html, retrieved January 12, 2011.

10. Steinbeck, J. (2008), *The grapes of wrath*, New York: Penguin. This novel was first published in 1939, p. 349.

11. de Waal, F. B. M. (2009), *The age of empathy: Nature's lessons for a kinder society*, New York: Harmony Books; Keltner, D. (2009), *Born to be good: The science of a meaningful life*, New York: W. W. Norton; McCullough, M. E. (2008), *Beyond revenge: The evolution of the forgiveness instinct*, San Francisco, CA: Jossey-Bass.

12. Baer, R. A. (Ed.) (2005), *Mindfulness-based treatment approaches: Clinician's guide to evidence base and applications*, New York: Academic; Diener, E., & Biswas-Diener, R. (2008), *Happiness: Unlocking the mysteries of psychological wealth*, New York: Wiley-Blackwell; Emmons, R. (2007), *Thanks! How the new science of gratitude can make you happier*, New York: Houghton Miffin Harcourt; Seligman, M. E. P. (2011), *Flourish: A visionary new understanding of happiness and well-being*, New York: Free Press.

13. See http://showcase.netins.net/web/creative/lincoln/speeches/1inaug.htm, retrieved August 1, 2012.

Chapter 1

1. Cited in Heider, F. (1958), *The psychology of interpersonal relations*, New York: John Wiley & Sons, p. 285.

2. Snyder, D. J. (1997), *The cliff walk*, New York: Little, Brown.

3. See http://www.nbc.com/saturday-night-live/, retrieved May 14, 2010.

4. Brickman, P., & Bulman, R. (1977), Pleasure and pain in social comparison, in J. M. Suls & R. L. Miller (Eds.), *Social comparison processes: Theoretical and empirical perspectives* (pp. 149–186), Washington, DC: Hemisphere; de Botton, A. (2004), *Status anxiety*, New York: Pantheon; Festinger, L. (1954), A theory of social comparison processes, *Human Relations*, 7, 117–140; Fiske, S. T. (2011), *Envy up, scorn down: How status divides us*, New York: Russell Sage Foundation; Frank, R. H. (1999), *Luxury fever*, New York: Free Press; Marmot, M. (2004), *The status syndrome*, New York: Times Books; Mussweiler, T. (2003), Comparison processes in social judgment: Mechanisms and consequences, *Psychological Review*, *110*, 472–489; Smith, R. H. (2000), Assimilative and contrastive emotional reactions to upward and downward social comparisons, in L. Wheeler & J. Suls (Eds.), *Handbook of social comparison: Theory and research* (pp. 173–200), New York: Kluwer Academic Publishers; Stapel, D., & Blanton, H. (Eds.) (2006), *Social comparison: Essential readings*, Brighton, NY: Psychology Press; Tesser, A. (1991), Emotion in social comparison and reflection processes, in J. M. Suls & T. A. Wills (Eds.), *Social comparison: Contemporary theory*

and research (pp. 115–145), Hillsdale, NJ: Erlbaum; Suls, J. M., & Wheeler, L. (Eds.) (2000), *Handbook of social comparison: Theory and research,* New York: Plenum Press.

5. See http://www.frasieronline.co.uk/episodeguide/season5/ep17.htm; and http://www.kacl780.net/frasier/transcripts/season_5/episode_17/the_perfect_guy.html, retrieved April 8, 2013.

6. Quoted in Baumol, W. J., & Blinder, A. S. (2010), *Economics: Principles and policy,* Mason, OH: Cengage Learning.

7. Summers, A., & Swan, R. (2006), *Sinatra: The life,* New York: Vintage Books, p. 81.

8. See http://www.youtube.com/watch?v=5QvSoRQrVJg, retrieved June 15, 2010.

9. Rousseau, J. (1984), *A discourse on inequality,* New York: Viking Penguin (orginally published in 1754; trans. Maurice Cranston).

10. Ibid., p. 114.

11. Much of this analysis was taken from Smith (2000).

12. Festinger (1954).

13. Fiske (2011).

14. Morse, S., & Gergen, K. J. (1970), Social comparison, self-consistency, and the concept of the self, *Journal of Personality and Social Psychology, 16,* 148–156.

15. Baumeister, R. F., & Bushman, B. (2008), *Social psychology and human nature* (1st ed.), Belmont, CA: Wadsworth; Kernis, M. H. (Ed.) (2006), *Self-esteem issues and answers: A sourcebook of current perspectives,* New York: Psychology Press; Tesser, A. (1988), Toward a self-evaluation maintenance model of social behavior, in L. Berkowitz (Ed.), *Advances in experimental social psychology,* vol. 21 (pp. 181–227), New York: Academic Press.

16. van Dijk, W., van Koningsbruggen, G. M., Ouwerkerk, J. W., & Wesseling, Y. M. (2011), Self-esteem, self-affirmation, and *schadenfreude, Emotion, 11,* 1445–1449.

17. van Dijk, W., Ouwerkerk, J. W., Wesseling, Y. M., & Koningsbruggen, G. M. (2011), Toward understanding pleasure at the misfortunes of others: The impact of self-evaluation threat on *schadenfreude, Cognition and Emotion, 25,* 360–368.

18. See http://www.quotationspage.com/quotes/François_de_La_Rochefoucauld, retrieved May 3, 2012.

19. Buss, D. (2012), *Evolutionary psychology: The new science of the mind* (4th ed.), New York: Allyn & Bacon. Also see a similar analysis in Smith (2000) and in Smith, R. H., & Kim, S. H. (2007), Comprehending envy, *Psychological Bulletin, 33*(1), 46–64.

20. Evolutionary perspectives also highlight that altruistic tendencies, especially toward kin, should be adaptive. It's not that the individual survives, but that his or her offspring survives. Offspring carry the individual's genetic material, and so tendencies that enhance the survival of kin should provide an evolutionary advantage.

21. Described in Fletcher, G. J. O. (2002), *The new science of intimate relationships,* Cambridge: Blackwell Publishers.

22. Frank (1999), pp. 135–136.

23. See Smith (2000) and Smith & Kim (2007).

24. de Botton (2004); Fiske (2011); Marmot (2004).

25. Buss (2012).

26. Brosnan, S. F., & de Waal, F. B. M. (2003), Monkeys reject unequal pay, *Nature*, *425*, 297–299.

27. See http://www.msnbc.msn.com/id/21773403/ns/technology_and_science-science/, retrieved November 28, 2009.

28. Boswell, J. (1904), *Life of Johnson*, Oxford: Oxford University Press (originally published in 1781).

29. Range, F., Horn, L., Viranyi, Z., & Hube, L. (2008), The absence of reward induces inequity aversion in dogs, *Proceedings of the National Academy of Sciences*, doi: 10.1073/pnas.0810957105, retrieved April 10, 2010.

30. Lindhom, C. (2008), Culture and envy, in R. H. Smith (Ed.), *Envy: Theory and research* (pp. 227–244), New York: Oxford University Press.

31. Alicke, M. D., & Govorun, O. (2005), The better-than-average effect, in M. D. Alicke, D. A. Dunning, & J. I. Krueger (Eds.), *The self in social judgment* (pp. 85–106), New York: Psychology Press. This effect is also referred to as the "Lake Wobegon effect" in reference to the imaginary community in Garrison Keiller's NPR show, *The Prairie Home Companion*, "where all the women are strong, all the men are good-looking, and all the children are above average." See http://prairiehome.publicradio.org/, retrieved May 5, 2012.

32. See http://www.digitaldreamdoor.com/pages/quotes/george_carlin.html, retrieved September 1, 2012.

33. Dunning, D. (2005), *Self-insight: Roadblocks and detours on the path to knowing thyself*, New York: Psychology Press; Taylor, S. E., & Brown, J. (1988), Illusion and well-being: A social psychological perspective on mental health, *Psychological Bulletin*, *103*, 193–210.

34. Baumeister, R. F. (1989), The optimal margin of illusion, *Journal of Social and Clinical Psychology*, *8*, 176–189.

35. I take many of the examples here about Crane's novel from a more extensive treatment in Smith (2000).

36. Crane, S. (1952/1895), *The red badge of courage*, New York: Signet, p. 21.

37. Ibid., p. 47.

38. Ibid., p. 92.

39. Ibid., p. 68.

40. Ibid.

41. Although *The Red Badge of Courage* is fictional, it has the feel of an absorbing documentary. Crane was in his early twenties when he wrote it and had no experience in battle,

but he was able to imagine the feelings a soldier might have and why. Indeed, this may have been one of his main goals in writing the book. During the period when he wrote it, he spent many hours in the New York studio of a painter friend, Corwin Linson, who saw him sift through many accounts of Civil War battles. See Linson, C. K. (1958), *My Stephen Crane*, Syracuse, NY: Syracuse University Press.

42. McCall, N. (1995), *Makes me wanna holler: A young black man in America*, New York: Vintage.

43. Ibid., p. 12.

44. Ibid., p. 13.

45. Ibid., p. 14.

46. Ibid., p. 17.

47. Ibid., p. 215.

48. Ibid., p. 263.

49. Ibid., p. 300.

50. Ibid., p. 351.

51. Ibid.

Chapter 2

1. Jones, G. (1996), *I lived to tell it all*, New York: Bantam Doubleday, p. 5.

2. Quoted in Sandage, S. A. (2005), *Born losers: A history of failure in America*, Cambridge: Harvard University Press, pp. 277–278.

3. See http://www.condenaststore.com/-sp/A-businessman-on-a-plane-thinks-it-s-not-enough-that-I-fly-first-class-New-Yorker-Cartoon-Prints_i8545335_.htm Leo Cullum, retrieved March 30, 2013.

4. See http://www.brainyquote.com/quotes/authors/g/george_carlin_2.html#CjVhwQkdRa8G3eEB.99, retrieved April 22, 2012.

5. See http://proof.blogs.nytimes.com/2008/12/15/drunkenfreude/, retrieved December 5, 2009.

6. Cheever also couched her *"drunkenfreude"* in the context of what she was able to learn from their behavior. She met many partygoers whose fine behavior left them unmemorable. It was the inebriated whose outrageous behavior was most instructive. She learned more about what *not to do* by watching those who embarrass themselves than she learned *to do* by watching the well-behaved and sober.

7. See http://proof.blogs.nytimes.com/2008/12/15/drunkenfreude/, retrieved December 5, 2009.

8. For an interesting empirical analogue, see Pyszczynski, T., Greenberg, J., & LaPrelle, J. (1985), Social comparison after success and failure: Biased search for information consistent with a self-serving conclusion, *Journal of Experimental Social Psychology, 21,*

195–211; Wills, T. A. (1981), Downward comparison principles in social psychology, *Psychological Bulletin, 90,* 245–271.

9. See http://kenlevine.blogspot.com/2007_12_01_archive.html, retrieved March 21, 2011.

10. See http://www.nj.com/entertainment/celebrities/index.ssf/2007/08/beauty_queens_map_quest.html, and http://www.theage.com.au/news/people/beauty-queen-left-searching-for-answers/2007/08/29/1188067160206.html, retrieved March 21, 2011.

11. See http://www.zimbio.com/Lauren+Caitlin+Upton/articles/IifvXCVcaBc/Caitlin+Upton+Miss+Teen+South+Carolina+Learns, retrieved March 21, 2011.

12. See http://www.nickburcher.com/2007/12/2007s-most-watched-best-youtube-clips.html, retrieved March 21, 2011.

13. See http://www.stupidityawards.com/Stupidest_Statement_of_the_Year.html, retrieved March 21, 2011.

14. See http://www.urbanmoms.ca/juice/2007/12/top-ten-quotes-of-2007.html, retrieved March 21, 2011; http://poplicks.com/2007/12/best-quotes-of-2007.html, retrieved March 21, 2011; and http://deathby1000papercuts.com/2007/12/the-27-most-outrageous-quotes-of-2007/, retrieved March 21, 2011.

15. http://www.boston.com/news/nation/gallery/121907_top10quotes?pg=3, and http://www.reuters.com/article/idUSN1959512020071219?loc=interstitialskip retrieved March 21, 2011.

16. See http://www.youtube.com/watch?v=lj3iNxZ8Dww, retrieved March 21, 2011.

17. See http://www.cincihomeless.org/content/downloads/Bumfights.pdf., retrieved December 5, 2009.

18. See http://vyuz.com/022706_Bumfights.htm, retrieved December 5, 2009.

19. Wills (1981).

20. Wert, S. R., & Salovey, P. (2004), A social comparison account of gossip, *Review of General Psychology, 8,* 122–137.

21. Wills (1981), p. 246.

22. Ibid.

23. Diener, E., Fraser, S. C., Beaman, A. L., & Kelem, R. T. (1976), Effects of deindividuation variables on stealing among Halloween trick-or-treaters, *Journal of Personality and Social Psychology, 33,* 178–183; Festinger, L., Pepitone, A., & Newcomb T. (1952), Some consequences of deindividuation in a group, *Journal of Abnormal and Social Psychology, 47,* 382–389; Postmes, T., & Spears, R. (1998), Deindividuation and anti-normative behavior: A meta-analysis, *Psychological Bulletin, 123,* 238–259; Zimbardo, P. G. (2007), *The Lucifer effect: Understanding how good people turn evil,* New York: Random House.

24. Wills (1981), p. 246.

25. Hobbes, T. (1968), *Leviathan*, Harmondsworth: Penguin, p. 35 (originally published in 1651).

26. Ibid.

27. Wills (1981), p. 260.

28. Ibid.

29. See http://www.guy-sports.com/humor/comedians/comedian_groucho_marx .htm, retrieved May 17, 2012.

30. See http://www.corsinet.com/braincandy/ins-fmen.html, retrieved May 17, 2012.

31. See http://www.thewrap.com/tv/column-post/jon-stewart-accept-it-gop-mitt-romneys-your-man-video-32710, retrieved November 13, 2011; another safe target is the self: there is no way to insult the audience if the focus is on the joketeller himself.

32. Gruner, C. R. (1997), *The game of humor: A comprehensive theory of why we laugh*, New Brunswick, NJ: Transaction Publishers, p. 8; see also Ferguson, M. A., & Ford, T. E. (2008), Disparagement humor: A theoretical and empirical review of psychoanalytic, superiority, and social identity theories, *Humor: Interrnational Journal of Humor Research, 21,* 283–312; La Fave, L., Haddad, J., Maesen, W. A. (1996/1976), Superiority, enhanced self-esteem, and perceived incongruity humor theory, in A. J. Chapman & H. C. Foot (Eds.), *Humor and laughter: Theory, research and applications* (pp. 63–91), New York: John Wiley & Sons; Zillman, D., & Cantor, J. R. (1976), A disposition theory of humor and mirth, in A. J. Chapman & H. C. Foot (Eds.), *Humor and laughter: Theory, research and applications* (pp. 93–116), London: Wiley.

33. As with Hobbes, Gruner also emphasizes that the laughter component of humor is related to suddenness of the victory.

34. For a recent evolutionary analysis, see Martens, J. P., Tracy, J. L., & Shariff, A. F. (2012), Status signals: Adaptive benefit of displaying and observing the nonverbal expressions of pride and shame, *Cognition and Emotion, 26,* 390–406.

35. See http://www.brainyquote.com/quotes/quotes/m/melbrooks161275 .html#J3q3MoD2rU1HwY8u.99, retrieved April 22, 2012.

36. For a review, see Ferguson, & Ford (2008).

37. Martin, R. A. (2007), *The psychology of humor: An integrative approach*, London: Elsevier.

38. Wills (1981), p. 260.

39. See http://www.harrypotterspage.com/category/j-k-rowling/, retrieved January 5, 2012. As Lev Goldman noted in a tribute to Wodehouse in *Time* magazine: "His subject was the foibles of the pre-war English aristocracy, which sounds limiting, but it was his subject the same way marble was Michelangelo's subject. He could do anything with

it." See http://entertainment.time.com/2011/11/23/in-praise-of-p-g-wodehouse/, retrieved January 5, 2012.

40. See http://www.booktv.org/Watch/8532/In+Depth+Christopher+Hitchens .aspx, retrieved January 5, 2012.

41. He designs ladies' underwear.

42. Wodehouse, P. G. (1938), *The code of the Woosters*, New York: Vintage Books, p. 166.

43. Ibid.

44. Ibid., p. 182.

45. Ibid., pp. 220–221.

Chapter 3

1. Orwell, G. (1950), *Shooting an elephant and other essays*, New York: Penguin.

2. See http://www.goodreads.com/author/quotes/370054.George_S_Patton_ Jr., retrieved May 26, 2012.

3. See http://www.condenaststore.com/-sp/It-s-not-enough-that-we-succeed-Cats-must-also-fail-New-Yorker-Cartoon-Prints_i8542217_.htm, retrieved February, 2012.

4. See http://thinkexist.com/quotes/billy_crystal/, retrieved April 22, 2012.

5. Von Neumann, J., & Morgensten, O. (1944), *Theory of games and economic behavior*, Princeton, NJ: Princeton University Press.

6. See http://boston.com/community/moms/blogs/parent_buzz/2012/07/aly_ raismans_parents_are_animated_in_the_stands_does_it_make_you_nervous_to_watch_ your_child_compete.html; and http://www.boston.com/sports/other_sports/olympics/ articles/2012/08/02/parents_of_olympians_arent_the_only_ones_who_feel_stress_ when_their_children_perform/; http://www.nbcolympics.com/video/gymnastics/chevy-top-moment-1-aly-raisman-s-mom-s-reaction.html, retrieved August 4, 2012.

7. Tajfel, H. (Ed.) (1978), *Differentiation between social groups: Studies in the social psychology of intergroup relations*, London: Academic Press.

8. Tajfel, H. (1970), Experiments in intergroup discrimination, *Scientific American*, *223*, 96–102.

9. Tajfel, H., & Turner, J. C. (1979), An integrative theory of intergroup conflict, in W. G. Austin & S. Worchel (Eds.), *The social psychology of intergroup relations* (pp. 94–109), Monterey, CA: Brooks-Cole; Tajfel, H., & Turner, J. C. (1986), The social identity theory of inter-group behavior, in S. Worchel & L. W. Austin (Eds.), *Psychology of intergroup relations* (pp. 2–24), Chicago: Nelson-Hall.

10. St. John, W. (2004), *Rammer jammer yellow hammer: A journey in the heart of fan mania*, New York: Crown.

11. Ibid., p. 125.

12. Ibid., pp. 98–99.

13. See http://www.wral.com/news/local/story/1245389/, retrieved June 21, 2010; and Taylor, S., & Johnson, K. C. (2008), *Until proven innocent: Political correctness and the shameful injustices of the Duke lacrosse rape case*, New York: St. Martin's Griffin.

14. Leach, C. W., Spears, R., Branscombe, N. R., & Doosje, B. (2003), Malicious pleasure: *Schadenfreude* at the suffering of another group, *Journal of Personality and Social Psychology, 84*, 932–943.

15. Empirical evidence for the nature of ingroup loyalty and outgroup distaste (and the potential for biased perceptions) goes as far back as the classic study examining Dartmouth and Princeton students' biased perceptions of film footage of a rough football game between the two schools. Hastorf, A. H., & Cantril, H. (1954), They saw a game: A case study, *Journal of Abnormal and Social Psychology, 49*, 129–134. A qualitative analysis of another football game from two perspectives is a documentary, *Havard Beats Yale, 29–29*, http://www.thedailybeast.com/newsweek/2009/01/23/when-harvard-beat-yale.html, retrieved April 19, 2013.

16. St. John (2004), p. 93.

17. Ibid., p. 94.

18. See http://www.fannation.com/si_blogs/for_the_record/posts/3541, retrieved August 10, 2010.

19. See http://sports.espn.go.com/espn/columns/story?columnist=ohlmeyer_don&id=4764245, retrieved May 26, 2012.

20. Wann D. L., Peterson R. R., Cothran C., & Dykes, M. (1999), Sport fan aggression and anonymity: The importance of team identification, *Social Behavior and Personality, 27*, 597–602; Wann, D. L., Haynes, G., McLean, B., & Pullen, P. (2003), Sport team identification and willingness to consider anonymous acts of hostile aggression, *Aggressive Behavior, 29*, 406–413.

21. Hoogland, C., Schurtz, R. D., Combs, D. J. Y., Cooper, C., Brown, E. G., & Smith, R. H. (2013), How does the severity of the misfortune affect *schadenfreude* in sports? Unpublished manuscript.

22. Cikara, M., Botvinick, M., & Fiske, S. T. (2010), Us versus them: Social identity shapes neural responses to intergroup competition and harm, *Psychological Science, 22*, 306–313.

23. Wildschut, T., Pinter, B., Vevea, J. L., Insko, C. A., & Schopler, J. (2003), Beyond the group mind: A quantitative review of the interindividual intergroup discontinuity effect, *Psychological Bulletin, 129*, 698–722.

24. See http://www.nbcsandiego.com/news/sports/James-Hahn-Gangnam-Style-Golf-Dance-Putt-PGA – 189662021.html, retrieved March 8, 2013.

25. See http://news.bbc.co.uk/2/hi/programmes/letter_from_america/464752 .stm, retrieved May 15, 2012.

26. See http://news.bbc.co.uk/sport2/hi/golf/3913453.stm, retrieved May 15, 2012; http://sportsillustrated.cnn.com/vault/article/magazine/MAG1017184/index .htm, retrieved May 15, 2012; http://www.youtube.com/watch?v=CxTbNTyWIvc, retrieved May 15, 2012; and http://news.bbc.co.uk/2/hi/programmes/letter_from_ america/464752.stm, retrieved May 15, 2012.

27. See http://news.bbc.co.uk/2/hi/programmes/letter_from_america/464752 .stm, retrieved May 15, 2012.

28. An example of politics as blood sport is the career of Lee Atwater, campaign manager for many Republican candidates and famous for his take-no-prisoners style. http://www.boogiemanfilm.com/; Brady, J. (1996), *Bad boy: The life and politics of Lee Atwater*, Cambridge, MA: Da Capo Press.

29. I take a number of examples in the section on politics and *schadenfreude* from Combs, D. J. Y, Powell, C. A. J., Schurtz, D. R., & Smith, R. H. (2009), Politics, *schadenfreude*, and ingroup identification: The sometimes funny thing about a poor economy and death, *Journal of Experimental Social Psychology*, *45*, 635–646.

30. See http://www.realclearpolitics.com/video/2012/02/23/obama_gop_licking_ their_chops_over_rising_gas_prices_they_root_for_bad_news.html, retrieved March 3, 2012.

31. Combs, Powell, Schurtz, & Smith (2009).

32. See http://www.rawstory.com/rs/2012/06/26/colbert-only-bad-economic- news-is-good-news-for-romney/, retrieved August 4, 2012.

33. Gay, P. (1998), *My German question*, New Haven: Yale University Press. Gay's father had originally arranged passage on another ship, but, concerned that the family get out of Gemany as soon as possible, using papers he had forged on his own, he found places on another ship that would leave two weeks earlier. The original ship ended up being one of those unlucky vessels that went from port to port seeking a country that would accept them. Less than a fourth of those passengers survived the Nazi net; Also see Portmann, J. (2000), *When bad things happen to other people*, New York: Routledge. pp. 54–55.

34. Gay (1998), p. 70.

35. Ibid., p. 83.

Chapter 4

1. James (1950), *Principles of psychology*, vol. 1, New York, Dover, p. 318 (originally published in 1890).

2. Swift, J. (1731), *Verses on the death of Dr. Swift, D.S.P.D.*, http://www.online-literature .com/swift/3514/, retrieved June 21, 2010.

3. Orwell (1950).

4. Nietzsche, F. (1967), *On the genealogy of morals* (trans. W. Kaufmann & R. J. Hollingdale), New York: Random House, p. 16 (originally published 1887).

5. James (1950), *Principles of psychology*, vol. 2, New York: Dover, p. 409 (originally published in 1890).

6. See http://www.slate.com/id/2208430/, retrieved December 14, 2010.

7. Baumeister, R. F., & Bushman, B. J. (2010), *Social psychology and human nature*, New York: Wadsworth Publishing.

8. James (1918), vol. 1, p. 318.

9. Swift (1731).

10. Jomini, A. H. (1827), *Vie politique et militaire de Napoléon*, vol. 2 (1827), p. 180; http://books.google.com/books?id+AJUTAAAAQAAJ&pg=PA180, retrieved May 24, 2012.

11. See http://www.theatlanticwire.com/politics/2012/10/jon-stewart-how-obama-allowed-romney-proceed-wall/58082/, retrieved December 3, 2012.

12. See http://www.dailykos.com/story/2012/11/30/1165769/-My-favorite-moment-of-2012-Please-proceed-governor, retrieved December 3, 2012.

13. See http://www.iep.utm.edu/psychego/, retrieved May 23, 2012; Batson, C. D. (2011), *Altruism in humans*, New York: Oxford University Press; Brown, S. L, Brown, R. M., & Penner, L. A. (Eds.) (2012), *Moving beyond self-interest: Perspectives from evolutionary biology, neuroscience, and the social sciences*, New York: Oxford University Press.

14. Hobbes (1968).

15. Freud, S. (1930), *Civilization and its discontents*, London: Hogarth.

16. Turchet, J. (Ed.) (1992), *La Rochefaucauld: Maximes*, Paris: Bordas.

17. Ibid.; see also http://www.quotationspage.com/quotes/Francois_de_La_Rochefoucauld.

18. Carnegie, D. (1964), *How to win friends and influence people*, New York: Simon & Schuster.

19. Ibid., p. 4.

20. Ibid., p. 50.

21. Ibid., p. 14.

22. Stengel, R. (2000), *You're too kind: A brief history of flattery*, New York: Touchstone.

23. Ibid.

24. See http://economictimes.indiatimes.com/opinion/interviews/today-corporate-traning-means-serious-business-growth-pallavi-jha-dale-carnegie-training-india/articleshow/13637502.cms, retrieved May 28, 2012.

25. See http://www.facebook.com/note.php?note_id=204703126222217, retrieved June 2, 2012.

26. Cialdini, R. B. (2009), *Influence: Science and practice* (5th ed.), Boston: Allyn & Bacon, p. xii.

27. Ibid.

28. Capote, T. (1966), *In cold blood*, New York: Random House.

29. Haas, A. (1984), *The doctor and the damned*, New York: St. Martin's Press, p. 232.

30. Brecht, B. (1973/1928). *Threepenny opera*, London: Eyre Methuen (trans. Hugh MacDiarmid), p. 46.

31. Becker. E. (1973), *The denial of death*, New York: Simon & Schuster, p. 3.

32. Ibid., pp. 3–4.

33. Smith, R. H., Eyre, H. L., Powell, C. A. J., & Kim, S. H. (2006), Relativistic origins of emotional reactions to events happening to others and to ourselves, *British Journal of Social Psychology, 45,* 357–371.

34. Smith, A. (2000), *The theory of moral sentiments*, Amherst, NY: Prometheus Books, p. 1. (originally published in 1759).

35. de Waal (2009); Keltner (2009); McCullough (2008).

36. Brown, Brown, & Penner (2012).

37. Brosnan & de Waal (2003).

38. See http://www.livescience.com/2044-monkeys-fuss-inequality.html, retrieved September 2, 2012.

39. Van den Bos, K., Peter, S. L., Bobocel, D. R., & Ybema, J. F. (2006), On preferences and doing the right thing: Satisfaction with advantageous inequity when cognitive processing is limited, *Journal of Experimental Social Psychology, 42,* 273–289.

40. Baumeister & Bushman (2010), p. 60.

41. Aristotle (1991), *The art of rhetoric*, London: Penguin Books (written c. 367–322 BC; trans. H. C. Lawson-Tancred, part I, chapter 5, p. 90.

42. Baumeister & Bushman (2010), pp. 60–61.

43. Bergson, H. (1911), *Laughter: An essay on the meaning of the comic*, London: Macmillan (quoted in Billig, M. [2005]), *Laughter and ridicule: Towards a social critique of humour,* London: Sage, p. 120.

Chapter 5

1. Cited in Portmann (2000), p. xii.

2. Rosten, L. (1968), *The joys of Yiddish*, New York: McGraw-Hill, p. 201.

3. Marable, M. (2011), *Malcolm X: A life of reinvention*, New York: Penguin Books.

4. Watts, A. E. (2008), *Laughing at the world: Schadenfreude*, social identity, and American media culture, unpublished dissertation, Northwestern University; Raney, A. A, & Bryant, J. (2002), Moral judgment and crime drama: An integrated theory of enjoyment, *Journal of Communication, 52,* 402–415.

5. De Palma, B. (Director) (1978), *The fury* [film], Chicago: Frank Yablans Presentations.

6. Portmann (2000); see also Ben-Ze'ev, A. (2000), *The subtlety of emotions*, Cambridge, MA: MIT Press.

7. Feather, N. T., & Sherman, R. (2002), Envy, resentment, *schadenfreude*, and sympathy: Reactions to deserved and undeserved achievement and subsequent failure, *Personality and Social Psychology Bulletin, 28*, 953–961; van Dijk, W. W., Ouwerkerk, J. W., Goslinga, S., & Nieweg, M. (2005), Deservingness and *schadenfreude, Cognition and Emotion, 19*, 933–939; van Dijk, W. W., Goslinga, S., & Ouwerkerk, J. W. (2008), The impact of responsibility for a misfortune on *schadenfreude* and sympathy: Further evidence, *Journal of Social Psychology, 148*, 631–636.

8. Feather, N. T. (2006), Deservingness and emotions: Applying the structural model of deservingness to the analysis of affective reactions to outcomes, *European Review of Social Psychology, 17*, 38–73; Feather, N. T. (1992), An attributional and value analysis of deservingness in success and failure situations, *British Journal of Social Psychology, 31*, 125–145; Hafer, C. L., Olson, J. M., & Peterson, A. A. (2008), Extreme harmdoing: A view from the social psychology of justice, in V. M. Esses & R. A. Vernon (Eds.), *Explaining the breakdown of ethnic relations: Why neighbors kill* (pp. 17–40), Malden, MA: Blackwell Publishing; Heuer, L., Blumenthal, E., Douglas, A., & Weinblatt, T. (1999), A deservingness approach to respect as a relationally based fairness judgment, *Personality and Social Psychology Bulletin, 25*, 1279–1292; van Dijk, Goslinga, & Ouwerkerk (2008).

9. See http://www.cbsnews.com/stories/2009/09/24/60minutes/main5339719 .shtml?tag=currentVideoInfo;segmentUtilities, retrieved February 9, 2010.

10. See http://www.reuters.com/article/ousiv/idUSTRE55P6O520090629, retrieved June 26, 2009.

11. Ibid.

12. Feather (1992); Darley, J. M., Carlsmith, K. M., & Robinson, P. H. (2000), Incapacitation and just deserts as motives for punishment, *Law and Human Behavior, 24*, 659–683; Hafer, Olson, & Peterson (2008); Heuer, Blumenthal, Douglas, & Weinblatt (1999).

13. See http://www.vanityfair.com/politics/features/2009/06/madoff200906, retrieved July 6, 2009.

14. See http://www.reuters.com/article/ousiv/idUSTRE55P6O520090629, retrieved July 30, 2009.

15. See http://www.nytimes.com/2009/06/30/business/30scene.html, retrieved July 12, 2009.

16. See http://www.nytimes.com/2009/02/27/business/27madoff.html, retrieved June 15, 2009.

17. See http://www.cnn.com/2009/CRIME/02/27/wiesel.madoff/index.html, retrieved May 15, 2009.

18. See http://www.businessinsider.com/bernies-cell-2009-3, retrieved May 20, 2009.

19. Some scholars argue that the more a misfortune seems deserved, the more the feeling produced in witnesses may shift from *schadenfreude* to a different category of emotion, a kind of impersonal, general satisfaction derived from the restoration of justice. In the case of the purely deserved, in part because the pleasure may produce no reproach from others. The emotion is, for lack of a needed term, "satisfied indignation," rather than *schadenfreude*. I think that this is an important distinction, but my preference, as I stated in the Introduction, is to opt for a broader, more inclusive view of *schadenfreude*. Otherwise, in this domain, we would be tempted to remove a sense of deservingness from any instances of *schadenfreude*. For examples of subtle treatments of these issues, see Kristjansson, K. (2005), *Justice and desert-based emotions*, Farnham, Surrey, UK: Ashgate Publishing; McNamee, M. (2003), *Schadenfreude* in sport: Envy, justice and self-esteem, *Journal of the Philosophy of Sport, 30*, 1–16; and Portmann (2000).

20. See http://www.abc.net.au/rn/science/mind/s680880.htm, retrieved April 5, 2010.

21. Portmann (2000), p. 114.

22. See http://www.ccel.org/ccel/edwards/works2.vi.ix.iii.html, retrieved May 23, 2012.

23. Seaman, A. R. (1999), *Swaggart: The unauthorized biography of an American evangelist*, New York: Continuum.

24. Ibid.

25. See http://www.time.com/time/magazine/article/0,9171,974120,00.html, retrieved May 13, 2010.

26. Charley Carlson, personal communication.

27. Baur, S. W. (2008), *The art of the public grovel: Sexual sin and public confession in America*, Princeton, NJ: Princeton University Press.

28. See http://www.miamiherald.com/2010/05/12/1624904_physician-heal-thyself.html, retrieved May 16, 2010.

29. I also use this example extensively in, Powell, C. A. J., & Smith, R. H. (in press), The inherent joy in seeing hypocrites hoisted with their own petards, *Self and Identity*.

30. See http://www.cnn.com/2009/US/01/29/lkl.ted.haggard/, retrieved March 13, 2009; and http://www.imdb.com/title/tt0486358/quotes, retrieved August 29, 2009.

31. Haggard, T., & Haggard, G. (2006), *From this day forward: Making your vows last a lifetime*, Colorado Springs, CO: Waterbook Press.

32. Jones, M. (2007), *I had to say something: The art of Ted Haggard's fall*, New York: Seven Stories Press, p. 145.

33. Ibid., p. 160.

34. See http://abcnews.go.com/GMA/story?id=2626067&page=1, retrieved April 2, 2009.

35. Amann, J. M., & Breuer, T. (2007), *The brotherhood of the disappearing pants: A field guide to conservative sex scandals*, New York: Nation Books.

36. See http://dorothysurrenders.blogspot.com/2006/11/fun-with-hypocrisy.html, retrieved January 15, 2009.

37. Jones (2007), p. 232.

38. Ibid., p. 9.

39. Wilde, O. (1891), *The picture of Dorian Gray*, Richmond: University of Virginia Library Electronic Text Center, p. 35.

40. Seaman (1999), p. 14.

41. Ibid.

42. See http://www.waynebrownministries.com/b2evolution/blogs/index.php/ 2010/ 05/06/ted-haggard-on-the-rekers-sex-scandal-we-are-all-sinners?blog=23, retrieved May 28, 2010.

43. See http://www.nytimes.com/2010/05/19/us/19rekers.html, retrieved May 28, 2010.

44. See http://www.washingtonmonthly.com/features/2003/0306.green.html, retrieved April 22, 2008; and http://www.slate.com/id/2082526/, retrieved May 12, 2008.

45. See http://www.nationalreview.com/goldberg/goldberg050503.asp, retrieved April 22, 2008.

46. See http://www.slate.com/id/2082526/, retrieved May 12, 2008.

47. King James Bible, Matthew 23:25, 27–28.

48. Cialdini (2009), p. 53.

49. Monin, B., Sawyer, P., & Marquez, M. (2008), The rejection of moral rebels: Resenting those who do the right thing, *Journal of Personality and Social Psychology, 95*, 76–93; Monin, B. (2007), Holier than me? Threatening social comparison in the moral domain, *International Review of Social Psychology, 20*, 53–68.

50. Monin (2007).

51. Heider (1958); Tripp, T. M., Bies, R. J., & Aquino, K. (2002), Poetic justice or petty jealousy? The aesthetics of revenge, *Organizational Behavior and Human Decision Processes, 89*, 966–987.

52. Powell & Smith (in press).

Chapter 6

1. Quoted in French, R. A. (2001), *The virtures of vengeance*, Lawrence: University of Kansas Press; *Agamemnon, The Oresteria* (trans. Robert Fagles), London: Penguin Books, 1975, p. 3.

2. See http://blog.al.com/live/2011/05/osama_bin_laden_death_brings_j.html, retrieved March 25, 2012.

3. See http://www.condenaststore.com/-sp/I-am-not-a-vengeful-man-but-I-do-enjoy-a-touch-of-retribution-now-and-then-New-Yorker-Cartoon-Prints_i8474436_.htm, retrieved June 2, 2012.

4. As I noted in Chapter 5, it can be argued that the more a misfortune seems deserved by objective standards, the more the feeling may seem qualitatively different from *schadenfreude*, and thus an impartial satisfaction derived from the restoration of justice. For my purposes, here, I opt for a broader view of *schadenfreude*, although I acknowledge that this is an important distinction.

5. Hafer, C. L., & Begue, L. (2005), Experimental research on just-world theory: Problems, developments, and future challenges, *Psychological Bulletin, 131,* 128–167; Lerner, M. J. (1980), *The belief in a just world: A fundamental delusion*, New York: Plenum Press; Lodewijkx, H. F. M., Wildschut, T., Nijstad, B. A., Savenije, W., Smit, M., & Nijstad, B. (2001), In a violent world, a just world makes sense: The case of "senseless violence" in the Netherlands, *Social Justice Research, 14,* 79–94.

6. Lerner, M. J., & Simmons, C. H. (1966). Observer's reaction to the "innocent victim": Compassion or rejection? *Journal of Personality and Social Psychology, 4,* 203–210.

7. See http://www.scu.edu/ethics/publications/iie/v3n2/justworld.html, retrieved May 20, 2008; and http://www.nytimes.com/1990/06/03/us/nature-of-clothing-isnt-evidence-in-rape-cases-florida-law-says.html, retrieved August 15, 2012.

8. Lerner (1980).

9. Alicke, M. D. (2000), Culpable control and the psychology of blame, *Psychological Bulletin, 126,* 556–574; Alicke, M. D., & Davis, T. L. (1989), The role of a posteriori victim information in judgments of blame and sanction, *Journal of Experimental Social Psychology, 25,* 362–377.

10. See http://blog.al.com/live/2011/05/osama_bin_laden_death_brings_j.html, retrieved March 23, 2012.

11. See http:// www.nytimes.com/2010/03/14/books/14dover.html, retrieved March 18, 2010; and http://www.guardian.co.uk/theguardian/2010/mar/08/sir-kenneth-dover-obituary, retrieved March, 2010.

12. Dover, K. (1994), *Marginal comment: A memoir*, London: Duckworth.

13. He decided to be unbothered if many of the things he wrote might seem unimportant to other people because "how can we know, so long as people are reticent through

fear of being thought vain if they speak of what is to their credit, or exhibitionists if it is discreditable, or, 'unbalanced' if they reveal how little things affects them and big thing did not?" Dover (1994), p. 2.

14. Dover (1994), p. 228.

15. See http://www.nytimes.com/1994/11/28/world/a-scholar-s-memoirs-raise-some-ghosts-at-oxford.html?pagewanted=all, retrieved May 2, 2010.

16. Dover (1994), p. 230.

17. According to an account in *The New York Times*, Dover's "level of moral culpability was roundly debated in British academic circles," and the publishing of his memoir some years later rekindled the debate and broadened it beyond academia; http:// www.nytimes.com/2010/03/14/books/14dover.html, retrieved March 18, 2010.

18. See http://www.nytimes.com/1994/11/28/world/a-scholar-s-memoirs-raise-some-ghosts-at-oxford.html?pagewanted=all, retrieved May 2, 2010.

19. Ibid.

20. Dover (1994), p. 230.

21. See http://www.guardian.co.uk/theguardian/2010/mar/08/sir-kenneth-dover-obituary, retrieved March 18, 2010.

22. Hareli, S., & Weiner, B. (2002), Dislike and envy as antecedents of pleasure at another's misfortune, *Motivation and Emotion*, 26, 257–277; Ortony, A., Clore, G., & Collins, A. (1988). *The cognition structure of emotions*. Cambridge: Cambridge University Press.

23. The German word was used in an ad campaign for Volkswagen in 1990. It meant "driving enjoyment." See http://www.urbandictionary.com/define.php?term=farfegnugen, retrieved May 26, 2012.

24. I rank his memoir, *The Doctor and the Damned*, as one of the most remarkable books that I have ever read. If I had unlimited funds, I would produce a 30-part television drama on it and include every detail. I appreciate, for example, the frank accounts of his feelings throughout.

25. Haas (1984), p. 284.

26. Ibid. I should note that other parts of his memoir suggest that Haas was not a vindictive man. Quite the opposite. He was fair-minded and compassionate—and resourceful. He was a survivor.

27. Manning, M. (2011), *Malcolm X: A life of reinvention*, New York: Penguin Books, p. 229.

28. See http://www.washingtonpost.com/wp-dyn/content/article/2005/09/20/AR2005092000201_pf.html, retrieved April 13, 2008.

29. See http://www.jewishfederations.org/page.aspx?id=108589, retrieved April 12, 2009.

30. "I'm doing this because I have to do it....I am not motivated by a sense of revenge. Perhaps I was for a short time in the very beginning....Even before I had had time to really think things through, I realized we must not forget. If all of us forgot, the same thing might happen again, in 20 or 50 or 100 years"; http://www.boston.com/news/world/europe/articles/2005/09/21/nazi_hunter_simon_wiesenthal_dies/, retrieved April 12, 2009.

31. See http://www.nytimes.com/2005/09/21/international/europe/21wiesenthal.html?pagewanted=all, retrieved March 26, 2012.

32. See http://www.boston.com/news/world/europe/articles/2005/09/21/nazi_hunter_simon_wiesenthal_dies/?page=full, retrieved March 23, 2012.

33. Carlsmith, K. M., & Darley, J. M. (2008), Psychological aspects of retributive justice, in M. P. Zanna (Ed.), *Advances in experimental social psychology* (vol. 40, pp. 193–236), San Diego, CA: Elsevier; Kim, S. H., & Smith, R. H. (1993), Revenge and conflict escalation, *Negotiation Journal, 9*, 37–43; McCullough (2008); Miller, W. I. (2007), *Eye for an eye*, New York: Cambridge University Press; Tripp, T. M., & Bies, R. J. (2009), *Getting even: The truth about workplace revenge—and how to stop it*, New York: Jossey-Bass.

34. Haas (1984), p. 291.

35. Ibid.

36. Ibid.

37. McCullough (2008).

38. Murphy, J. G. (2003), *Getting even: Forgiveness and its limits*, New York: Oxford University Press.

39. Murphy, J. G. (2002), Vengeance, justice and forgiveness, *Canyon Institute for Advanced Studies, 2* (1), 1.

40. Kleist, M. (2007), *Michael Kohlhaas: A tale from an old chronicle* (trans. Frances H. King), New York: Mondial (originally published in 1811).

41. Murphy (2002), p. 1.

42. Lester, M. L. (Director) (1985), *Commando* [film]. Available at http://www.script-o-rama.com/movie_scripts/c/commando-script-transcript-arnold-schwarzenegger.html, retrieved March 12, 2013.

43. Auden, W. H. (1976), *Collected poems*, New York: Random House.

44. Kim & Smith (1993).

45. Cited in Kim, S. H. (2005), The role of vengeance in conflict escalation, in I. W. Zartman & G. O. Faure (Eds.), *Escalation and negotiation in international conflicts* (pp. 141–162), Cambridge: Cambridge University Press.

46. See, for example, Lotto, D. (2006). The psychohistory of vengeance, *Journal of Psychohistory, 34*, 43–59.

47. King James Bible, Paul's letter to the Romans 12:19.

48. Carlsmith, K. M., Wilson, T. D., & Gilbert, D. T. (2008), The paradoxical consequences of revenge, *Journal of Personality and Social Psychology, 95,* 1316–1324.

49. Ibid., p. 1324.

50. This fits with other empirical work showing that rumination about prior mistreatment from others tends to prolong and aggravate negative feelings. When people ruminate about their mistreatment, they get more angry and remain angry longer; Mor, N., & Winquist, J. (2002), Self-focused attention and negative affect: A meta-analysis, *Psychological Bulletin, 128,* 638–662. When people ruminate about someone who has harmed them, they become more aggressive than when they distract themselves; Rusting, C. L., & Nolen-Hoeksema, S. (1998), Regulating responses to anger: Effects of rumination and distraction on angry mood, *Journal of Personality and Social Psychology, 74,* 790–803. Moreover, they are less likely to forgive an offense; Bushman, B. J. (2002), Does venting anger feed or extinguish the flame? Catharsis, rumination, distraction, anger and aggressive responding, *Personality and Social Psychology Bulletin, 28,* 724–731.

51. Kim (2005).

52. Ben-Ze'ev (2000). I largely agree with scholars such as Aaron Ben-Ze'ev who emphasize that *schadenfreude* proper is passive. If we take an active role in someone else's misfortune, something more complex is occurring. However, I would not make such a hard-and-fast distinction. Action complicates the picture, but in my view does not remove all traces of *schadenfreude*.

53. Sides, H. (2002), *Ghost soldiers: The epic account of World War II's greatest rescue mission,* New York: Anchor.

54. See Baumeister, R. F. (1997), *Evil: Inside human cruelty and violence,* New York: W. H. Freeman. Sadism involves delight in cruelty, especially excessive cruelty. It doesn't imply other motives aside from the pleasure in the cruelty. Also, it is generally active rather than passive. Sadistic people hurt others and enjoy inflicting the harm. The line between extreme forms of *schadenfreude* and sadism, as I conceive the two, is blurry. People could feel *schadenfreude* because they perceive that a suffering person deserves to suffer. A witness to this pleasure might find it sadistic because he or she does not think the suffering deserved. When *schadenfreude* is active, its overlap with sadism is most difficult to delineate because its active features link it closely with the raw enjoyment of cruelty rather than with other motives, such as deservingness.

55. Shakespeare, W. (1963), *Hamlet: An authoritative text, intellectual backgrounds, extracts from the sources, and essays in criticism,* New York: W. W. Norton (written approximately in 1599), Act III, sc. 4, lns 210–211.

Chapter 7

1. See http://archive.dailycal.org/article/13978/berkeley_junior_shot_down_in_american_idol_tryout, retrieved April 19, 2012.

2. Gandhi, M. K. (1983/1948), *Autobiography: The story of my experiments with truth*, New York: Dover, p. 99.

3. James (1918), vol. 2, p. 414.

4. See http://www.asianweek.com/2008/08/27/breakfast-is-out-to-lunch/, retrieved December 12, 2010.

5. See http://yellow-face.com/, retrieved December 12, 2010.

6. Perhaps this explains why public speaking is considered a singularly widespread and intense fear: Gibson, J. W., Gruner, C. R., Hanna, M. S., Smythe, M. J., & Hayes, M. T. (1980), The basic course in speech at U.S. colleges and universities: III, *Communication Education, 29,* 1–9.

7. Goffman, E. (1952), On cooling the mark out: Some aspects of adaptation to failure, *Psychiatry, 15,* 451–463, p. 463.

8. See http://www.youtube.com/watch?v=vqmy5qrvaVQ, retrieved May 21, 2012.

9. Ibid.

10. Watts (2008).

11. Booker, S., & Waite, B. M. (2005, May), *Humilitainment? Lessons from 'The Apprentice': A reality television content analysis*, presented at the 17th Annual Convention of the American Psychological Society, Los Angeles; Waite, B. M., Bendezu, J., & Booker, S. (2004, May), *Why do we like reality television? A personality analysis*, presented at the 16th Annual Convention of the American Psychological Society, Chicago.

12. See http://www.nbc.com/howie-do-it/, retrieved March 10, 2011.

13. See http://www.nbc.com/howie-do-it/about/, retrieved March 10, 2011.

14. See http://www.nbc.com/howie-do-it/, retrieved March 10, 2011.

15. See http://orwell.ru/library/essays/joys/english/e_joys, retrieved August 15, 2012; Orwell, G. (1953), *Such, such were the joys*, New York: Harcourt, Brace and Company.

16. See http://www.democraticunderground.com/discuss/duboard.php?az=view_all&address=389x276680, retrieved March 3, 2013.

17. See http://www.msnbc.msn.com/id/10912603/ns/dateline_nbc-to_catch_a_predator/, retrieved August 15, 2012.

18. Shakespeare, *Othello, the Moor of Venice*, Act II, Scene III, 242–244.

19. See http://www.mediabistro.com/tvnewser/nbcs-chris-hansen-busts-homer-simpson_b33598, retrieved March 10, 2011; and http://www.imdb.com/title/tt0905647/, retrieved March 10, 2011.

20. See http://www.sfgate.com/cgi-bin/article.cgi?f=/c/a/2007/08/08/ DDEGREAI31.DTL&ao=all; and http://articles.sfgate.com/2007-08-08/ entertainment/17255578_1_sexual-solicitations-nbc-s-predator-reality, retrieved May 17, 2012.

21. Adler, A. M. (2010), "To catch a predator," New York University Public Law and Legal Theory Working Papers, Paper 229, retrieved March 10, 2011; and http://lsr .nellco.org/nyu_plltwp/229, retrieved March 10, 2011.

22. See http://www.tvrage.com/Jimmy_Kimmel_Live/episodes/582351, retrieved March 11, 2001.

23. Terry, K.T. (2005), *Sexual offenses and offenders: Theory, practice, and policy*, New York: Wadsworth Publishing.

24. Trammell, R., & Chenault, S. (2011), "We have to take these guys out": Motivations for assaulting incarcerated child molestors, *Symbolic Interaction, 32*, 334–350; http://abcnews.go.com/US/story?id=90004#.T3d4nHi4L0c, retrieved March 31, 2012; http://www.slate.com/articles/news_and_politics/explainer/2011/11/jerry_ sandusky_out_on_bail_are_child_molesters_tormented_in_american_prisons_.html, retrieved, March 31, 2012; and http://www.nytimes.com/2003/08/28/opinion/ prisoners-of-hate.html, retrieved March 31, 2012.

25. See http://www.cjr.org/feature/the_shame_game.php?page=all, retrieved April 21, 2013.

26. See http://www.pollyklaas.org/, retrieved May 28, 2012.

27. Book, A. S. (1999), Shame on you: An analysis of modern shame punishment as an alternative to incarceration, *William & Mary Law Review, 40*, 653–686; Ziel, P. (2004–2005), Eighteenth century public humiliation penalties in twenty-first century America: The shameful return of scarlet letter punishments in U.S. v. Gementera, *BYU Journal of Public Law, 19*, 499–522. There are exceptions, such as http://www.thedailyaztec. com/2011/01/public-shaming-is-an-effective-alternative-to-prison/, retrieved August 15, 2012; http://www.publicengines.com/blog/2009/11/09/creative-sentencing- public-humiliation/, retrieved, August 15, 2012; and http://lawvibe.com/get-caught- stealing-and-face-public-humiliation/, retrieved August 15, 2012.

28. See http://www.cjr.org/feature/the_shame_game.php?page=all, retrieved April 21, 2013.

29. See http://www.youtube.com/watch?v=TgwOu1IlWuY, retrieved March 4, 2013.

30. Ibid.

31. Hansen, C. (2007), *To catch a predator: Protecting your kids from online enemies already in your home*, New York: Dutton Adult, p. 5.

32. One case involved an army sergeant who begged Hansen to take pity on him. He said, "Sir, please I don't want you to ruin my life." He then went down on his knees and put his hands behind his head, as if had just been captured by an enemy soldier. This pleading failed to awaken Hansen's sympathy. As Hansen wrote, "On his knees, you could almost feel sorry for the guy, but remember this is the same man who typed more than fifty pages of often explicit chats to a girl he thought was fourteen years old." Ibid., p. 211.

33. Reiss, S. & Wiltz, J. (2004), Why people watch reality TV, *Media Psychology, 6,* 363–378.

34. See http://www.ew.com/ew/article/0,,399467,00.html, retrieved March 10, 2011.

35. Whitman, J. Q. (1998), What is wrong with inflicting shame sanctions? *Faculty Scholarship Series,* Paper 655, http://digitalcommons.law.yale.edu/fss_papers/655, retrieved March 11, 2011.

36. See http://en.allexperts.com/q/U-S-History-672/2008/8/Puritan-Women-punishment.htm, retrieved March 12, 2011.

37. Ibid.

38. McTiernan, J. (Director) (1988), *Die Hard* [Film]. Los Angeles: 20th Century Fox.

39. Ibid.

40. For extensive statistics and analysis, see information at the Crimes Against Children Research Center at http://www.unh.edu/ccrc/, retrieved June 12, 2012; Finkelhor, D. (2008), *Childhood victimization: Violence, crime, and abuse in the lives of young people,* New York: Oxford University Press.

41. Snyder, Howard N. (2000, July), *Sexual assault of young children as reported to law enforcement: Victim, incident, and offender characteristics,* retrieved from http://bjs.ojp.usdoj.gov/content/pub/pdf/saycrle.pdf, June 2, 2012; Crimes Against Children Research Center, http://www.unh.edu/ccrc/, retrieved June 12, 2012.

42. See http://www.huffingtonpost.com/jesse-wegman/dateline-to-kill-a-predat_b_41911.html, retrieved June 2, 2012.

Chapter 8

1. Cited in Griffin, A. K. (1931), *Aristotle's psychology of conduct,* London: Williams and Norgate, p. 78.

2. Spinoza, B. (2008), *The ethics,* New York: Bibliolife, p. 138 (originally published in 1677).

3. See http://www.snpp.com/episodes/7F23.html, retrieved April 5, 2010.

4. Smith & Kim (2007).

5. Forman, M. (Director) (1984), *Amadeus* (film based on a play by Peter Shaffer [2001], *Amadeus: A play by Peter Shaffer*, New York: Harper Perennial). There is little evidence that Salieri actually envied Mozart in the way depicted in the play or film or that he engineered Mozart's death. See Borowitz, A. I. (1973), Salieri and the "murder" of Mozart, *The Musical Quarterly, 59*, 268–279.

6. Fiske (2011).

7. Harris, L. T., & Fiske, S. T. (2006), Dehumanizing the lowest of the low: Neuro-imaging responses to extreme outgroups, *Psychological Science, 17*, 847–853; Harris, L. T., Cikara, M., & Fiske, S. T. (2008), Envy as predicted by the stereotype content model: A volatile ambivalence, in R. H. Smith (Ed.), *Envy: Theory and research* (pp. 133–147), New York: Oxford University Press.

8. Fiske (2011), p. 32; Botvinick, M. M., Cohen, J. D., & Carter, C. S. (2004), Conflict monitoring and anterior cingulate cortex: An update, *Trends in Cognitive Sciences, 8*, 539–546.

9. Mitchell, J. P. (2008), Contributions of functional neuroimaging to the study of social cognition, *Current Directions in Psychological Science, 17*, 142–146.

10. Harris, Cikara, & Fiske (2008); Harris, L.T., McClure, S. M., van den Bos, W., Cohen, J. D., & Fiske, S. T. (2007), Regions of the MPFC differentially tuned to social and non-social affective evaluation, *Cognitive and Behavioral Neuroscience, 7*, 309–316; van den Bos, W., McClure, S. M., Harris, L. T., Fiske, S. T., & Cohen, J. D. (2007), Dissociating affective evaluation and social cognitive processes in ventral medial prefrontal cortex, *Cognitive and Behavioral Neuroscience, 7*, 337–346.

11. Smith, R. H., Turner, T. J., Garonzik, R., Leach, C. W., Urch-Druskat, V., & Weston, C. M. (1996), Envy and *schadenfreude, Personality and Social Psychology Bulletin, 25*, 158–168.

12. See http://thetenbest.net/gorevidalquotes/, retrieved March 10, 2010.

13. Twain, M. (2000), *Life on the Mississippi*, Toronto: Dover, p. 22 (originally published in 1883); I also use this example in a similar way in Powell, C. A. J., Smith, R. H., & Schurtz, D. R. (2008), *Schadenfreude* caused by an envied person's gain, in R. H. Smith (Ed.), *Envy: Theory and research* (pp. 148–164), New York: Oxford University Press.

14. Percy, W. (2000), *Lost in the cosmos*, New York: Picador, p. 65. I also make extended and similar use of this example in Powell, Smith, & Schurtz (2008).

15. Percy (2000), p. 65.

16. Ibid.

17. Smith, Turner, Garonzik, Leach, Urch-Druskat, & Weston (1996).

18. Takahashi, H, Kato, M., Matsuura, M., Mobbs, D., Suhara, T., & Okubo, Y. (2009), When your gain is my pain and your pain is my gain: Neural correlates of envy and *schadenfreude, Science, 13*, 937–939.

19. See http://www.nytimes.com/2009/02/17/science/17angi.html?_r=1, retrieved May 15, 2010.

20. Cuddy, A. J. C., Fiske, S. T., & Glick, P. (2007), The BIAS map: Behaviors from intergroup affect and stereotypes, *Journal of Personality and Social Psychology, 92*, 631–648; Fehr, E., & Fischbacher, U. (2005), The economics of strong reciprocity, in H. Gintis, S. Bowles, R. Boyd, & E. Fehr (Eds.), *Moral sentiments and material interests: The foundations of cooperation in economic life* (pp. 151–191), Cambridge: MIT Press; Kirchsteiger, G. (1994), The role of envy in ultimatum games, *Journal of Economic Behavior and Organization, 25*, 373–389; Smith & Kim (2007). Recent evidence suggests that there are two types of envy: a benign and a malicious type. *Schadenfreude* is most related to malicious envy: see van de Ven, N., Zeelenberg, M., & Pieters, R. (2009), Leveling up and down: The experience of malicious and benign envy, *Emotion, 9*, 419–429.

21. Fortunately, the boy survived the explosion. Twain probably would not have recounted the story so enthusiastically otherwise. And yet, even the boy's survival created mixed feelings. Twain noted that "when he came home the next week, alive, renowned, and appeared in church all battered up and bandaged, a shining hero, stared at and wondered over by everybody, it seemed to us that the partiality of Providence for an undeserving reptile had reached a point where it was open to criticism." Twain (2000), p. 22.

22. Beckman, S. R., Formby, J. P., Smith, W. J., & Zheng, B. H. (2002), Envy, malice and Pareto efficiency: An experimental examination, *Social Choice and Welfare, 19*, 349–367; Zizzo, D. J. (2003), Money burning and rank egalitarianism with random dictators, *Economics Letters, 81*, 263–266; Zizzo, D. J., & Oswald, A. J. (2001), Are people willing to pay to reduce others' incomes? *Annales d'Economie et de Statistique, 63–64*, 39–62.

23. Smith, R. H. (1991), Envy and the sense of injustice, in P. Salovey (Ed.), *The psychology of jealousy and envy* (pp. 79–99), New York: Guilford Press; Smith, R. H., Parrott, W. G., Ozer, D., & Moniz, A. (1994), Subjective injustice and inferiority as predictors of hostile and depressive feelings in envy, *Personality and Social Psychology Bulletin, 20*, 705–711.

24. van de Ven, Zeelenberg, & Pieters (2009).

25. Cited in Portmann (2000), p. 139.

26. Burke, E. (1987), *A philosophical enquiry into the origin of our ideas of the sublime*, Oxford: Basil Blackwell, p. 46 (originally published in 1756); the credibility of *The National Enquirer* is probably tarred by the wacky fictions of the other publications. However, *The National Enquirer* articles, often dismissed as malicious lies by those who are the focus of the articles, often end up being largely true; see http://www.slate.com/id/2102303/, retrieved May 15, 2010.

27. Chang, J., & Halliday, J. (2005), *Mao: The unknown story*, New York: First Anchor Books, p. 14.

28. Ibid.

29. Boucher, K., & Smith, R. H., (2010), unpublished data.

30. See http://www.slate.com/id/2067667, retrieved May 15, 2010.

31. Byron, C. (2002), *Martha Inc.: The incredible story of Martha Stewart Living Omnimedia*, New York: Wiley.

32. See http://www.slate.com/id/2067667, retrieved May 15, 2010.

33. See http://www.newyorker.com/archive/2003/02/03/030203fa_fact?current Page=all, retrieved March 3, 2010.

34. Ibid.

35. Ibid.

36. Ibid.

37. Aronson, E., Willerman, B., & Floyd, J. (1966), The effect of a pratfall on increasing interpersonal attractiveness, *Psychonomic Science 4*, 227–228.

38. See http://www.chevychasecentral.com/trivia.htm, retrieved September 4, 2012.

39. See http://www.parade.com/celebrity/sunday-with/2012/05/20-jay-leno-comic-highs-lows-cars-secrets-successful-marriage.html, retrieved May 20, 2012.

40. Sundie, J. M., Ward, J., Beal, D. J., Chin, W. W., & Oneto, S. (2009), *Schadenfreude* as a consumption-related emotion: Feeling happiness about the downfall of another's product, *Journal of Consumer Psychology, 19*, 356–373; Sundie, J. M., Kenrick, D. T., Griskevicius, V., Tybur, J. M., Vohs, K. D., & Beal, D. J. (2011), Peacocks, Porsches, and Thorstein Veblen: Conspicuous consumption as a sexual signaling system, *Journal of Personality and Social Psychology, 100*, 664–680; Veblen, T. (1989), *The theory of the leisure class*, New York: Macmillan.

41. See http://www.dailydot.com/video/lamborghini-crash/, retrieved May 25, 2012; and http://www.reddit.com/r/videos/comments/tn1y4/lamborghini_tries_to_ show_off_ends_up_crashing/, retrieved May 25, 2012.

42. See http://www.dailydot.com/video/lamborghini-crash/ retrieved May 24, 2012; and http://www.imdb.com/title/tt0145487/quotes, retrieved May 24, 2012.

43. See http://www.youtube.com/all_comments?v=1pgm8I0B8bY, retrieved May 24, 2012.

44. Hareli & Weiner (2002).

45. Swift (1731).

46. See http://www.newyorker.com/archive/2003/02/03/030203fa_fact?current Page=all, retrieved March 3, 2010; Byron (2002).

47. See http://www.newyorker.com/archive/2003/02/03/030203fa_fact?current Page=all, retrieved March 3, 2010.

48. See http://www.snpp.com/episodes/7F08.html, retrieved April 5, 2010.

49. Ibid.

Chapter 9

1. Pushkin, A. (1964), *The poems, prose, and plays of Alexander Pushkin*, New York: Modern Library, p. 430.

2. Shakespeare, W. (1963), *Julius Caesar*, New York: The New American Library p. 40, (originally published 1599).

3. Goethe, J. W. (1906), *The maxims and reflections of Goethe*, New York: Macmillan.

4. Farber, L. (1966), *The Ways of the will*, New York: Basic Books; Foster, G. (1972), The anatomy of envy, *Current Anthropology, 13*, 165–202; Smith & Kim (2007); Vidaillet, B. (2009), Psychoanalytic contributions to understanding envy: Classic and contemporary perspectives, in R. H. Smith (Ed.), *Envy: Theory and research.* (pp. 267–289), New York: Oxford University Press.

5. I take some of the examples in this chapter from Powell, Smith, & Schurtz (2008); Smith, R. H., & Kim, S. H. (2008), Introduction, in R. H. Smith (Ed.), *Envy: Theory and research* (pp. 3–14), New York: Oxford University Press; and Smith & Kim (2007).

6. Alicke & Govorun (2005); Dunning (2005); Freud, A. (1937), *The ego and the mechanisms of defense*, London: Hogarth Press and Institute of Psycho-Analysis; Gilovich, T. (1993), *How we know what isn't so: The fallibility of human reason in everyday life*, New York: Simon & Schuster; Paulhus, D. L., Fridhandler, B., & Hayes S. (1997), Psychological defense: Contemporary theory and research, in S. Briggs, R. Hogan, R. Goode, & J. W. Johnson (Eds.), *Handbook of personality psychology* (pp. 543–579) Boston: Academic Press; Vaillant, G. E. (1992), *Ego mechanisms of defense: A guide for clinicians and researchers*, Arlington, VA: American Psychiatric Publishing.

7. Duffy, M. K., Shaw, J. D., & Schaubroeck, J. (2008), *Envy in organizational life*, in R. Smith (Ed.), *Envy: Theory and research* (pp. 167–189), New York: Oxford University Press; Elster, J. (1998), *Alchemies of the mind: Rationality and the emotions*, Cambridge: Cambridge University Press; Foster, G. (1972), The anatomy of envy, *Current Anthropology, 13*, 165–202; Schoeck, H. (1969), *Envy: A theory of social behavior*, New York: Harcourt, Brace, and World; Silver, M., & Sabini, J. (1978), The perception of envy, *Social Psychology Quarterly, 41*, 105–117; Smith & Kim (2007).

8. Elster (1998); Foster (1972), Schoeck (1969); Silver, & Sabini (1978). H. Also see Powell, Smith, & Schurtz (2008); Smith & Kim (2007).

9. King James Bible, Exodus 20:17.

10. Schimmel, S. (2008), Envy in Jewish thought and literature, in R. H. Smith (Ed.), *Envy: Theory and research* (pp. 17–38), New York: Oxford University Press.

11. King James Bible, Genesis 4:1–16.

12. Milton, J. (1962), *Paradise lost and selected poetry and prose*, New York: Holt, Rinehardt, and Winston, p. 126 (originally published in 1667).

13. Alighieri, D. (1939), *The divine comedy* (trans. John D. Sinclair), New York: Oxford University Press (originally published in 1308–1321).

14. See http://www.etymonline.com/index.php?term=envy, retrieved April 12, 2010.

15. Aquaro, G. R. A. (2004), *Death by envy: The evil eye and envy in the Christian tradition*, Lincoln, NE: Universe; Smith & Kim (2007).

16. King James Bible, Matthew 19:24.

17. Smith & Kim (2007).

18. Unamuno, M. (1996), *Abel Sanchez and other short stories*, New York: Gateway Editions p. 103 (originally published in 1917); cited by Foster, (1972), p. 173; Smith & Kim (2007).

19. Elster (1998), p. 165.

20. Ibid., p. 172.

21. Smith & Kim (2007).

22. Ben-Ze'ev (2000); Smith (1991); Smith, Parrott, Ozer, & Moniz (1994).

23. Heider (1958), p. 287.

24. Aristotle (1941), Rhetoric, in R. McKeaon (Ed.), *The basic works of Aristotle*, New York: Random House (originally published in 322 BC); Salovey, P., & Rodin, J. (1984), Some antecedents and consequences of social-comparison jealousy, *Journal of Personality and Social Psychology*, 47, 780–792; Schaubroeck, J., & Lam, S. K. (2004), Comparing lots before and after: Promotion rejectees' invidious reactions to promotees, *Organizational Behavior and Human Decision Processes*, 94, 33–47.

25. Forrester, J. (1997), *Dispatches for the Freud wars*, Cambridge, MA: Harvard University Press; Kristjansson (2005).

26. Smith (1991).

27. Khayyám, O. (1952). *The rubáiyát of Omar Khayyám* (E. Fitzgerald, Trans.) Garden City, NY: Doubleday, p. 170 (originally published in 1858); I also use this and other similar examples in Smith, R. H. (1990), Envy and the sense of injustice, in P. Salovey (Ed.), *Psychology perspective on jealousy and envy* (pp. 79–99), New York: Guilford.

28. Heider (1958), p. 289.

29. Hill, S. E., & Buss, D. M. (2008), The evolutionary psychology of envy, in R. H. Smith (Ed.), *Envy: Theory and research* (pp. 60–70), New York: Oxford University Press, p. 60.

30. Quoted in Leach, C. W., & Spears, R. (2008), "A vengefulness of the impotent": The pain of ingroup inferiority and *schadenfreude* toward successful outgroups, *Journal of Personality and Social Psychology*, 95, 1383–1396, p. 1384; Nietzsche (1967), p. 37.

31. Krizan, Z., & Johar, O. (2012), Envy divides the two faces of narcissism, *Journal of Personality, 80*, 1415–1451.

32. Hotchkiss, S. (2003), *Why is it always about you?: The seven deadly sins of narcissism,* New York: Free Press, p. 16.

33. Forman (1984).

34. See Smith (2004) for another extended example of transmuted envy, this taken from Shakespeare's *Julius Caesar.*

35. Elster (1998); Smith (2004); Simth & Kim (2007); Sundie, Ward, Beal, Chin, & Oneto (2009).

36. Russo, R. (2008), *Bridge of sighs,* New York: Vintage.

37. Ibid., p. 86.

38. Ibid.

39. Stephen Thielke, personal communication. Instead, envy would be of the "benign" kind. See van de Ven, Zeelenberg, & Pieters (2009).

Chapter *10*

1. Marrus, M. R. (1997), *The Nuremberg War Crimes Trial 1945–46: A documentary history,* New York: Bedford Books, p. 207.

2. Gilligan, J. (1996), *Violence: Reflections on a national epidemic,* New York: Vintage Books.

3. Twain, M. (1898), Concerning the Jews, *Harper's Magazine,* March 1898; http://www.fordham.edu/halsall/mod/1898twain-jews.asp, retrieved April 20, 2013.

4. Here is a sample: Bauer, Y. (1982), *A history of the Holocaust,* New York: Franklin Watts; Browning, C. R. (1993), *Ordinary men: Reserve police battalion 101 and the final solution in Poland,* New York: Harper Perennial; Evans, R. J. (2003), *The coming of the Third Reich,* New York: Penguin; Evans, R. J. (2005), *The Third Reich in power,* New York: Penguin; Evans, R. J. (2008), *The Third Reich at war,* New York: Penguin; Gilbert, M. (2000), *Never again: The history of the Holocaust,* New York: Universe; Goldhagen, D. J. (1997), *Hitler's willing executioners: Ordinary Germans and the Holocaust,* New York: Vintage; Hildberg, R. (2003), *The destruction of the European Jews,* New Haven: Yale University Press (originally published in 1961); Prager, D., & Telushkin, J. (2003), *Why the Jews? The reason for anti-Semitism,* New York: Touchstone; Rosenbaum, R. (1998), *Explaining Hitler: The search for the origins of his evil,* New York: Random House; Wistrich, R. S. (2010), *A lethal obsession: Anti-Semitism from antiquity to the global jihad,* New York: Random House.

5. Kubizek, A. (1955), The young Hitler I knew; http://www.faem.com/books/, retrieved June 14, 2012.

6. Hitler, A. (1925), *Mein kampf* (trans. Ralph Manheim), Boston, MA: Houghton Mifflin, p. 55.

7. Ibid., p. 52.

8. Ibid., p. 52.

9. Ibid. p. 10.

10. Epstein, J. (2003), *Envy: The seven deadly sins*, New York: Oxford University Press, p. 60.

11. Hitler (1925), p. 58.

12. Ibid., p. 56.

13. Ibid., p. 58. The Jewish population of Vienna, absorbed by Germany in the spring of 1938, was larger than in German cities proper.

14. Ibid., p. 57.

15. Ibid., p. 61.

16. Ibid., p. 62.

17. Ibid.

18. Ibid., p. 63.

19. *People Magazine* interview, April 12, 1976, vol. 5, no. 14. Also, in his memoirs, *Inside the Third Reich*, Speer described Adolf Hitler's sense of humor to be almost entirely based on *schadenfreude*. "Hitler had no humor. He left joking to others, although he could laugh loudly, abandonedly, sometimes literally writhing with laughter. Often he would wipe tears from his eyes during such spasms. He liked laughing, but it was always laughter at the expense of others," Speer, A. (1969), *Inside the Third Reich* (trans. Richard and Clara Winston), Bronx, NY: Ishi Press, p 123.

20. Kubizek (1955).

21. Ibid.

22. Freud, S. (1939), *Moses and monotheism*, New York: Random House, p. 116.

23. Toland, J. (1976), *Adolf Hitler*, New York: Bantam Doubleday Dell, p. 701.

24. Hitler ended his account of how he came to hate the Jews by writing: "Eternal Nature inexorably avenges the infringement of her commands. Hence today I believe that I am acting in accordance with the will of the Almighty Creator: *by defending myself against the Jews, I am fighting for the work of the Lord*," Hitler (1925), p. 65.

25. The role of envy in anti-Semitism has been addressed by many. For example, the French scholar Bernard Lazare, who became heavily involved in the Dreyfus affair, wrote what is considered to be a remarkably impartial analysis of anti-Semitism and included envy as an important factor. Here is a selection from his book, *Antisemitism: Its history and causes*: "Everywhere they wanted to remain Jews, and everywhere they were granted the privilege of establishing a State within the State. By virtue of these privileges and exemptions, and immunity from taxes, they would soon rise above the general condition of the citizens of the municipalities where they resided; they had better opportunities for trade and accumulation of wealth, whereby they excited jealousy and hatred. Thus, Israel's

attachment to its law was one of the first causes of its unpopularity, whether because it derived from that law benefits and advantages which were apt to excite envy, or because it prided itself upon the excellence of its Torah and considered itself above and beyond other peoples," pp. 6–7, http://www.archive.org/details/Anti-semitismItsHistoryAndC ausesByBernardLazare. Freud suggests the distinctiveness of Jews and then notes: "The second peculiarity has an even more pronounced effect. It is that they defy oppression, that even the most cruel persecutions have not succeeded in exterminating them. On the contrary, they show a capacity for holding their own in practical life and, where they are admitted, they make valuable contributions to the surrounding civilization. The deeper motives of anti-Semitism have their roots in times long past; they come from the unconscious, and I am quite prepared to hear that what I am going to say will at first appear incredible. I venture to assert that the jealousy which the Jews evoked in other peoples by maintaining that they were the first-born, favourite child of God the Father has not yet been overcome by those others, just as if the latter had given credence to the assumption," Freud (1939), p. 116. Freud argued that the notion of Jews being a chosen people led to jealous and rivalrous feelings in non-Jews. Nietzsche, despite his influence on so many Nazi beliefs, was appalled by anti-Semitism, and wrote: "The struggle against the Jews has always been a symptom of the worst characters, those more envious and more cowardly. He who participates in it now must have much of the disposition of the mob." Quoted in Santaniello, W. (1997), A post-holocaust re-examination of Nietzsche and the Jews, in J. Golomb (Ed.), *Nietzsche and Jewish culture* (pp. 21–54), New York: Routledge. More recent examples are Prager & Telushkin (2003); Patterson, C. (2000), *Anti-Semitism: The road to the holocaust and beyond*, Lincoln, NE: iUniverse.com; Aly, G. (2011), *Warum die Deutschen? Warum die Juden? Gleichheit, Neid und Rassenhass 1800 1933*, Frankfurt: Fischer Verlag; Gilder, G. (2009), *The Israel test*, New York: Richard Vigilante Books; McKale, D. M. (2006), *Hitler's shadow war: The Holocaust and World War II*, New York: Taylor Trade Publishing.

26. Prager & Telushkin (2003), p. 30.

27. Also see Aly (2011).

28. Cuddy, A. J. C., Fiske, S. T., & Glick, P. (2008), Warmth and competence as universal dimensions of social perception: The Stereotype Content Model and the BIAS Map, in M. P. Zanna (Ed.), *Advances in experimental social psychology* (vol. 40, pp. 61–149), Thousand Oaks, CA: Academic Press; Fiske, S. T., Cuddy, A. J. C., Glick, P., & Xu, J. (2002), A model of (often mixed) stereotype content: Competence and warmth respectively follow from perceived status and competition, *Journal of Personality and Social Psychology*, 82, 878–902; Glick, P. (2002), Sacrificial lambs dressed in wolves' clothing: Envious prejudice, ideology, and the scapegoating of Jews, in L. S. Newman & R. Erber (Eds.), *Understanding genocide: The social psychology of the Holocaust* (pp. 113–142), Oxford: Oxford University Press; Glick, P. (2008), When neighbors blame neighbors: Scapegoating and

the breakdown of ethnic relations, in V. M. Esses & R. A. Vernon (Eds.), *Explaining the breakdown of ethnic relations: Why neighbors kill* (pp. 123–146), Malden, MA: Blackwell.

29. Cuddy, Fiske, & Glick (2008); Fiske, Cuddy, Glick, & Xu (2002). Interestingly, this group is not the prototype of the kind usually focused on when we think of prejudice. Anti-black prejudice by majority whites, for example, stereotypically assumes low status and perhaps some degree of competition, if resources are being taken away, say, through affirmative action. But this condition predicts feeling ranging from pity to contempt, as perceived threat increases. These are very different feelings from envy, and the implications are profound. Hitler may have been disgusted by Gypsies, but he hated the Jews.

30. Segel, B. W. (1996), *A lie and a libel: The history of the Protocols of the Elders of Zion,* R. S. Levy (Ed.) (trans. R. S. Levy), Lincoln: University of Nebraska Press.

31. The classic example is a white person in the previously segregated South who feels threatened by a loss in status and therefore develops hatred toward blacks.

32. Bachrach, S., & Luckert, S. (2009), *State of deception: The power of Nazi propaganda,* New York: W. W. Norton.

33. Epstein (2003). No wonder, as Joseph Epstein points out, that anti-Semitism "has historically taken two forms; one in which the Jews are castigated for being inferior, and another in which they are resented for being superior," p. 165; Epstein, J. (2002), *Snobbery: The American version,* New York: Houghton Mifflin.

34. Glick makes the point that few Germans would admit to having hostile envy toward Jews. It is the nature of envy to find other plausible causes to justify ill will. Here, conveniently, the other stereotypes of clever, underhanded, dirty, and so on now combine with the perception of threat, both to the country's national goals and purity of race. Thus, the use of terms suggesting "cleverness" rather than the kind of intelligence to be admired.

35. Evans (2005).

36. Cikara, M., & Fiske, S. T. (2012), Stereotypes and *schadenfreude*: Affective and physiological markers of pleasure at outgroups' misfortune, *Social Psychological and Personality Science, 3*, 63–71.

37. Metaxas, E. (2010), *Bonhoeffer: Pastor, martyr, prophet, spy,* Nashville, TN: Thomas Nelson, p. 176.

38. Toland (1976), p. 505.

39. Goldhagen (1996); Klee, E., Dressen, W., & Riess, V. (1991) (Eds.), *"The good old days": The Holocaust as seen by its perpetrators and bystanders* (trans. Deborah Burnstone), Old Saybrook, CT: Konecky & Konecky; Billig, M. (2005), *Laughter and ridicule: Towards a social critique of humour,* London: Sage.

40. McKale (2006), p. 147.

41. Spears, R., & Leach, C. W. (2008), Why neighbors don't stop the killing: The role of group-based *schadenfreude*, in V. Esses & R. A. Vernon (Eds.), *Explaining the breakdown of ethnic relations: Why neighbors kill* (pp. 93–120), Malden: Blackwell Publishing.

42. Cikara, M., & Fiske, S. T. (2011), Bounded empathy: Neural responses to out-groups' (mis)fortunes, *Journal of Cognitive Neuroscience, 23*, 3791–3803.

43. Farber, L. (1966), *Ways of the will*, New York: Basic Books, p. 36.

44. Fiske (2011).

45. Ibid.

46. Quoted in Patterson (2000), p. 79; McKale (2006).

47. Cesarani, D. (2004), *Eichmann: His life and crimes*, London: W. Heinemann.

48. Peter Longerich, "The Wannsee Conference in the Development of the 'Final Solution,'" available online at the *House of the Wannsee Conference: Memorial and educational site website*, http://www.ghwk.de/engl/kopfengl.htm, retrieved August 27, 2012.

49. McKale (2006), p. 242.

50. Roseman, M. (2002), *The Wannsee Conference and the final solution: A reconsideration*, New York: Picador.

51. Quoted in Roseman (2002), p. 144, from Eichmann trial, session 79, June 26, 1961; session 107, July 24, 1961.

52. Ibid., p. 149.

53. Ibid., p. 148.

54. Ibid., p 165.

55. Pierson, F (Director) (2001), *Conspiracy* [film].

56. Aly (2011); Arendt, H. (1963), *Eichmann in Jerusalem: A report on the banality of evil*, New York: Viking Press; Browning, C. (1992), *Ordinary men: Reserve Police Battalion 101 and the Final Solution in Poland*, New York: HarperCollins; Cohen, R. (2005), *Soldiers and slaves: American POWs trapped by the Nazis' final gamble*, New York: Knopf; Haas (1984); Hilberg, R. (1961), *The destruction of the European Jews*, 3rd ed., New Haven: Yale University Press; Goldhagen (1997); McKale (2006); Klee, Dressen, & Riess (1991), p. 76.

57. Cohen (2005).

58. Many American troops were taken prisoner. The Germans, in violation of the Geneva Conventions, singled out some of this group to be sent to Berga, in effect, to work them to their deaths; see Cohen (2005).

59. *Schadenfreude* from the guards' point of view; sadistic laughter from the prisoners' perspective.

60. Cohen (2005), p. 137. I cannot emphasize enough what a remarkable book this is.

61. Ibid.

62. Ibid., pp. 137–138.

63. Ibid., p. 54.

64. Cohen emphasizes that some of the Christian families resisted this treatment and offered the Jewish families food as they waited for the next stage in the Germans' plans. Generally, this compassion did not appear to last, however.

65. Cohen (2005), p. 55.

66. Ibid.

67. Adding to the sense that envy permeated the attitude of the Germans and their complicit Hungarian counterparts was the general concern over status in relation to the Jews. Hauer remembered, for example, the head of the Hungarian gendarmerie verbally abused Hauer's father simply because he committed the "effrontery" of wearing a hat in his presence. The Germans insisted on being treated with respect by their prisoners, which meant appropriate servility. In fact, one of the reasons GI's were selected for Berga, even if they were not Jewish, was when they didn't cooperate in this regard. The best example was Private Hans Kasten, a remarkably courageous man who refused to go along with the Germans' insistence that GI's reveal who was Jewish among them. Cohen's book is worth reading for his account of Kasten's actions alone.

68. And, more perversely still, if the Germans treated the prisoners so harshly, then it must be correspondingly deserved. Only people who were so thoroughly depraved could be treated this way.

69. Cohen (2005), pp. 184–185.

70. Ibid., p. 258.

71. Ibid., p. 207.

Chapter 11

1. Baker, J. A. (2006), *"Work hard, study…and keep out of politics!": Adventures and lessons from an unexpected public life*, New York: G. P. Putnam, p. 44.

2. King James Bible, John 8:3–11.

3. Fitzgerald, F. S. (1925), *The great Gatsby*, New York: Scribner, p. 1.

4. "If," by Rudyard Kipling in; Kipling, R. (1999), *The collected poems of Rudyard Kipling*, New York: Wordsworth.

5. This may help explain why we have hundreds of trait labels (e.g., rude, inconsiderate, arrogant, narcissistic… "jerk" and so on) to understand the actions we observe in others, but an impoverished set of imprecise labels to describe situations (e.g., a tough or difficult situation). Sometimes, people really are jerks, but a large swath of everyday behaviors are probably more a result of situational factors.

6. See http://www.nytimes.com/2005/09/27/health/psychology/27muse.html?_r=1, retrieved May 3, 2012.

7. Milgram, S. (1983), *Obedience to authority*, New York: Harper Perennial, p. 25.

8. Ibid.

9. Ibid.

10. Ross, L. (1977), The intuitive psychologist and his shortcomings: Distortions in the attribution process, in L. Berkowitz (Ed.), *Advances in experimental social psychology* (vol. 10, pp. 173–220), New York: Academic Press.

11. Milgram (1983), p. 31.

12. Ibid.

13. Gilbert, D. T., Pelham, B. W., & Krull, D. S. (1988), On cognitive busyness: When person perceivers meet persons perceived, *Journal of Personality and Social Psychology, 54,* 733–740; Gilbert, D. T., McNulty, S. E., Giuliano, T. A., & Benson, E. J. (1992), Blurry words and fuzzy deeds: The attribution of obscure behavior, *Journal of Personality and Social Psychology, 62,* 18–25.

14. The term "fundamental attribution *error*" can be misleading. Clearly, the true and full explanation for anyone's behavior, whether it is explaining why a particular man showed up at the sting site or why a particular father lost his patience with a nurse, will depend on the details of each event. If you've had a chance to watch *Predator,* I think you would agree that some of these men deserve much less sympathy than others. Some are clearly hardcore, repeat offenders who have a record of committing sexual violence without an apparent trace of guilt feelings. They needed little bait to lure them into their explicit conversations with the decoy and no cajoling to arrange a meeting. To attribute their behavior to dispositional causes would hardly be an "error." Some others, however, were probably engaged in more of a fantasy exchange at first and would not have showed up at the site if not for the persistent, creative strategies employed by the Perverted Justice staff. A multitude of possible situational factors may have heavily influenced their actions. Of course, let me emphasize that none of such factors, singularly or collectively, exonerates their showing up at the site—even though these factors may affect our moral evaluations of these men and affect whether we conclude their humiliation is fully deserved and is therefore pleasing.

15. See http://www.historycooperative.org/journals/jala/3/thomas.html, retrieved May 3, 2012.

16. Ibid.

17. Oates, S. B. (1994), *With malice toward none: A life of Lincoln,* New York: Harper Perennial.

18. See http://quotationsbook.com/quote/38116/, retrieved April 4, 2012.

19. The event is featured prominently in Dale Carnegie's book *How to win friends and influence people,* for example.

20. See http://www.civilwarhome.com/lincolnmeadeletter.htm, retrieved April 4, 2012.

21. Oates (1994), p. 19.

22. Quoted in http://www.mrlincolnandfriends.org/inside.asp?pageID=23& subjectID=1, retrieved May 3, 2012; Douglas L. Wilson & Rodney O. Davis, editor, *Herndon's Informants*, p. 259 (letter from John McNamar to William H. Herndon, May 23, 1866).

23. See http://www.historycooperative.org/journals/jala/3/thomas.html, p. 30, retrieved May 3, 2012.

24. Donald, D. H. (1995), *Lincoln*, New York: Simon & Schuster, p. 259.

25. Ward Hill Lamon, a fellow Illinois lawyer, recounted a time early on in their friendship when he had embarrassed himself in court. Lamon had been wrestling with someone outside the courthouse, which caused a big tear in the rear of his pants. But before he had time to change, he was called into court to start a case. Lamon later wrote:

> The evidence was finished. I, being the Prosecuting Attorney at the time, got up to address the jury,…Having on a somewhat short coat, my misfortune was rather apparent. One of the lawyers, for a joke, started a subscription paper which was passed from one member of the bar to another as they sat by a long table fronting the bench, to buy a pair of pantaloons for Lamon,—"he being," the paper said, "a poor but worthy young man." Several put down their names with some ludicrous subscription, and finally the paper was laid by someone in front of Mr. Lincoln, he being engaged in writing at the time. He quietly glanced over the paper, and immediately taking up his pen, wrote after his name, "I can contribute nothing to the end in view."

This was, certainly, a kind of enjoyment of another's "misfortune" but hardly mean-spirited. From Ward Hill Lamon, *Recollections of Abraham Lincoln*, pp. 16–17. Quoted in http://www.mrlincolnandfriends.org/inside.asp?pageID=23&subjectID=1, retrieved May 3, 2012.

26. The historian Benjamin Thomas relates this story:

> "Lincoln spoke of a man who accosted him on a train, saying: 'Excuse me, sir, but I have an article in my possession which rightfully belongs to you.' 'How is that?' asked Lincoln in amazement. Whereupon the stranger produced a jack-knife and explained: 'This knife was placed in my hands some years ago, with the injunction that I was to keep it until I found a man uglier than myself. Allow me now to say, sir, that I think you are fairly entitled to it.'" (see http://www.historycooperative.org/journals/jala/3/thomas.html, p. 41, retrieved May 3, 2012).

27. Oates (1994), p. 116.

28. Ibid.

29. Ibid., p. 126.

30. See http://www.brainyquote.com/quotes/quotes/a/abrahamlin104175.html, retrieved April 4, 2012.

31. Donald (1995), p. 567.

Conclusion

1. Bellow, S. (1964), *Herzog*, New York: Penguin, p. 23.

2. James (1918), vol. 2, p. 413.

3. See http://www.forbes.com/2004/03/18/cx_ld_0318nike.html, retrieved June 15, 2010.

4. See http://www.pbs.org/newshour/bb/sports/jan-june10/tiger_04-08.html, retrieved June 15, 2010.

5. See http://sportsillustrated.cnn.com/vault/article/magazine/MAG1009257/index.htm, retrieved June 15, 2010.

6. See http://articles.orlandosentinel.com/2009-11-29/sports/os-bk-tiger-woods-accident_1_ocoee-in-serious-condition-million-mansion-friday-evening-elin-nor-degren-woods, retrieved June 15, 2010.

7. See http://www.nytimes.com/reuters/2009/12/02/arts/entertainment-us-golf-woods.html?scp=2&sq=Tiger%20Woods%20Enquirer&st=cse, retrieved June 15, 2010.

8. See http://www.nytimes.com/2009/12/03/sports/golf/03woods.html?_r=1&scp=17&sq=tiger%20woods&st=cse, retrieved June 15, 2010.

9. See http://www.ajc.com/sports/text-of-tiger-woods-314300.html, retrieved June 15, 2010.

10. See http://www.nationalenquirer.com/celebrity/67747, retrieved June 15, 2010.

11. See http://abcnews.go.com/Sports/wireStory?id=9198393, retrieved June 15, 2010; http://www.sfgate.com/cgi-bin/article.cgi?f=/n/a/2009/12/12/sports/s062742S18.DTL, retrieved June 15, 2010; http://www.nytimes.com/2009/12/03/sports/golf/03woods.html?_r=1&scp=17&sq=tiger%20woods&st=cse, retrieved June 15, 2010; http://www.waggleroom.com/2009/12/2/1181429/tiger-woods-is-americas-new-bill, retrieved June 15, 2010; http://sportsillustrated.cnn.com/2010/writers/frank_deford/03/29/Tiger.Woods.return.Masters/index.html, retrieved June 15, 2010; http://www.esquire.com/the-side/tiger-woods-scandal, retrieved June 15, 2010; http://www.golf.com/golf/tours_news/article/0,28136,1948231,00.html, retrieved June 15, 2010; and http://hubpages.com/hub/Why-do-we-like-it-when-people-fail, retrieved June 15, 2010.

12. See http://www.jokes4us.com/celebrityjokes/tigerwoodsjokes.html, retrieved May 11, 2012.

13. See http://www.huliq.com/8059/89384/tiger-woods-cheetah-eyes-tabloid-news, retrieved May 11, 2012.

14. See http://media.www.ecollegetimes.com/media/storage/paper991/news/2010/05/06/Top10s/Top-10.Tiger.Woods.Jokes-3917903.shtml#5, retrieved June 15, 2010.

15. See http://sports.espn.go.com/espn/columns/story?columnist=ohlmeyer_don&id=4764245, retrieved June 15, 2010; and http://sports.espn.go.com/espn/news/story?id=4327128, retrieved May 12, 2012.

16. See http://sports.espn.go.com/espn/columns/story?columnist=ohlmeyer_don&id=4764245, retrieved May 12, 2012.

17. See http://www.golf.com/golf/tours_news/article/0,28136,1990399,00.html, retrieved June 15, 2010.

18. See http://sports.espn.go.com/golf/usopen10/columns/story?columnist=harig_bob&id=52671, retrieved June 15, 2010.

19. See http://sports.espn.go.com/golf/usopen10/columns/story?columnist=harig_bob&id=5267152, retrieved June 15, 2010.

20. See http://www.frontporchrepublic.com/2010/03/an-apologia-for-tiger-woods/, retrieved June 15, 2010.

21. See http://www.knoxnews.com/news/2010/feb/20/geoff-calkins-time-will-tell-if-tiger-woods-apolog/, retrieved June 15, 2010.

22. See http://www.golf.com/golf/tours_news/article/0,28136,1888274,00.html, retrieved June 15, 2010.

23. See http://blogs.golf.com/presstent/2010/02/tiger-rules-hell-talk-friday.html, retrieved June 15, 2010.

24. See http://www.usatoday.com/sports/golf/story/2012-07-22/ernie-els-wins-british-open/56415126/1, retrieved August 20, 2012.

25. See http://www.supergolfclubs.net/tiger-calls-out-ernie-els-not-a-big-worker-physically/, retrieved May 30, 2012.

26. See http://www.thesun.co.uk/sol/homepage/sport/golf/4444156/Ernie-Els-to-celebrate-Open-win-with-Nelson-Mandela.html, retrieved August 20, 2012; and http://www.sbnation.com/golf/2012/7/22/3176267/ernie-els-2012-british-open-speech-video, retrieved August 20, 2012.

27. See http://www.buzzingolf.co.uk/matchmaker-jesper-parnevik-angry-at-tiger-woods/617, retrieved June 15, 2010; and http://sports.espn.go.com/golf/news/story?id=4924113, retrieved May 12, 2012.

28. See http://www.snpp.com/episodes/7F23.html, retrieved April 5, 2010.

29. Ibid.

30. Why the German language has a word for this concept, and English does not is hard to say. Some languages do (e.g., *leedvemaak* in Dutch); some don't (e.g., French).

31. Ben-Ze'ev (2000); Portmann (2000).

32. See http://chronicle.com/article/The-Pleasure-of-Seeing-the/125381, retrieved January 12, 2011.

33. Ibid.

34. See http://chronicle.com/article/article-content/125621/, retrieved January 12, 2012.

35. See http://strangebehaviors.wordpress.com/2007/07/12/the-elusive-etymology-of-an-emotion/, retrieved June 27, 2010.

INDEX

CPSIA information can be obtained
at www.ICGtesting.com
Printed in the USA
BVHW060257170223
658463BV00001B/4